T0353448

Certifiable Software Applications 3

I thank my wife Nadège and my children
Geoffrey, Adrien, Marie and Jeanne for their love and support.

Certifiable Software Applications 3

Downward Cycle

Jean-Louis Boulanger

First published 2018 in Great Britain and the United States by ISTE Press Ltd and Elsevier Ltd

ISTE Press Ltd
27-37 St George's Road
London SW19 4EU
UK

www.iste.co.uk

Elsevier Ltd
The Boulevard, Langford Lane
Kidlington, Oxford, OX5 1GB
UK

www.elsevier.com

Notices

Knowledge and best practice in this field are constantly changing. As new research and experience broaden our understanding, changes in research methods, professional practices, or medical treatment may become necessary.

Practitioners and researchers must always rely on their own experience and knowledge in evaluating and using any information, methods, compounds, or experiments described herein. In using such information or methods they should be mindful of their own safety and the safety of others, including parties for whom they have a professional responsibility.

To the fullest extent of the law, neither the Publisher nor the authors, contributors, or editors, assume any liability for any injury and/or damage to persons or property as a matter of products liability, negligence or otherwise, or from any use or operation of any methods, products, instructions, or ideas contained in the material herein.

For information on all our publications visit our website at http://store.elsevier.com/

British Library Cataloguing-in-Publication Data
A CIP record for this book is available from the British Library
Library of Congress Cataloging in Publication Data
A catalog record for this book is available from the Library of Congress
ISBN 978-1-78548-119-2

Printed and bound in the UK and US

Contents

Introduction   xiii

Chapter 1. Realization of a Software Application   1

1.1. Introduction.   1
1.2. Implementation process   2
1.3. Quality control   3
   1.3.1. Introduction   3
   1.3.2. Software quality assurance plan   4
1.4. Conclusion   6

Chapter 2. Requirements Management   7

2.1. Introduction.   7
2.2. Three key concepts   8
   2.2.1. Introduction   8
   2.2.2. Process requirement   9
   2.2.3. Requirement   9
   2.2.4. Attributes.   13
   2.2.5. Allocation versus refinement   15
   2.2.6. Traceability   18
2.3. Process   21
   2.3.1. Introduction   21
   2.3.2. Two approaches.   23
   2.3.3. Implementation of tools   24
2.4. Conclusion   26

Chapter 3. Documentation Structure   29

3.1. Introduction.   29
3.2. Documentation   29
   3.2.1. Introduction   29

3.2.2. Formalization of documents   30
3.2.3. Signature and acceptance   30
3.3. Quality control   31
3.3.1. The company's quality process   31
3.3.2. Project quality control   32
3.4. Implementation process   35
3.5. Configuration management   36
3.6. Defect and non-conformity management   37
3.6.1. Presentation   37
3.6.2. Defect formalization   37
3.6.3. Impact of changes   38
3.7. Conclusion   41

Chapter 4. Requirements Specification of a Software Application .   43

4.1. Introduction   43
4.2. Requirements management   44
4.2.1. Presentation   44
4.2.2. Requirements manager   45
4.3. Specification know-how   46
4.4. Quality characteristics of a software product   48
4.5. Objectives of the software requirements specification phase   50
4.6. Risk assessment   55
4.7. System requirements specification document: SwRS   56
4.7.1. Presentation   56
4.7.2. Characterization of the content of the SwRS   57
4.7.3. Identification of software boundaries   58
4.7.4. Identification of the operation modes   60
4.7.5. Identification of parametrization data   63
4.7.6. Identification of services/functions   64
4.7.7. Behavior description   64
4.8. Specifications formalization   67
4.8.1. Modeling for verification   67
4.8.2. Text specification versus graphical specification   69
4.8.3. Formal method   70
4.9. Considering COTS and reused components   70
4.10. Specification verification   71
4.11. Conclusion   71
4.12. Appendix: SwRS template   72

Chapter 5. Modeling   75

5.1. Introduction   75
5.2. Modeling   76
5.2.1. Presentation   76

5.2.2. Model.   76
5.2.3. Different types of modeling.   81
5.3. Model transformation.   82
5.3.1. Presentation   82
5.3.2. Different types of transformation   82
5.3.3. Abstraction.   84
5.3.4. Implementation   85
5.3.5. Element transformation   87
5.3.6. Code generation.   88
5.3.7. Summary.   89
5.4. Model refinement   91
5.5. Methods.   93
5.5.1. Semiformal method.   93
5.5.2. Structured method   94
5.5.3. Formal method   95
5.5.4. Computer-aided specification tools   96
5.5.5. Summary.   96
5.6. Conclusion   96

Chapter 6. Formalization   97

6.1. Introduction.   97
6.2. Approach example.   97
6.2.1. Context diagram   98
6.2.2. Structured method   102
6.2.3. Modeling.   106
6.2.4. Formal method and/or technique.   121
6.2.5. Synthesis   142
6.3. Model verification.   143
6.4. Setting up of formal methods   144
6.5. Implementation of formal methods.   146
6.5.1. Conventional processes   146
6.5.2. Process taking formal methods into account   147
6.5.3. Issues   149
6.6. Software application maintenance   151
6.7. Conclusion   151

Chapter 7. Software Specification Verification Stage   155

7.1. Introduction.   155
7.2. Verification.   156
7.2.1. Presentation   156
7.2.2. Verifications of the software requirement specification   156
7.2.3. Overview.   170
7.3. Conclusion   171

Chapter 8. Component Versus Module 173

8.1. Introduction. 173
8.2. Reusability, maintainability and continuity of service. 174
8.3. Module and component. 176
  8.3.1. Presentation 176
  8.3.2. Module 176
  8.3.3. Component. 179
  8.3.4. Data encapsulation versus information hiding 181
8.4. Conclusion 181

Chapter 9. Software Application Architecture 183

9.1. Introduction. 183
9.2. Objective of the architecture phase of a software application 184
9.3. Software architect 186
9.4. Software architecture description document 187
  9.4.1. Introduction 187
  9.4.2. Constraint on the methodology. 187
  9.4.3. Description of the interfaces with the environment 188
  9.4.4. Typical architecture 189
  9.4.5. Component, module and interface 191
  9.4.6. Architecture principle 193
  9.4.7. Description of the software application architecture 204
9.5. Verification of the software application architecture 208
9.6. Consideration of COTS and reused components 209
  9.6.1. Introduction 209
  9.6.2. Preexisting component. 210
  9.6.3. COTS 210
  9.6.4. Reusability. 212
9.7. Model approach 212
9.8. Conclusion 214

Chapter 10. Software Application Architecture Verification 215

10.1. Introduction 215
10.2. Verification 216
  10.2.1. Reminder 216
  10.2.2. Software application architecture verifications. 216
  10.2.3. Synthesis 230
10.3. Conclusion 230

Chapter 11. Software Application Design. 231

11.1. Introduction 231
11.2. Component 231
11.3. Purpose of the design phase 232

11.4. Designer 234
11.5. Software component specification document 234
11.5.1. Objective 234
11.5.2. Constraint on the methodology 235
11.5.3. Methodology characteristic 236
11.6. Software component specification document 237
11.6.1. Principles 237
11.6.2. Functional decomposition 240
11.6.3. Modular or programming unit decomposition 241
11.6.4. Data description 241
11.6.5. Description of the algorithms 242
11.6.6. Requirement traceability 243
11.7. Design verification 245
11.8. Consideration of COTS and reused components 246
11.8.1. Introduction 246
11.8.2. Preexisting code 247
11.8.3. COTS 247
11.9. Conclusion 248

**Chapter 12. Software Application Component Design Phase
Verification** 249

12.1. Introduction 249
12.2. Verification 249
12.2.1. Reminder 249
12.2.2. Software application component design phase verifications 250
12.2.3. Synthesis 259
12.3. Conclusion 260

Chapter 13. Software Application Coding 261

13.1. Introduction 261
13.2. Coding phase objective 262
13.3. IMPlementer 264
13.4. Code production 264
13.4.1. Manual coding or automatic generation 264
13.4.2. Executable generation sequence 266
13.5. Principles to be implemented in the context of the coding phase . . . 267
13.5.1. Compliance with the SwCD 267
13.5.2. Programming rules 268
13.6. The choice of design language 271
13.6.1. Introduction 271
13.6.2. Essential properties 271
13.6.3. Analysis of languages 273

13.7. Consideration of COTS and reused components   284
13.8. Coding phase verification.   284
13.9. Conclusion   284

Chapter 14. Programming Rules   287

14.1. Introduction   287
14.2. Characteristics of programming rules.   287
  14.2.1. Introduction   287
  14.2.2. General rules   290
  14.2.3. Compilation rules   290
  14.2.4. Formatting rules   291
  14.2.5. Documentation conventions.   292
  14.2.6. Software engineering conventions   292
  14.2.7. Object names.   294
  14.2.8. Variables management   296
  14.2.9. Rules related to safety principles   299
14.3. Programming rules verification   300
14.4. Conclusion   301

Chapter 15. Coding Verification   303

15.1. Introduction   303
15.2. Verification   303
  15.2.1. Reminder   303
  15.2.2. Methodology.   304
  15.2.3. Compliance with coding rules.   306
15.3. Dead code and unreachable code   307
  15.3.1. Introduction   307
  15.3.2. Unreachable code   309
  15.3.3. Dead code   309
  15.3.4. Inhibited code   310
15.4. Conclusion   310

Chapter 16. Version Sheet of the Software Application   311

16.1. Introduction   311
16.2. Generating the executable   311
  16.2.1. Principles   311
16.3. Identification of the executable   314
  16.3.1. Introduction   314
  16.3.2. Identification of the executable   314
  16.3.3. Executable protection.   314
16.4. Version datasheet of the application software   315
  16.4.1. Presentation of the need   315
  16.4.2. Implementation   315

16.4.3. Compatibility 317

16.4.4. Summary 317

16.5. Conclusion 317

16.6. Appendix: SwVS 318

Conclusion 319

Glossary 321

Bibliography 329

Index 339

Introduction

This introduction is shared across the different volumes of this series on the development of *certifiable* software applications.

Developing a software application is a difficult process that requires teamwork. The complexity of software applications is ever increasing and the amount has grown from a few tens of thousands to a few million. In order to be able to manage this complexity, development teams are of significant importance. The involvement of development teams in a software application, the internationalization of companies for a better distribution of work teams (multisite companies, use of outsourcing, etc.) – all these factors combined make it difficult to manage the complexity of a software application.

The complexity of developing a software application is further intensified by the race to obsolescence. The obsolescence of the hardware components entails the implementation of specific strategies (saving equipment, repository of tool sources, etc.) and mastering reproducibility and maintainability of the software application.

Another challenge is the requirement to demonstrate the safety of a software application. The demonstration of safety relies on the development of specific techniques (diversity, redundancy, fault tolerance, etc.) and/or controlling defects in the software application.

Even though the relationships related to systems and hardware architectures are introduced in these volumes, only the software aspect shall be discussed in detail [BOU 09a].

This book series is a concrete presentation of the development of a critical software application. This approach is based on quality assurance as defined in ISO 9001 [ISO 08] and various industry standards such as DO 178 (aeronautics), IEC 61508 (programmable system), CENELEC 50128 (railway), ISO 26262 (automotive) and IEC 880 (nuclear). It must be noted that this book series is only a complement to other existing books such as the one written by Ian Sommerville [SOM 07].

Reader's guide

Volume 1 [BOU 16] is dedicated to the establishment of quality assurance and safety assurance. The concept of a software application and the relationship with the system approach are addressed here. This chapter, therefore, discusses the fundamentals including the management of requirements.

Volume 2 [BOU 17] describes the support processes, such as qualification tools, configuration management, verification and validation. Volume 2 is essential to understand what is necessary to develop a certifiable software application.

Volume 3 describes all the activities to be performed in the downward phase of the V cycle to produce a version of the software application. Activities such as specification, the establishment of an architecture and design of a software application are discussed here. This volume concludes with the presentation of production code of software application.

Volume 4 [BOU 19] discusses the ascending phase of the V cycle along with a description of various stages of testing (unit tests, modular tests, component testing, integration tests and testing of the entire software) and various other associated tests. All these activities lead to the production of a version of the software application.

Acknowledgments

This book is a compilation of all my work carried out with the manufacturers to implement systems that are safe and secure for people.

Realization of a Software Application

1.1. Introduction

It should be recalled that this book (Volume 3) follows the first two volumes [BOU 16, BOU 17]. In order to have an independent book, we will remember the key concepts and constraints of the implementation of a software application (see Definition 1.1).

DEFINITION 1.1 (Software Application).– *Set of programs, processes and rules and possibly the documentation relating to the operation of an information processing system.*

The implementation of a software application involves the definition of a strategy, which is to be formalized within a software quality assurance plan (SQAP). This implementation strategy must be considered within the context of system implementation.

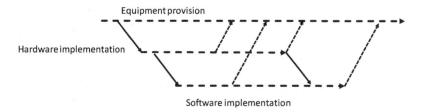

Figure 1.1. *Example of a dependency relationship between implementation processes*

1.2. Implementation process

In Volume 1 [BOU 16], we discussed the fact that a software application could be parametrized by means of data. There are thus two processes (see Figure 1.2) that have to be put in place for the implementation of a software application.

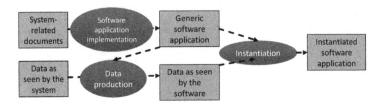

Figure 1.2. *Instantiated software application*

In Figure 1.2, the first process aims to implement the software application (for more details, see Figure 1.3), which is then said to be generic, and the second process is designed to perform the parametrization process.

The parametrization process is set up on the basis of the knowledge of the generic software application and the identification of the characteristics that may change during system operation.

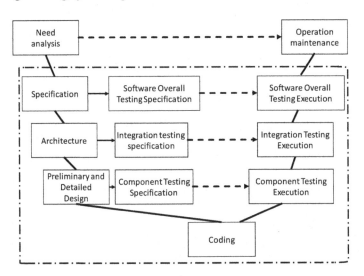

Figure 1.3. *V-model*

The implementation process of the software application may follow different cycles (waterfall, V-model, etc.) but as a general rule, it is the V-model (see Figure 1.3) that is chosen. It is worth noting that the V-model is not a monolithic cycle but a set of Vs in parallel where an iterative and/or incremental approach has to be taken into account (see Chapter 11 of Volume 2 [BOU 17]).

The parametrization process includes the implementation of parametrization means and the definition of the instantiation process of the generic software application for configuration. This process was discussed in Chapter 14 of Volume 2 [BOU 17].

1.3. Quality control

1.3.1. *Introduction*

The implementation process of a certifiable software application has to be formalized. To this end, a repository quality (quality management system) is first necessary within the company in which the processes being implemented are formalized through business processes (describing the means implemented and the method), models (describing the content of the different deliverables) and guides (which are generally necessary to explain the operation of a tool, the characteristics of the languages used, etc.). To learn more about quality assurance, see Volume 2 [BOU 17].

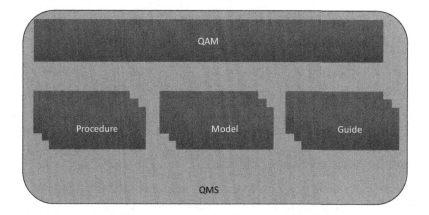

Figure 1.4. *The quality management system*

It is important to recall that in the context of software development, the minimum process to be implemented is the IOS 9001 through its specialization (International Organization for Standardization [ISO] 90003), and then a certain area proposes a standard, which is a superset of the ISO 9001 [ISO 15] + ISO 90003 [ISO 14]. In ISO 9126 [ISO 04], some main properties for software are presented and defined, such as maintainability, security and testability.

1.3.2. Software quality assurance plan

In order to build a software application, a SQAP has to be implemented. The quality of the software assurance plan defines the organization and the means that have to be implemented to design and develop the software application by specifying the role of each component involved.

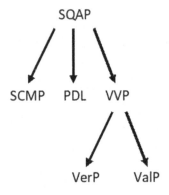

Figure 1.5. *Plan hierarchy*

The SQAP may be divided into several documents, as shown in Figure 1.5. The SQAP must also describe the management of changes and non-conformities that might appear during software production or operation.

Topics to be covered are as follows:

– Section 1: identification of standards and mandatory regulations. The purpose of this section is to identify the set of standards and regulations to be followed during software development. It is necessary to properly identify titles, references and versions of these documents. In this section, one can find the ISO 9001:2015 for quality control, depending on the International Electro-technical Commission (IEC) 61508:2010 standard, DO 178:C, ISO 26262 standard or the European Committee for Electro-technical Standardization (CENELEC) 50128:2011 standard, IEC 62279:2014, etc.

– Section 2: the project organization (software aspects), the demonstration of independences and the justification of skills (which may rely on a process local to the project and on the company's human resource management).

– Section 3: a presentation of the perimeter of the software to be built.

– Section 4: a presentation of quality mastery and control (metrics, control points, audit, etc.).

– Section 5: a presentation of the software delivery cycle (V-model, etc.) and of each phase. For each one, a subsection should describe input and output elements, the activities to be performed, human resources, the technical means (tools, testing environments, laboratories, etc.) as well as acceptance and control criteria of the end of phase.

– Section 6: a presentation of configuration management (tool, process, version identification, identification of the components to be managed, etc.). It will be necessary to explain how the software version data sheet is produced.

– Section 7: a presentation of anomalies, change requests and corrections management processes.

– Section 8: a presentation of the tools management process (identification, configuration management, etc.) and, more specifically, tools qualification management.

– Section 9: a list of the documents to be produced during software development is necessary.

– Section 10: compliance with the standards identified in Section 1 has to be demonstrated, and more specifically with business processes such as the IEC 61508 standard, the DO 178:C, the ISO 26262 or the CENELEC 50128 (or IEC 62279) standard. Compliance with this type of standard must not only be based on the tables in the appendices but on the entire standard. As a matter of fact, the body of the standard is normative, and a few topics are not covered by Appendices Tables of these standards. For example, in the 2001 version of the CENELEC 50128 standard [CEN 01], testing coverage is not addressed by an Appendix table but by a sentence in the body of the document. For the 2011 version of the CENELEC 50128 standard [CEN 11], it is the qualification of the tools that is not covered by an Appendix Table.

1.4. Conclusion

The purpose of this chapter was not to resume the entirety of the first two volumes but to provide concepts for understanding this book. Therefore, we have presented the implementation process of a software application by presenting the content of the SQAP.

2

Requirements Management

2.1. Introduction

In Chapter 10 of Volume 1 [BOU 16], we introduced the process of requirements management (for more information on requirements engineering, see also [BOU 14, HUL 05, POH 10]). The purpose of this chapter is to recall the essential concepts for understanding this book.

One has to bear in mind that requirements engineering is a central element for the implementation of applications known as critical. The general IEC 61508[1] standard [IEC 08] and business standards such as the CENELEC 50126, 50128 [CEN 01, CEN 11] and 50129, the DO 178 [DO 11] and the ISO 26262 [ISO 14] all recommend establishing requirements engineering.

Requirements engineering does not concern numbering portions of text but writing down and managing requirements. Requirements represent a need, a constraint and/or a goal to be reached (Definition 2.1). It is therefore necessary to properly formulate requirements.

DEFINITION 2.1 (Requirement).– *A requirement is a statement that reflects a need and/or constraints (techniques, costs, delays, etc.). This statement is written in a language that can be natural, mathematical, etc.*

---

1 It should be noted that the general standard introduces the notion of prescription instead of the notion of requirement.

2.2. Three key concepts

2.2.1. *Introduction*

Requirements engineering is an addition to systems engineering. It focuses on an essential concept in the implementation of systems engineering, i.e. need. Need can be equally linked to the process or to the product, as shown in Figure 2.1.

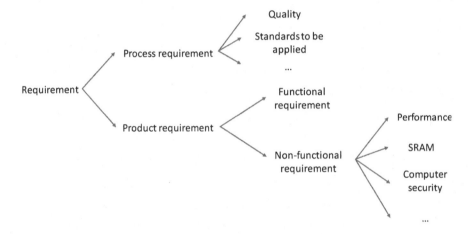

Figure 2.1. *Different families of requirements*

Need should be identified and traced until its conclusion (in the sense taken into account). To this end, it is important to formalize need (see Definition 2.1) and to define it for each design stage. This is then referred to as requirement. There are notions of customer requirement, design requirement, testing requirement, etc.

Since this need should be defined during each production stage and that its impact has to be shown, the need to implement *traceability* ought to be identified.

The last essential concept is a way to characterize a requirement. These are attributes. An attribute is a means to inform the user about priority, safety level, etc., and/or about the reasons that justify the requirement.

2.2.2. *Process requirement*

Table 2.1 illustrates the notion of process requirement. Process requirements must be covered by the project quality plans, such as the SQAP, SVVP, and SCMP.

Ref.	Description
REQ_1	The development of the software application must follow the DO 178 standard version C
REQ_2	The software application development should follow an ISO 9001-type process
REQ_3	The set of elements of the software application must be managed in the configuration

Table 2.1. *Examples of requirements*

Table 2.1 introduces an example of some requirements that may have an impact on the process.

2.2.3. *Requirement*

2.2.3.1. *Introduction*

Definition 2.1 defines the concept of requirement and Table 2.2 defines the basic attributes that characterize a requirement.

Attributes	Description
ID	Unique identifier
TEXT	Requirement text
SOURCE	Element that has enabled this requirement to be introduced

Table 2.2. *Examples of requirements*

2.2.3.2. *Identification*

A requirement must be uniquely identifiable; this is generally why an identifier is associated with each requirement. This identifier must be unique. In order not to confuse it with other items that can be numbered (list items, etc.), the identifier is built using a label (for example, EXI) and a unique number (xxxx). We then have an identifier of the form EXI_xxxx:

[EXI_0001]

It should be possible to update the software.

[PROJECT] AAAA

[DOCUMENT] DDD

A requirement is associated with a project and especially with a document. It is thus possible to have an identifier of the form EXI_AAAA_DDDD_xxxx with AAAA representing the project number, DDDD the reference of the document and xxxx the requirement number.

The management of the project reference and the documentary reference can now be integrated with the identifier or be seen as an attribute:

[EXI_AAAA_DDD_0001]

It should be possible to update the software.

In order to make the identifier unique, it is necessary not to reassign requirement numbers in case a requirement is suppressed. For the same reason, one should avoid putting in place a mechanism for automatic identification (such as the autonumbering function of the program Word).

Concerning the identification of a requirement, it can be difficult to detect the end of a requirement; this is why it proves useful to define an identification in the form of tags, see the following example:

[EXI_0002]

A software cycle must be executed in 100 ms.

[FIN_EXI]

2.2.3.3. *Some important features*

Before defining requirements, a set of criteria has to be put in place. These criteria should provide a means to qualify requirements. A literature review (scientific and/or normative) can enable us to identify criteria that relate to a requirement and others concerning a set of requirements.

For each requirement, the following criteria are most frequently encountered:

– atomic: the requirement is an identifiable element and cannot be broken down; it expresses a single fact;

– concise: when it is described in natural language, a requirement should be written in the form of a single sentence that does not exceed a few lines;

– clear: one reading of the requirement should be enough to understand it; the sentence structure is simple and does not make use of literary subtleties;

– precise: all the elements employed in the requirement are identifiable and completely characterized (no pending questions such as: what is the unit used?);

– abstract: a requirement is at the appropriate level of abstraction; it does not impose a solution (technical or functional) but only describes the need;

– unambiguous: reading the requirement must allow for understanding the need with only one possible interpretation; it is important not to use turns of phrase or words that can have several interpretations or that can make the requirement more difficult to understand;

– updated: the requirement reflects the current state of the system/its knowledge;

– comprehensive: all of the concepts used in the requirement have to be defined and no information must be missing;

– verifiable: there must be a possible (and reasonable) way to verify the requirement;

– consistent: it is necessary to verify that the requirement presents a consistent form (the terms used in the requirement are the same and have the same meaning);

– coherent: the requirement is not in conflict (the requirement does not state one thing and its opposite), employs consistent terminology and is coherent with the glossary;

– correct: it corresponds to a real need of one of the intervening actors (external coherence);

– traceable: it is necessary to trace the source, the development, the impact and the usage of the requirement.

Other criteria may be necessary, for example the fact that a requirement must be feasible, in other words, an implementation is possible according to cost, time and production constraints.

In the end, even if it is possible to add other criteria, those presented above already provide a good basis for building a methodology.

There are two main rules for understanding the requirements:

– make short sentences and short paragraphs (generally three lines);

– formulate one and only one requirement per sentence.

2.2.3.4. *Characterization of a set of requirements*

For a set of requirements, the main criteria concern consistency, completeness and non-redundancy.

A set of requirements must be:

– comprehensive: there is no missing requirement and all are complete. The completeness of the set of requirements is a difficult point, because it is linked to a comprehensive identification of needs. For example, it is usual to easily forget to describe the behavior of software in a specification during unwanted events (hardware failures, errors in the data entered by the user, etc.). In such situations, the developer is not responsible for inventing what the program will do during implementation. When identifying the requirements, it is necessary to verify that the requirements cover:

- all of the manipulated objects;

- all the states of manipulated objects;

- all usage conditions;

- all operation scenarios that have been considered;

- all applicable standards and occupational standards, etc.

The best way to evaluate the completeness of a set of requirements is to establish a document template;

– coherent: there is no ambiguity, no internal inconsistency in the list of requirements; there are no contradictions between requirements, there is a unique identification of the document. The consistency of a set of requirements concerns the proper definition of the concepts on all the requirements; in other words, every word has to be used in the same way for each requirement;

– non-redundant: it is important that there are no redundancies in all of the requirements, the same information and/or the same need must not appear more than once.

2.2.4. Attributes

From a process perspective, every requirement has to be:

– identifiable: each requirement has to be associated with a unique identifier (see the first attribute in Tables 2.2 and 2.3);

– verifiable: it is necessary to ensure that all requirements are verifiable. The verification can be a new reading, a model, a specific analysis and/or a test (see the fourth attribute in Table 2.3);

– adaptable: one must be able to manage changes to requirements throughout the lifecycle of the system (implementation, production, commissioning, maintenance, withdrawal); for this purpose, a configuration or version management process must be implemented (see the fifth attribute).

Attributes	Description
ID	Unique identifier
TEXT	Requirement text
SOURCE	Element that enabled this requirement to be introduced
VERIFICATION	Associated verification activity
VERSION	Version associated with the requirement

Table 2.3. *List of attributes characterizing a requirement*

Table 2.3 introduces a second identification of the attributes that describe a requirement. We will complete this description as we move forward through the chapter.

It is possible to complete this list of attributes with attributes allowing for the qualification of the requirement:

– family (functional, reliability, availability and maintainability (RAM)[2], safety, security, performance, etc.);

– requirement status: in progress, to be validated, approved, implemented, etc;

– priority (to be defined depending on the project);

– verifiable (yes/no);

– verification type (new reading, specific analysis, simulation, etc.);

– testable (yes/no);

– test type;

– source (who, when, etc.);

– status (to be processed, analyzed, rejected, etc.);

– document type;

– version;

– effort;

– allocation.

Attributes	Description	Values
ID	Unique identifier	EXI_AAAA_DDDD_xxxx
TEXT	Requirement text	
SOURCE	Element that enabled this requirement to be introduced	
FAMILY		FUNC, RAM, S[3], PERF
VERIFIABLE		Yes/No
VERIFICATION	Associated verification activity	design review/walkthrough computation unit tests integration tests ...
VERSION	Version associated with the requirement	xx.yy

Table 2.4. *List of attributes characterizing a requirement (supplement)*

2 RAM for reliability, availability and maintainability.
3 S for Safety

The definition of the attributes is to be done in the early stages of the project and it is necessary to define them properly (see Table 2.5).

Attribute name	Version
Attribute semantic	Version associated with the requirement
List of possible values	x.y
Value semantic	x is the major index y is the minor index
Unit	Without object

Table 2.5. *Definition of attribute*

2.2.5. *Allocation versus refinement*

The implementation of a product (in particular, a software application) is a process that is based on requirements. On the basis of need (which is expressed in the form of requirements), it is necessary that the requirements that characterize the product for every stage of the production cycle be defined.

Therefore, between every stage of the production cycle, traceability has to be implemented (see Definition 2.2 and the following section) as a means of demonstrating that nothing has been forgotten and that nothing has been added.

DEFINITION 2.2 (Traceability).– *Traceability consists of creating a link between two objects.*

Traceability makes it possible to manage the explicit links between the requirements of each stage. Within each stage, the requirements of the previous stage are specialized and/or implemented; this is referred to as requirement refinement.

Refinement consists of having an approach in which the level of detail is refined at every stage. A requirement can be refined through one or more requirements at the downstream level, and a requirement may refine one or more upstream level requirements. However, a requirement may be identical to an upstream level requirement: this is refinement that is referred to as direct allocation. The different types of traceability are presented in Figure 2.4. Section 5.4 of Chapter 5 will present the notion of refinement more formally.

DEFINITION 2.3 (Refinement Process).– *The process aims to shift from an abstract to a concrete level, and the requirements are broken down and specialized in order to transform the need for implementation.*

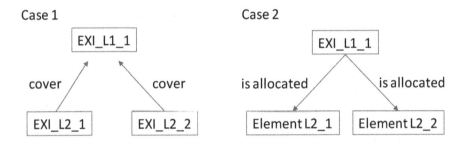

Figure 2.2. *Refinement versus allocation*

In many projects, as a result of misunderstanding requirements engineering, the refinement process is replaced by a process of allocation of the requirements.

Case 1 of Figure 2.2 shows an example of a process of requirements refinement; the requirement EXI_L1_1 is broken down into two requirements. While case 2 shows an example of the allocation process, in which a requirement is allocated onto different elements.

DEFINITION 2.4 (Allocation Process).– *The process aims to identify* a priori *the components of the product to be implemented that will assume the requirement.*

As indicated by Definition 2.4, the allocation process allows making an *a priori* link between a requirement and an element of the product. This link can be useful in the implementation process to direct production and to control complexity (and therefore the load).

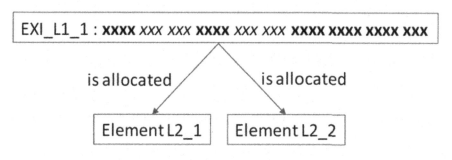

Figure 2.3. *Allocation. For a color version of this figure, see www.iste.co.uk/boulanger/applications3.zip*

Figure 2.3 shows an example of allocation; the bold part is allocated to element L2_1 and the red part to element L2_2. Given that this example is very simple, one can imagine the difficulty with a real project.

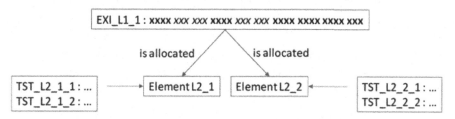

Figure 2.4. *Allocation and testing traceability. For a color version of this figure, see www.iste.co.uk/boulanger/applications3.zip*

Tools do not make it possible to address this type of issue (memorization of the allocated portions of text) but in addition it is necessary to be able to manage this information in the event of a change of requirement. For each element, it is necessary to implement traceability between the element tests and requirements, which will be quite difficult to achieve and maintain (see Figure 2.4).

2.2.6. *Traceability*

Traceability is the main tool used to manage requirements (see Definition 2.2). Traceability must be two-way, and one must be able to establish:

– vertical traceability: trace a requirement from its highest level to the lowest level; the aim is to show that regardless of the level, all requirements are related to a need;

– horizontal traceability: trace a requirement through the phases of the development and implementation process; the objective is to show that a requirement is met.

Figure 2.5 shows how a customer's recommendations can be defined onto the system and how the process can proceed until software and hardware types of elements. Within the context of the verification phase of level n_i, it has to be demonstrated that the requirements of this level are related to the above level n_{i-1}. This relationship is established through the implementation of a traceability action.

The implementation of traceability (see Definition 2.2) involves the definition of at least one link between two objects. As part of the requirements, traceability links must be able to show that a requirement of level n_i is related to a need of the previous level n_{i-1}. The reverse link is a means to show that no requirement has been forgotten during the implementation process.

Ideally, all information included in a requirement of an input document (referred to as upstream requirement) should be refined in at least one requirement of the current document (referred to as downstream requirement) except for requirements that should not be allocated to this document (for example a requirement related to the hardware will not be taken into account at the software level) and any information existing in a downstream requirement must be the refinement of information existing in an upstream requirement, except for information that is specific to the document level being considered (choice of programming language of the order of execution of certain actions for which no constraint is provided at the upstream level, etc.).

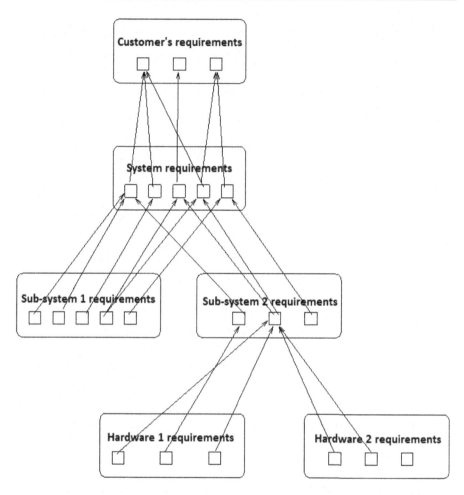

Figure 2.5. *Partial traceability between customer's
requirements and requirements related to the hardware*

As shown in Figure 2.6, there are several basic requirement
transformations. Among these, two cases are particularly interesting: adding
and relinquishing a requirement; in either case, one must definitely attach a
justification to the requirement.

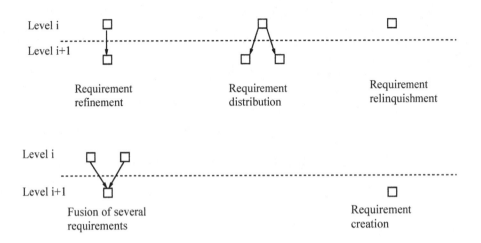

Figure 2.6. *Basic requirements traceability*

Traceability aims to define relationships between requirements. As shown in Figure 2.7, the basic link establishes a relationship between two requirements that belong to two different and consecutive levels.

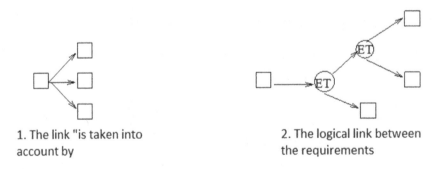

Figure 2.7. *Link between requirements*

The requirements are then associated with the functionality of the system, subsystem, equipment, software or hardware. A functionality is an expected behavior of the system, subsystem, equipment, software or hardware.

The term functionality is used because at the system level, there is not necessarily a service in the sense of function but rather a global service expected (which is the result of a range of actions). Naturally, this process will have to be derived onto subsystems, equipment, as well as into hardware and software aspects.

Figure 2.8 presents a traceability matrix that enables establishing the link between requirements and functions but also between requirements and derived requirements.

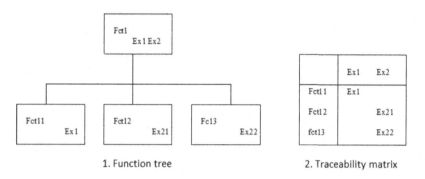

1. Function tree   2. Traceability matrix

Figure 2.8. *Requirements traceability matrix*

The left part of Figure 2.8 shows the functional relationship and the association of the requirements on both levels. Thus, function Fct1 is derived from three subfunctions. As shown in the right part of the figure, the requirement E2 has been broken down into two requirements (Ex21 and Ex22) that are associated with two subfunctions (Fct12 and Fct13) of the function Fct1.

2.3. Process

2.3.1. *Introduction*

Requirements are used to make the link between documents (specification documents, design documents, coding documents) but also as testing objectives. The different testing categories (unit, software–software integration, software–hardware integration, functional and acceptance) can be put in relation with the requirements based on the attribute "verification type". We thus obtain a requirements management process that establishes the link between the initial needs, the choices made during implementation and validation phases (see Figure 2.9).

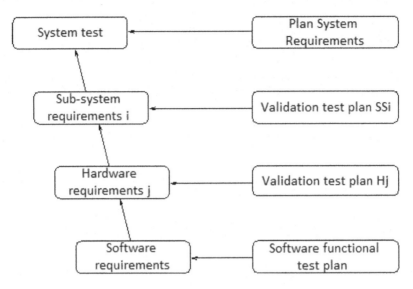

Figure 2.9. *Links between activities*

The verification phase consists of verifying the coverage of the requirements and the consistency of the links that have been put in place. From a project perspective, the coverage of requirements management allows the quantification of the work achieved and the remaining work to do.

Control of requirements management development and the analysis of impacts on linked requirements and products are the key points of requirements engineering. It should be indicated that the real difficulty of requirements engineering is development control.

As a summary, we can mention that requirements management requires the implementation of simple mechanisms such as:

– the introduction of identifiers management;

– the description of requirements;

– the definition of the traceability table.

2.3.2. *Two approaches*

Requirements management is currently implemented based on two approaches; the first is database-centric (section 2.3.2.1) and the second is document-centric (section 2.3.2.2).

2.3.2.1. *Database-centric approach*

The first approach, known as database-centric, involves gathering all of the requirements (and associated elements) within a database and establishing the set of all the links within this database.

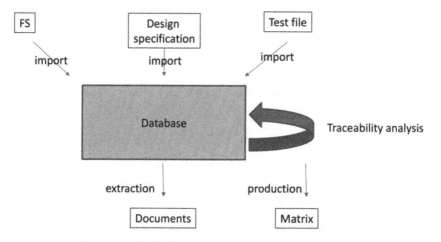

Figure 2.10. *Database-centric approach*

The implementation of this approach requires the import all of the elements (documents, models, source files, test scenarios, test results, etc.) into this database. It will be then possible to produce traceability matrices and to examine any links between requirements (impact analysis, management changes, etc.).

Centralization within a database is a disadvantage for several reasons:

– the size of the database depends on the size of processed documents;

– in the event of any changes in the source document, it has to be imported again into the database; and it is however generally quite difficult to automate the reintegration of information related to the requirements.

2.3.2.2. Document-centric approach

The second approach, known as document-centric, involves introducing information within documents concerning the links between objects (documents, models, source files, test scenarios, test results, etc.). This information consists of tags, attributes and links.

The implementation of this approach requires that it will be possible to add information and to capture it by means of queries.

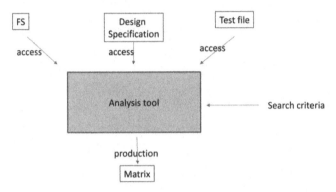

Figure 2.11. *Document-centric approach*

This approach has the advantage of not changing the process put in place for implementing the project and instead merely appends to the documents.

2.3.3. Implementation of tools

In [STA 01], the authors mention that implementing an environment for requirements management is the best way to manage a strong impact on the success of a project. The definition of a minimum set of requirements makes it possible to have a base that can be managed, the tool then being a vehicle for communication between teams.

A tool such as a text editor[4] (table, identifier management, link between documents, etc.) should thus be enough to process one or several documents.

---

4 As part of the double validation established by the RATP for the SAET-METEOR that operates on line 14 of the Paris metro, by means of the text processor INTERLEAF, it has been possible to define and manage the set of requirements (of the system up to the three software programs written with the formal language called B-method).

In the context of complex systems, the number of documents and the number of steps (see Figure 2.9) involve establishing a requirements management process that will be based on tooling.

However, it is absolutely necessary that a requirements management process be associated with this equipment.

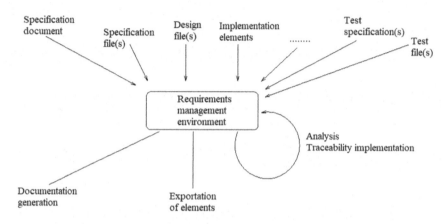

Figure 2.12. *Outline of a requirements management environment*

Choveau and de Chazelles [CHO 01] present the approach known as CARE (Common Airbus Requirements Engineering) that has been designed to enable the development of the Airbus A380 airliner. This approach is rooted in the definition of a comprehensive methodology, which originates in the standard EIA632 [IBD 98], which is also equipped.

Requirements engineering is supported by tools that enable the acquisition of requirements, the implementation of traceability, reporting and documentation generation. This list contains, for example, DOORS (distributed by the IBM company), RTM (Integrated Chipware Inc.) and Requisite Pro from Rational or Reqtify (DASSAULT's tool is dedicated to traceability aspects). One of the difficulties of the implementation of the tools lies in the ability to integrate them within the existing business processes of the company.

2.4. Conclusion

Requirements engineering is a process on its own, which is why it is essential to produce a requirements management plan that will aim to describe:

– the organization put in place to manage the requirements of the project during every stage (from the acquisition phase of the need to the withdrawal phase);

– the notion of requirements: syntax, notation principle, list of attributes, etc.;

– the means implemented to manage requirements: tools and processes;

– management and document production principles;

– the management process of changes (identification of changes, impact analysis, non-regression analysis).

During the formulation of requirements, it is important to be very careful with the properties that we have introduced in sections 2.2.2.2 and 2.2.2.3. Moreover, the primary stumbling blocks of requirements management are incompleteness and inconsistency. It is not always possible to automatically verify this kind of property.

In order to facilitate the verification, it may be useful to implement requirement templates.

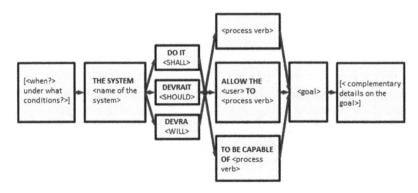

Figure 2.13. *Example of a template for requirement formulation*[5]

---

5 Source translated from [POH 10].

The formulation template is an effective tool for drafting a requirement. Using a requirement template will help prevent common mistakes during the outlining of requirements in natural language.

The template is an excellent teaching tool, particularly effective during the learning phase. It is a guide for the syntactic structure of a unit requirement and is well suited to drafting the functional requirements. An example of a template is shown in Figure 2.13.

By combining the glossary and the drafting template, we will be able to reduce the ambiguities introduced by natural language.

3

Documentation Structure

3.1. Introduction

As indicated in Chapter 1 concerning the implementation of a software application, an implementation process has to be defined that is based on a development cycle (waterfall, V-cycle, etc.) and that will enable the software application to be produced. Although the final product is one (or more) executable(s), a large number of elements produced are part of the documentation but also contain source files, test scenarios, test results and other software analysis results. The purpose of this chapter is to review these elements of documentation.

3.2. Documentation

3.2.1. *Introduction*

The certification of a system is based on items of evidence that are made available to the people in charge of the evaluation. These items of evidence are formalized by means of records (log files, test files, test results, specific analysis, etc.) and documents (specifications, architecture and design documents, version sheets, etc.).

The notion of a document requires a sufficient level of formalization and a model (or template).

3.2.2. *Formalization of documents*

The model template for documents must contain certain essential sections such as:

– a description of the document;

– a table of contents;

– a table of changes;

– a section describing the strategy implemented to manage changes in the document;

– a list of documents on input (list of applicable documents and reference documents);

– a list of acronyms and terms used in the document. This list may rely on a company glossary or a project glossary. The glossary is an important inclusion; it helps ensure the use of a common and uniform vocabulary that will prevent errors. One common error in projects is related to vocabulary ("same word, different meaning").

The cover page of the document should contain information such as the title, the reference and the version, but also information about the author, the reviewer(s) and the approver.

On each page of the document, the following information should be present:

– the reference;

– the version;

– the current page number over the number of total pages.

3.2.3. *Signature and acceptance*

There must be a process of acceptance for documents. This acceptance process is based on the verification process, but it must be completed with formalization of the acceptance by the author, reviewer(s) and approver.

The approver has the responsibility to provide means to the reviewers and to the author for the drafting. The reviewer's acceptance means that the document has been verified and that it is considered as being correct.

The formalization of acceptances can be achieved through different mechanisms:

– a paper signature: accompanied by an electronic version that will be easier to manage in time than in paper form;

– an electronic signature: accompanied by a process that ought to ensure that a previous electronic signature will not be reused for a following version (consider the example of the cross placed on the front page which will still remain visible during the preparation of the following version);

– acceptance by mail: it is possible to manage immaterial acceptance but a process has to be defined to record the evidence of this acceptance;

– all other combination where approval is recorded.

3.3. Quality control

3.3.1. *The company's quality process*

As it has been mentioned, the implementation of a software application with virtually no flaws involves a quality control stage. To this end, a quality methodological repository must be implemented based on standards such as the ISO 9001 [ISO 15], the Capability Maturity Model for Integration (CMMI[1]) or Software Process Improvement and Capability Determination (SPICE, see [ISO 04a]).

In this series of books, the working basis that we will assume is the ISO 9001 standard (version 2008 or 2015), which will be supplemented with the ISO 90003 [ISO 14] standard that takes into account the specificities of software applications.

As shown in Figure 3.1, the quality standard of a company is based on culture, objectives and standards. This standard consists of, at least, a Quality Assurance Manual (QAM) and a set of methodological documents (models, guides, manuals and procedures) to be applied to projects carried out by the company.

1 The CMMI is a maturity model dedicated to the software industry that includes a set of best practices to be implemented in development projects. For more information, see the website of the Software Engineering Institute: www.sei.cmu.edu/cmmi.

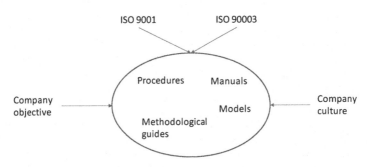

Figure 3.1. *Quality standard*

One of the important points concerns the existence of a set of models that make it possible to align the methodology implemented in projects. It is always difficult to start from scratch.

The benefit of quality assurance is to ensure a regular application of the same process, which should enable an increase in quality of the work. Furthermore, knowledge of rules and their applications can contribute to improving the quality of the work done. To have rules does not mean that it is not possible to adapt the process but if the adaptation is beneficial, it deserves to be reintroduced within the quality standard.

Concerning standards related to quality, we tended to use more dedicated versions, for example:

– International Railway Industry Standard (IRIS[2]): a combination of ISO 9001 [ISO 15] and CENELEC 50126 [CEN 00], 50129 [CEN 03] and 50128 [CEN 11] dedicated to railways;

– A-SPICE [VDA 17]: a dedicated version of the SPICE standard [ISO 04a] for the automotive domain.

3.3.2. *Project quality control*

The quality control applied to the implementation of a software application involves the production of a software quality assurance plan (SQAP). This SQAP is intended to derive the quality control process of the company onto this development.

---

2 IRIS is the International Railway Industry Standard. For more information, see http://www.iris-rail.org.

An SQAP can be:

– a generic document applicable to any software application development or can be restricted to a product family;

– a generic document that will be supplemented by a specific document explaining the peculiarities of the project;

– a specific document applicable to a particular project.

Figure 3.2. *Plan organization*

In section 1.3.2, we have presented the structure and typical content of an SQAP. As shown in Figure 3.2, the SQAP is in general based on other plans for managing configuration management, development, and verification and validation (V&V).

These plans (software development plan [SDP], software configuration management plan [SCMP], software verification and validation plan [SVVP]) are the responsibility of other teams that have to maintain an independent position as does, for example, the V&V team.

The SDP describes the implementation process of the software application. It should describe

– the organization: organizational setup for the development of the software and list of functions (name of the function, responsibility and required skills);

– human resources: who is in charge and a demonstration that required skills are assumed (training, competencies, experiences, etc.);

– hardware resources: lists of tools and a demonstration that the tools are adequate (qualification see Chapter 13 of Volume 2 [BOU 17]);

– activities to be performed: for each activity, the elements on input, the functions involved, the actions to be implemented and the elements on output have to be described.

Configuration management was presented in Chapter 7 of Volume 2 [BOU 17]. The SCMP will be introduced in section 3.5.

As feedback, we have noticed that in many projects (see section 3.2.2), at the beginning of each document there is a list of reference documents and of applicable documents and that in general their versions are established. Generally, applicable documents such as standards and contracts do not change, but reference documents such as plans are subject to changes during the whole duration of the project, and this leads to changing a lot of documents without any real impact.

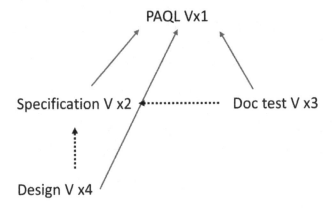

Figure 3.3. *Referencing links*

Figure 3.3 shows that documents such as plans are referenced in several documents of the project. In the event of a change in the version of a plan, it is necessary to update all the documentation of the project. Figure 3.3 brings forward two types of link. The solid arrows represent links to general documents, therefore changes can have no effect on the document; the dotted arrows represent links to documents characterizing the activity to be performed, and so a change requires updating the document.

Project:	Version:	
Doc name	Doc reference	Doc version
Software quality assurance plan	1234	A1

Software verification and validation plan	1235	A2
....		
Software release note	2000	A3
PDL status:		

Table 3.1. *PDL example*

In most projects, a new document can be seen to emerge that is the project documentation list (PDL). The objective of the PDL is to identify (by title and reference) all documents to be produced and their status. The PDL is a means to have a document that is the reference of the project and subsequently any change to a document will be reported in the PDL along with an analysis of the actions to be taken on all related documents.

The SVVP must describe all of the V&V activities implemented as part of the development of the software application.

Chapter 11 of Volume 2 [BOU 17] introduces the verification process to be implemented (Volume 4 [BOU 19] presents more specifically the various verification techniques and their implementation). The SVVP must define the organizational setup and the activities to be carried out. There are several types of activities of the V&V team:

– verification by means of a new reading of all the documents produced;

– verification by analysis (verification of programming rules, verification of metrics, testing code coverage verification, etc.) of generated elements;

– verification through specification and test execution.

3.4. Implementation process

Figure 3.4 is a representation of the implementation process in the form of a V-model. This V-model generates a number of documents that will have to be produced in the context of the software application implementation.

Moving down through the V–model, design documents can be seen to emerge, such as the software requirement specification (SwRS), the software architecture document (SAD), the software design document (SDD), and the code.

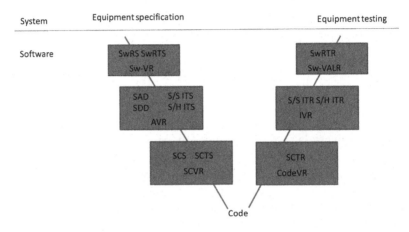

Figure 3.4. *V-model for the implementation of a software application*

Each design document is associated with a testing specification document (SRTS, software/software integration testing specification [S/S ITS], software/hardware integration testing specification [S/H ITS] and software component testing specification [SCTS]) and each phase is completed by a verification activity formalized through a verification report (Sw-RSVR, Sw-ADVR and SwCVR).

3.5. Configuration management

The implementation of an application known as certifiable requires the production of a number of proofs of different natures; this is the reason that configuration management is essential.

The SCMP allows identifying the management process of the configuration management of all elements necessary for the production of the software application.

Chapter 7 of Volume 2 [BOU 17] introduces the basic principles of configuration management. These are several types of elements and may require different configuration managements. Within these elements, we can identify

– tools: support media management (CD, DVD, etc.), self-extracting executable management, downloads versioning management, etc.;

– documents: native document (Word, Excel, text–only, etc.) and PDF versions (signed document, signed cover page, etc.);

– sources and all other files needed for the generation of the executable;

– the archives produced by development environments that manage their workspace (see, for example, the tools associated with programmable logic controllers).

Tools are a big challenge; they provide the means to ensure that the same tool can be executed in the future with a different computer, a different operating system version, etc. Furthermore, software virtualization is an opportunity that can be of great assistance.

3.6. Defect and non-conformity management

3.6.1. *Presentation*

Within the framework of dependability (D), a fault is the existing element that, if activated, can result in failure. In the software world, this is referred to as a software error or *bug*. One of the only certainties about software application is that they contain an unquantifiable number of defects. Software defects are constant; they are part of the software world.

One of the main reasons behind the ongoing development of a software application is defect correction. As a matter of fact, it is possible to develop the behavior of the software application following client's requests (adding functionality, addition of a message, etc.) but the primary cause behind change remains the correction of defects in order to obtain a behavior that meets its specification.

3.6.2. *Defect formalization*

At the time of implementing a software application – and particularly during V&V activities – abnormalities can be detected. Each anomaly should be formalized. Table 3.2 describes the content of an anomaly sheet.

Id_anomaly		Date opened:
Title:		
Anomaly description:		
Attachments:		
Person in charge of the analysis	Priority:	Status: Open/Postponed
Anomaly analysis:		
Attachments:		
Person in charge of the verification	Date:	Status: Analyzed
Elements related to the verification:		
Attachments:		
Person in charge of closure	Date	Status: Verified
Elements related to closure:		
Closure date:		Status: Closed

Table 3.2. *Description of an anomaly*

3.6.3. *Impact of changes*

The defect management cycle consists of several phases: identification, analysis of their effects (impact on safety and/or reliability of the software application), selection of anomalies to be corrected, anomaly analysis, implementation of corrections and verification of corrections (in general, the verification of the correct implementation of changes involves a series of tests, but it will be necessary to verify that no additional change has been implemented). Figure 3.5 shows the analysis process of a defect.

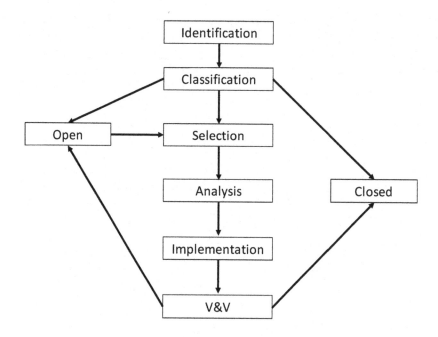

Figure 3.5. *V-model for the implementation of a software application*

Change analysis (correction of anomalies, change management) is achieved through impact analysis (Definition 3.1) and non-regression analysis (Definition 3.2). In some cases, non-regression is said to be comprehensive, and thus, it is then important to rerun the set of all tests of one or all the phases. The objective of non-regression analysis is to minimize the cost of a new version.

DEFINITION 3.1 (Impact Analysis).– *The impact analysis of an anomaly consists of identifying the changes to be made during the descending phase (impact on documents, impact on code, impact on the description and on the implementation of tests) of the implementation.*

DEFINITION 3.2 (Non-regression Analysis).– *Non-regression analysis is intended to determine a set of tests capable of demonstrating that the change that was carried out has no effect on the rest of the software application*[3].

---

3 It is worth noting that non-regression analysis can be performed on the software application or on a more significant element such as hardware, a subsystem and/or a system.

As shown in Figure 3.6, it is possible to achieve the impact analysis based on the modified requirements. To this end, one extracts the cone originating in the modified requirement and going toward the code; this code makes it possible to identify the requirements of the lower levels that are potentially affected by the change, and the associated test cases.

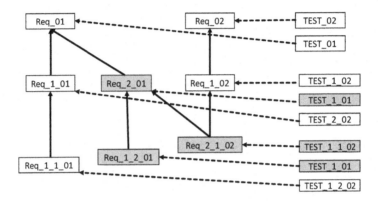

Figure 3.6. *Impact analysis*

The second analysis (see Figure 3.7) consists of carrying out the non-regression analysis. The non-regression analysis involves building a cone that starts from the modified requirement and moves up to the requirements of the input specification. At the base of the requirement cone, the regression tests to be re-executed can be selected to show that the change has no impact on the needs of the system.

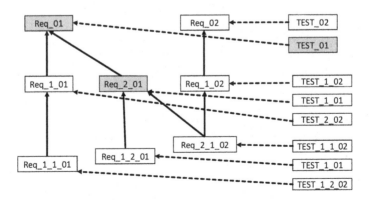

Figure 3.7. *Non-regression analysis*

3.7. Conclusion

The purpose of this chapter is to present quality elements necessary to the implementation of a software application while focusing on a particular aspect, which is required to produce documents and maintain them throughout the implementation of the software application.

There is often a lack of understanding concerning the need for documentation. The documentation of a project has two major objectives:

– facilitating the development of future, similar applications if necessary;

– the possibility of maintaining it for a rather long period of time (from 15 to 50 years)[4].

It is therefore important to generate documentation of the best quality. Since documentation is seen as a constraint, there is a temptation to do two things:

– to combine several documents into a single one;

– to automatically generate the documentation (for example through information extraction from the code).

In both cases, the documentation will become increasingly complex and this will have an impact on the maintenance of the software application.

Another significant topic of documentation management is the need to ensure requirement traceability (implementation of requirement-based management throughout the lifecycle) as well as documentation traceability (list of input documents).

---

4 In the automotive sector, a car is produced for 15 years and European regulation requires for 15 years of maintenance. This totals 30 years for the automotive industry. In the nuclear sector, the American authority requires 50 to 80 years.

Requirements Specification of a Software Application

4.1. Introduction

In this chapter, we are going to clarify what a specification is and what the underlying difficulties in establishing a good specification are. The specification of a system, subsystem, equipment and/or a software application describes what is expected of the element to be implemented in terms of the *services* and *conditions* under which they are provided. In the following, we will focus on the implementation of a specification of a software application even if several aspects and/or concepts are applicable to any type of specification.

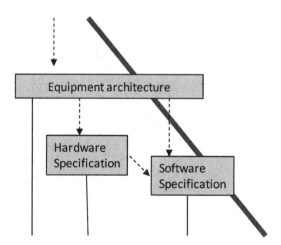

Figure 4.1. *Input of the requirements specification of a software application*

As shown in Figure 4.1, the specification of a software application takes on input elements such as the architecture of the system, the hardware specification and the specification of the external interfaces.

DEFINITION 4.1 (Interface).– *An interface is a device that allows for exchanges and interactions between different parts of the product.*

The notion of an interface is important for the system implementation (see Meinadier [MEI 02]). At the specification document level, interfaces are called external because they make it possible to describe the exchanges of the system with its environment. During the decomposition of the system into subsystems and equipment, the so-called internal interfaces are introduced that can define the exchanges and interactions between the various components of the system. The interfaces can be of different types (mechanical, electrical, pneumatic, etc.).

As soon as the software level is reached, interfaces are either physical (point of exchange between software and hardware) or logical (point of exchange between 2 software components).

4.2. Requirements management

4.2.1. *Presentation*

In order to implement a software application that is consistent with the need stated by the customer, one should describe what the software application must satisfy through a so-called *prescriptive* model. These models can be described in the form of requirements [HUL 05, POH 10, BOU 14].

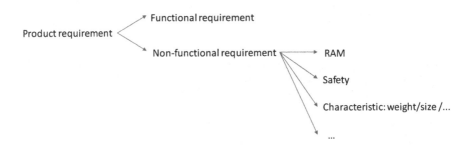

Figure 4.2. *Different types of product requirement*

As shown in Figure 4.2, it is possible to split the requirement set into a functional requirement set (what should the system do) and a non-functional requirement set (safety, reliability, performance, etc.).

Label	Description of user's requirement
REQ_1	The final product should cost less than 100 euros each
REQ_2	The software is classified SSIL2
REQ_3	The C code of the software must respect the MISRA C: 2012 standard

Table 4.1. *Example of a process requirement*

Within the framework of systems based on software with no dependability constraint, services characterize the reactions of the system according to the demands of the environment. In the context of systems subject to safety requirements (safety and/or confidentiality), the specification must clearly identify what must not happen. For this purpose, it must describe safe states[1] and/or confidential information, etc.

4.2.2. *Requirements manager*

As indicated in Chapter 4 of Volume 2 [BOU 17], the activities related to the software requirements specification are carried out by the requirements manager (which we will refer to as RQM for ReQuirement Manager). The RQM is part of the design team. Table 4.2 specifies responsibilities and the main skills of the RQM.

Role: Requirements manager: RQM

Responsibilities are as follows:
    – responsible for specifying the requirements related to the software;
    – owner of the software requirements specification;
    – establish and maintain traceability to and from system level requirements;
    – ensure that the requirements related to the specifications and software are taken into account in change and configuration management, including the status, version and approval status;

---

1 In this series, we focus on safety aspects, but we will be able to extend safety aspects to security-confidentiality/integrity.

– ensure consistency and completeness in the software requirements specification (with reference to the user's requirements and the final application environment); – develop and maintain the requirements documents relative to the software.

Main skills are as follows:
    – proficient in requirements engineering;
    – experienced in the scope of application;
    – holds experience of safety criteria in the application scope;
    – understands the overall role of the system and the application environment;
    – understands the analytical techniques and their results;
    – understands the applicable regulations;
    – understands the requirements domain standards[2] applicable to the project and/or the company.

Table 4.2. *Requirements manager[3]*

4.3. Specification know-how

As shown in all the studies, one of the most sensitive phases of designing a software application, but also of a complex system, consists of writing the specification.

This phase is an acquisition phase of need but it is also a phase for verifying that the need is attainable/feasible.

When writing a specification, there are several difficulties that should be avoided such as:

– *overspecification*: when writing a specification, only the need stated should be considered and it is important to avoid completing the description or embellishing it with complementary needs;

– *underspecification*: the specification must include the set of needs identified in the previous step (drafting of specifications, acquisition phase, etc.). Each item in the specification must be detailed;

---

2 ISO 26262, CENELEC EN 50128, DO 178, IEC 61508, etc.
3 This description of the role of the RQM is extracted from the CENELEC 50128 :2011 [CEN 11] standard.

– *inconsistency*: the specification document can be of variable size; it is necessary to verify that all the elements are consistent with one another;

– *incompleteness*: the specification must describe all the needs, and all the information necessary for understanding must be presented or referenced;

– *providing a solution*: a specification should focus on the need and introducing hints of a solution must absolutely be avoided.

This first series of pitfalls could be further augmented, but it seems preferable to define criteria allowing us to characterize good specifications:

– *clarity*: specifications should be unambiguous. This means that all individuals involved in the project must be able to have the same understanding of the requirements;

– *correction*: this means that, like any element participating in the implementation of the system, specifications should be verified and validated. This process should take change management into account;

– *completeness*: incomplete specifications are at the basis of a large number of accidents. A specification will be complete if the reader is able to distinguish between acceptable and unacceptable behavior;

– *concision*: the specifications should only contain what is necessary. It is absolutely necessary that one focuses on the *what* and that any proposal of a solution (*how*) be avoided;

– *feasible*: we have to show that we are capable of implementing this specification. To demonstrate feasibility, the software requirements testing specification has to be prepared at the earliest stage possible. If a software application is testable, it is thus implementable;

– *testability*: this is essential and it must be planned for. To this end, the software application has to be observable. Observability is a property that guarantees access to essential data for understanding the behavior of the software application. It is therefore necessary to identify at the earliest stage possible data and means of accessing these data. The access to data introduces the need to put in place data encapsulation as a programming rule.

A specification that meets the previous criteria will enable proper communication between those involved in the project. However, as we have mentioned before, we can see the notion of good and bad behavior emerge.

These behaviors are directly related to the expression (safety requirement) and to the taking into account of the risks[4] and mitigations associated with the specification.

Regarding the railway sector, the CENELEC EN 50128 [CEN 01, CEN 11] standard refers to the *software requirements specification* and not to the *software needs specification*. The expected requirements concern: functionality (including scaling and the expected performance), reliability, maintainability, safety, effectiveness, usability and portability (see the ISO 9126 [ISO 04] standard).

Standards require the production of a software specification in the form of a set of requirements. Vertical and horizontal traceabilities underlie the notion of requirement and are in fact recommended in the railway standard [CEN 01, CEN 11] but also in standards such as the IEC 61508 [IEC 08], the ISO 26262 [ISO 11] and the DO-178 [ARI 92, RTC 11].

4.4. Quality characteristics of a software product

The ISO 9126 [ISO 04] standard, "Software engineering: product quality", defines and describes a series of quality characteristics of a software product (internal and external characteristics, usage characteristics). These characteristics can be used to specify customers and users's functional and non-functional requirements.

The characteristics identified by the ISO/IEC 9126 [ISO 04] are as follows:

– *Functional capability*: is the software satisfying the expressed functional needs?

This property is essential and will be verified during the V&V stage that will be implemented.

---

4 As indicated in Chapter 3 of Volume 1 [BOU 16], at the system level, several risk analyses are implemented in order to study the risks and the impact of failures on the system. These studies are inputs for the implementation of the software application.

– *Reliability*: does the software maintain its service level under specific conditions and for a determined period?

For so-called critical software applications, the notion of reliability is related to the ability to detect errors and to ensure safe behavior in the event of an error (for example, by shifting to a safe state).

– *Usability*: does the software require little effort during utilization?

Under the framework of so-called safety software applications which should be certifiable, this notion does not make any sense. This is due to the fact that the object is usually of an embedded software application (within a more or less complex system) and that there is very little direct access to the functions of the software on the part of an operator. This notion of usability is more relevant for so-called offline maintenance tools and control applications.

– *Efficiency*: does the software require cost-effective and proportional scaling of the hosting platform in light of the other requirements?

With regard to so-called safety software applications that should be certifiable, this notion is related to the notion of performance requirement. Performance requirements allow us to characterize, at least, the software application memory footprint and the CPU load.

– *Maintainability*: does the software require little effort during its development with respect to the new needs?

Software maintainability is quite complex to be characterized, but in all of the standards, concepts such as modularity, abstraction, encapsulation and/or complexity control can be identified. These concepts are designed to limit the impact of a change on the overall software application.

– *Portability*: can the software be transferred from one platform or environment to another?

With regard to the so-called safety software applications which should be certifiable, portability is replaced by the notion of *low adherence*. Definition 4.2 serves as a reminder that a software application is never independent of the runtime environment (hardware and software).

DEFINITION 4.2 (Adherence of a Software Component).– *The adherence of an element of a software application is defined by the list of components of the software application and/or of the environment of this software application (hardware, driver, etc.), which are necessary for the execution of this component.*

Adherence is a means to characterize the impact of changes in the runtime system on the software application. For example, an application may be designed for a processor of the INTEL or AMD type. It is possible to have an application running on 16 bits, 32 bits or 64 bits. The application can be dependent on the numbers or addressing memory representation, etc.

Adherence may take values as very low, low, strong and very strong. Very low guarantees that little impact is ensured in case of change of the hardware and very strong indicates the need to revalidate the software application in the event of development of the runtime platform.

The notion of adherence will be resumed in the following section.

4.5. Objectives of the software requirements specification phase

Figure 4.3 illustrates the repositioning of the software requirements specification in its context. The software requirements specification stage can start once the hardware architecture has been identified.

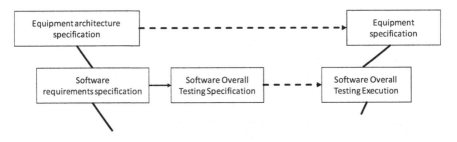

Figure 4.3. *Positioning of the specification stage*

To be a little more specific, we can say that the software requirements specification stage starts once the requirements of the upper level have been distributed onto a hardware architecture. This notion of distribution is interesting and means that at the system architecture level, an allocation process is to be implemented.

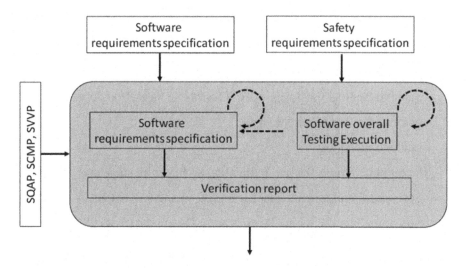

Figure 4.4. *Software application specification stage*

Figure 4.4 is a synthesis of the specification stage of a software application. It allows the identification of elements incoming and exiting the stage.

For the software application specification stage, the inputs are:

– Plans:

- Software Quality Assurance Plan (SQAP);

- Software Verification and Validation Plan (SVVP).

– Project documents:

- System Requirements Specification Document[5] (SyRS);

- System Architecture Description Document (SyAD);

- safety requirements list[6];

---

5 Based on the architecture of the product, a system can be replaced by a subsystem, hardware or product.
6 Safety requirements can be included in the SyRS but in many cases, they are found in the safety team document.

- project glossary[7] (GL).

– Methodological guides:

- guide to writing a software specification document;

- guide to writing a software overall testing specification document;

- guide to writing requirements;

- guide to modeling.

– The outputs of the software application architecture stage are:

- Software Requirements Specification Document (SwRS);

- Software Overall Testing Specification Document (SwOTS);

- project glossary[8] (GL);

- verification report (SS_VR).

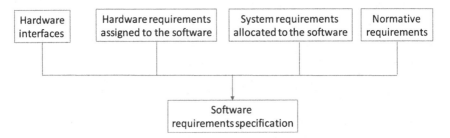

Figure 4.5. *Software application specification inputs*

In the case of the implementation of a complex system, on input of the specification phase of a software application (see Figure 4.5), we will find:

---

7 Making a glossary available for the project and/or the company is a strong point that should not be overlooked. Requirements engineering introduces the notion of common vocabulary. This common vocabulary allows avoiding misunderstandings and errors. The glossary is an essential part of good project management.

8 The project glossary is to be updated throughout the implementation of the software application, since new concepts may appear at every level.

– a system specification(SyRS)[9]: it must identify

- the set of needs that the system must meet through requirement (functional and non-functional) and operational scenarios;

- the set of elements interfacing with the system;

– a system architecture (SyAD): it must enable the identification of the separation between hardware architecture and software application. The general safety principles of the hardware architecture must be identified as well as the impacts on the software application. The system architecture must identify all of the software in interaction as well as interfaces between software and hardware components;

– a hardware architecture specification: based on the architecture, the hardware architecture specification must describe the architecture principles, the effective safety principles, the interfaces and usage constraints;

– a safety study set: the system specification and the system architecture analysis must make it possible to do some safety studies (FTA, FMEA, etc.) and to identify safety requirements that the various components (hardware and software) have to follow. The hardware architecture analysis should identify the safety constraints that the software application must meet so that every component complies with those safety requirements. In general, during this phase, we introduce the concept of safety. The concept of safety means the safety principle that guarantees that safety is achieved.

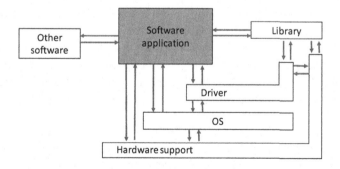

Figure 4.6. *Dependency between the software application and the hardware platform*

---

9 In this book, it will be considered that the system is reduced to a hardware architecture along with a software application, but according to the type of decomposition, it is possible to have a system, subsystem or hardware.

The software application requires a hardware platform for its execution (see Figure 4.6). This is the reason why one has to be able to identify the boundaries of the software application in the implementation input elements. These boundaries are characterized by physical interfaces (data exchange with the hardware) and interfaces which are of two types of logic interfaces (data exchange between software).

NOTE.– During the implementation of a software application, one might easily think that it is possible to create an application that is independent of the hardware platform. In order for a software application to be executable on a different runtime environment, it is necessary to have low adherence between the software and the hardware (see Definition 4.2).

The implementation of a software application ought to take into account the characteristics of the hardware architecture (hardware, operating system, driver, firmware, middleware, etc.), which will constitute the platform.

At the very least, adhesion concerns the hardware platform (processor, memory and bus). This adhesion means that if these elements change there will be an impact on the behavior of the software application. This impact can be related to the execution time, to the depth of the stack being used or simply to the functionality (instruction with different behaviors). However, the minimal impact will have effects on the system.

For example, consider a hardware architecture that contains two boards (a main motherboard and a communication board). A memory change on the communication board causes a small delay that does not affect the results of the software application. During the hardware boot-up time, the motherboard is master and waits for the communication board to complete its start-up, but as it takes a little bit more time, the watchdog is triggered and the hardware shifts into a safe state; this is of course in a systematic way.

AUTOSAR[10] and the IMA[11] [RAH 08] are attempts to propose a solution aiming to obtain low adhesion. These are two architectures whose objective is the development of software applications independently of the hardware platform. This low adhesion involves the definition of abstraction layer and a demonstration of conformity of the hardware components.

---

10 AUTOSAR for AUTomotive Open System ARchitecture. For more information see https://www.autosar.org/.
11 IMA for Integrated Modular Avionics.

When the system is safety critical, it is necessary to define the concept of safety at the hardware level. The concept of safety describes the mechanisms put in place to achieve a safety goal.

The concept of safety (see works by Boulanger [BOU 09a, BOU 11c] for more information) can be based on:

– a redundant architecture (2oo2[12], 2oo3, NooM) with or without diversity and with or without a vote;

– a protection mechanism for the data exchanged (CRC[13], Checksum, hamming code, etc.);

– some self-tests;

– watchdog (for time management).

4.6. Risk assessment

The fact of identifying system risks that should be achieved at the earliest makes it possible to introduce them in the specifications (and especially in the software requirements specification) and thus to facilitate demonstrations related to RAMS[14] requirements (safety for example).

Therefore, within the specification, it is required to introduce:

– the notion of state by putting in place a partition between proper operating states, regression states and dangerous states;

– the notion of correct behavior and dangerous behavior;

– the notion of safety-related requirement. This type of requirement must allow for characterizing dangerous behaviors;

– the software safety integrity level (sometimes noted DAL[15] or SIL).

---

12 2oo2 or 2 out of 2, the same happens for the architectures NooM and 2oo3.

13 The CRC (Cyclic Redundant Code), hamming codes and/or checksums are means to protect one or more data; for more information, see Boulanger [BOU 09a].

14 RAMS for Reliability, Availability Maintainability and Safety.

15 Depending on the area, the notion of SIL (Safety Level Integrity) or DAL (Design Assurance Level) will be used to characterize the safety integrity level of the software application.

The second important point introduced by the above-mentioned criteria concern *verification and validation* aspects of the specification. Verification and validation activities can only be carried out if the specification is formalized.

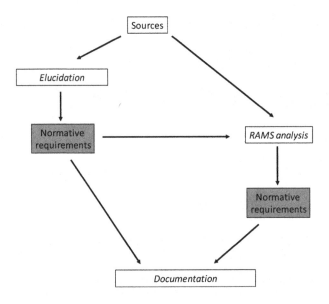

Figure 4.7. *Specification development*

Figure 4.7 shows the proposed method. A first analysis of the specifications provided by the customer must be able to identify the functional requirements. At the same time, it is possible to begin the analyses related to dependability, which are designed to define non-functional requirements: safety requirements but also availability and reliability requirements and others.

4.7. System requirements specification document: SwRS

4.7.1. *Presentation*

The specification stage makes it possible to produce the software requirements specification document (that we will denote by SwRS), which is an input for the following phases. The software specification document should thus describe all of the items that have been presented in the previous sections.

The title of the document suggests that the content of the SwRS is centered on the notion of requirement. This is a very important point because this is the current direction for the different areas (rail, aerospace and automotive). The software requirements specification document must describe a complete set of software requirements. This set of requirements has to meet the needs that have been set up at the top level.

The software requirements specification document is a document intended for the people involved in the implementation of the software application; its completeness is a means to avoid the manipulation of other documents.

4.7.2. Characterization of the content of the SwRS

The software requirements specification document must express the need characterizing the software application being implemented. The set of procedures to put in place to implement the application is not included in the scope of this software but must be part of the SQAP.

Regarding the characterization of the need, one must describe:

– the boundaries of the application software and must properly identify the interfaces;

– the software application modes of operation: initialization phase, normal phase, maintenance phase, etc.;

– features: features can be defined through a requirement list, a model and/or a text description;

– non-functional characteristics such as performance and/or scaling;

– parametrization data;

– performance targets: targets related to the memory footprint of the software application and/or these data, targets related to the CPU load, targets in terms of numbers of messages, etc;

– maintainability objectives[16];

---

16 In some standards or areas, the notion of reliability goals may appear but we consider (by means of feedback) that it makes no sense in the context of a software application (see Baufreton *et al.* [BAU 10]).

– safety objectives: identifying safety functions and the levels associated with them is required.

4.7.3. *Identification of software boundaries*

Based on the documents on input of the specification phase, the interfaces between the software application and the environment have to be identified. These interfaces can be either software application inputs or interfaces between the software application and the hardware (input/output port, memory addresses, AON[17] input/output, watchdog, access to a CAN bus, etc.).

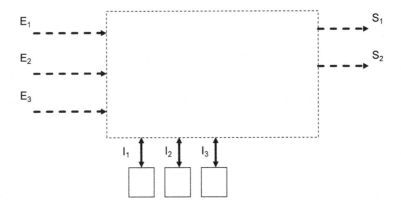

Figure 4.8. *Software application environment*

Figure 4.8 shows a software application environment that consists of three input interfaces (E_i), two output interfaces (S_j) and three physical interfaces (I_k) with hardware resources (for example access to a specific memory address).

DEFINITION 4.3 (Software Interface).– *At the software application level, an interface is a device that allows exchanges and interactions between different parts of the software application. In the context of this book, it refers to exchanges between software components.*

---

17 AON for "All or Nothing".

The software interface is thus a way to pair software components. If the software component is a library, this is referred to as an Application Programming Interface (API).

The identification of interfaces with other systems must take into account the internal or external elements of the equipment being implemented. Among these interfacing systems, one must not forget to take operators into account. It is worth noting that the interface with the operators may be necessary for the operation of the hardware, for maintenance and/or for removing the equipment.

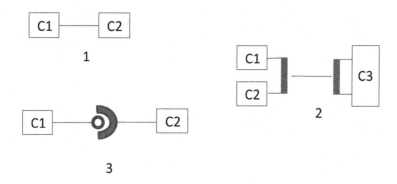

Figure 4.9. *Example of the representation of an interface*

Figure 4.9 illustrates three examples of graphical representation of software interfaces. Representation 1 is the simplest – two elements are connected. Representation 2 brings forward the notions of a bus and data multiplexing. Representation 3 allows us to identify the ability to connect and disconnect an interface.

The main difficulty with the notion of interface derives from the fact that at the specification level there is a link between different elements, but at the code level, the interface mechanism does not exist; it will be built on the basis of the mechanisms of the computing language utilized.

From Definition 4.3, an interface can be pictured as a data stream between the software application and an external element. It is important to characterize this data flow.

For an interface *I*, one has to describe at least:

– the list of data exchanged and for each data element:

  - the name;

  - the family and/or the type;

  - units (if necessary);

  - the range of acceptable values;

  - values identifying an error;

– real-time characteristics (time constraint, protocol, etc.);

– error handling:

  - Is the interface capable of detecting errors during exchanges?

  - If yes, what are the associated behaviors?

  - Is there an exception handling mechanism?

– memory management:

  - Is there memory allocation?

  - Is there a buffer? If yes, what happens when it is full?

  - If there is no memorization mechanism, what happens if several data elements are received at the same time?

The description of interfaces is paramount in order to ensure the integration, the testability and the maintenance of the software application.

4.7.4. *Identification of the operation modes*

Concerning the software application, it is necessary to identify the different modes of operation and behaviors applicable to each of these modes of operation.

For example, the first question that arises during the implementation of a software application for a so-called critical system is: what happens during the initialization of the application software? As a matter of fact, the default output value having an impact on the safety of the system is essential. This value will depend on the type of logic used at the system level: positive (energy is needed for activation) or passive (no energy is needed for activation) activation.

DEFINITION 4.4 (Operating Mode).– *The mode of operation is defined by a certain number of variables called state variables. The operating mode makes it possible to characterize a particular situation.*

Operating modes (see Definition 4.4) are directly related to the concept of safety. For example, in the *initialization* mode, it is necessary to carry out self-tests. If an anomaly is detected, the *failure* mode is started where, usually, the only way out is to reboot the computer.

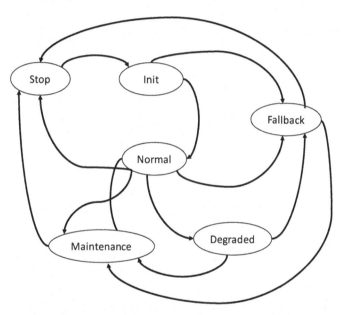

Figure 4.10. *Example of a graph illustrating the operating mode*

Figure 4.10 shows an example of a graph of the operating mode for a software application. It is worth noting that the mode *Stop* (or *PowerOff*) must be identified in order to have a complete graph.

There is no degraded mode existing in every software application, but there is a strong demand from customers for the mission to continue as long as possible, even if it means having lower performance (speed limitation) or even losing features (this is called graceful degradation).

Graceful degradation is now a requirement to take into account and during the system design phase and in the software requirement specification we need to introduce the needs of graceful degradation. It is possible to have two different inputs (two antennas, two networks, etc.) to introduce some redundancy. This redundancy is not for safety but for availability. The software can manage two inputs and can decide which input to use; if one of the inputs fails, the software can send a warning and continue.

One of the special modes is the *maintenance* mode: this mode enables the connection to the maintenance tool, which will make various processes, such as downloading a version of the software application, available, retrieving the installed versions, recovering or resetting the file containing operation records (the log file).

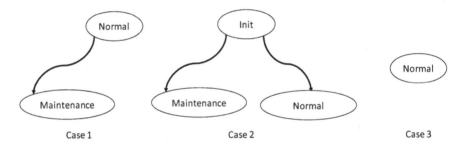

Figure 4.11. *Mode for the transition to "maintenance" mode*

As shown in Figure 4.11, for the maintenance mode, there are several possibilities of behavior. Case 1 indicates that at any time, it is possible to switch from normal mode to maintenance mode, for instance, by detecting the connection of the maintenance tool to a specific port. Case 2 indicates that during the initialization stage on a specific user action, it is possible to shift to maintenance mode. In case 3, in normal mode, all of the maintenance information is sent into a dedicated port whether the maintenance tool is or is not connected to it.

The identification of the operation modes is an activity necessary for controlling the behavior of the software application. It should be recalled that the operation modes of the software application must be consistent with the operation modes of the hardware.

4.7.5. Identification of parametrization data

In Chapter 14 of Volume 2 [BOU 17], we introduced the notion of the parametrization of a software application. The software requirements specification must contain an identification of the parameters that the software application will use.

Figure 4.12 introduces the three options for parametrization that can be implemented. Case 1 consists of identifying constants at the software application level that are directly accessible by the application software. Case 2 consists of inserting the set of parameters in a library that is linked to the executable during compilation. Cases 1 and 2 require the generation of the executable if the parameters change. Case 3 introduces a separation between the executable and parameters. There are two distinct memory regions. Case 3 allows for greater flexibility and the capability to change the parameters without generating a new executable.

Figure 4.12. *Software and parameters*

Concerning the modification of the parameters, there are several possibilities:

– the data can be on a dongle (including an EEPROM) or in a buffer (EEPROM hence more or less physical coding) and the replacement of the buffer/dongle provides a new parameter set;

– data can be found on an EEPROM that is loaded at startup and which can be updated through the maintenance tool;

– data can be received through a network during the initialization stage.

For each parameter of the software application, it is necessary to describe:

– the name;

– the nature (topological data, train characteristic, etc.);

– the family (speed, distance, etc.);

– the functional domain of the parameter;

– the unit;

– the precision;

– the structure (if it is a complex datum).

4.7.6. *Identification of services/functions*

Once the environment of the software application has been identified, the main services that make it possible to generate the outputs based on the inputs have to be identified.

Every software application is composed of a set of so-called functional services. The implementation of a functional service is provided by a group of compilation units (sometimes called module or component. This point will be detailed in Chapter 8).

DEFINITION 4.5 (Service).– *The service is a functionality provided by a software component to ensure a particular task.*

This identification of the main functions of the main application must be achieved based on the functional analysis carried out at the hardware level and through the analysis of the input requirements of the specification phase.

4.7.7. *Behavior description*

For each service function, it is necessary to identify the requirements characterizing the associated behavior. The requirements characterizing the services of the software application may be functional requirements (description of the behavior) and/or non-functional requirements: safety-related requirements, performance-related requirements, etc.

For each requirement, one has to identify:

– the link (traceability) with the requirements at the phase input;

– the safety attribute (yes or no);

– the verification attribute that indicates whether the requirement is testable or if a specific analysis is required.

With respect to requirements testability, it is necessary to recall that the requirements should be verifiable and that some are testable.

Label	Description of user requirement
UR1	The level crossing must be a distributed system.
UR2	The level crossing should be based on radio communication.
UR3	The objective of a level crossing is to manage the intersection of a railway line and a road.
UR4	The railway line is a single line.
UR5	The intersection of the road and the railway line is called the danger zone.
UR6	Therefore, in order to avoid collision, it is necessary to avoid that a train and a road user cross the danger zone at the same time.
UR7	The level crossing is equipped with gates.
UR8	The level crossing is equipped with traffic lights.
UR9	There are two traffic lights associated with a level crossing, one red and one amber.
UR10	When the amber light is on, it means that road users (cars, cyclists, pedestrians, drivers, etc.) must stop at the limit of the crossing if possible.
UR11	The red light indicates that the crossing is closed to road traffic and that it is forbidden to move forward.
...	
UR23	The main components can communicate with each other through a radio communication system.
UR24	The transmission times of the radio communication system are not fixed and may vary.
UR25	The messages transiting through the radio communication system can be lost.
...	
UR37	Failures must be taken into account to achieve a safe level crossing.
UR38	The main causes for failure are associated with sensors and actuators.
...	
UR43	Failures can occur at any time.
...	
UR45	A list of potential failures: – light failures; – gate failures; – train sensors failures; – communication failures: delays, message loss, message alteration, etc.
...	

Table 4.3. *Requirement example*

In Chapter 2 of Ramachandran [RAM 09] and Chapter 3 of Ramachandran [RAM 11], we have presented examples of requirements management in automotive and railway areas.

SyRS	SwRS
SyRS_EX_1	SwRS_EX_11, SwRS_EX_12, SwRS_EX_13
SyRS_EX_2	-
SyRS_EX_3	SwRS_EX_11

Table 4.4. *Example of "input document"/SwRS traceability*

Table 4.4 shows an example of traceability between "input documents" and the SwRS. The purpose of this traceability is to demonstrate that all the top-level requirements have been taken into account. In this example, there is a requirement which has not been included; an explanation has to be added that justifies that requirement SyRS_EX_2 is fully taken into account during the previous phases of the hardware analysis.

As a general rule, a requirement associated with a component at the "hardware" level must be covered by requirements at the software application specification level. However, it may happen that this requirement is related to mechanical, electric, electronic, etc. aspects and that it does not impact the software application.

Table 4.4 is not sufficient because software requirements that are not traceable must be identified (in the aeronautics field, this is referred to as derived requirements). It is therefore necessary to add reverse traceability (Table 4.5).

SwRS	SyRS
SwRS_EX_11	SyRS_EX_1, SyRS_EX_3
SwRS_EX_12	SyRS_EX_1
SwRS_EX_13	SyRS_EX_1
SwRS_EX_14	–

Table 4.5. *Example of SwRS/"input document" traceability*

Table 4.5 shows an example of traceability between the SwRS and the "hardware" level. The objective of this traceability is to demonstrate that there is no element introduced during the specification phase that is not traceable with a need.

In our example, one must justify that the SwRS_EX_14 requirement is included for a reason and that it has no impact on safety at the software application specification level.

In the aeronautics field, this type of requirement (without traceability) is named "derived requirement" and in railway engineering it is called a "non-traceable requirement". In both cases, this means that there is no associated behavior at the system level and thus no system-level test or verification covers this requirement, hence the need to demonstrate that it has no impact on system safety.

4.8. Specifications formalization

4.8.1. Modeling for verification

Regarding the completeness of the software requirements specification, it is not possible to achieve this property by simple document analysis. For consistency in the specification, it would be preferable to perform a two-by-two comparison of the requirements, which is not always possible. Due to these two problems, it is recommended that a model be made. Creating a model makes it possible to establish the completeness and consistency analysis on the development and analysis of the model.

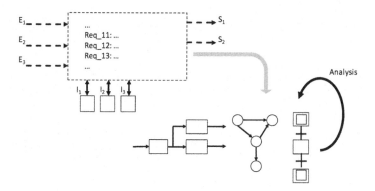

Figure 4.13. *Modeling for verification*

As shown in Figure 4.13, based on the boundary of the software application and requirements, it is possible to develop one or more models that can prove to be helpful in the analysis of requirements consistency and completeness (see Boulanger [BOU 99, BOU 06a]).

For example, Figure 4.14 is a three-state automaton (A, B, C) with three transitions (*t1, t2* and *t3*). It was possible to produce this automaton in order to verify requirements. It can be noted that from state *A*, we have transitions *t1* and *t3* that allow changing state. But the question remains, can transitions *t1* and *t3* be executable at the same time? If so, we are faced with non-determinism and there is thus an inconsistency in the software requirements specification. By analyzing the model, it can be seen that state *C* is a sink state. This may be a desired situation but it can also be an incompleteness in the software requirements specification.

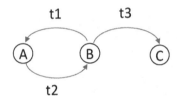

Figure 4.14. *Modeling for verification*

We have presented an example of graphic modeling, but it is possible to achieve models with mathematical languages (see Figure 4.15) like the B-method [ABR 96]. For examples of an industrial application of the B-method, see Boulanger [BOU 13].

```
MACHINE
    Exemple
SETS
        TRAIN ; POSITION
VARIABLES
        Domaine
INVARIANT
        Domaine : TRAIN - - >POW(POSITION)
    &    !(t1,t2). ((t1,t2: TRAIN*TRAIN) => ((Domaine(t1) ∧ Domaine(t2) = {}) & (t1/=t2)))
INITIALISATION
    Domaine :( Domaine : TRAIN - - >POW(POSITION)
            & !(t1,t2). ((t1,t2: TRAIN*TRAIN) => ((Domaine(t1) ∧ Domaine(t2) = {}) & (t1/=t2)))
            )
END
```

Figure 4.15. *Example of a B-model*

4.8.2. *Text specification versus graphical specification*

In the beginning, specifications were conducted in the form of texts in natural language that described the expected behaviors of the software application. These descriptions contained different types of information: descriptive text of behaviors, text describing the processes to achieve and explanatory text which was redundant with the previous texts.

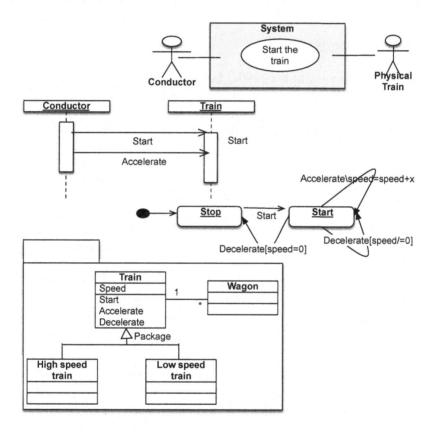

Figure 4.16. *Modeling for verification*

Information redundancy and difficulty in identifying the need for blah-blah (explanatory text providing no information), generated errors in the implementation (many faults were discovered during the validation phase) and difficulties in maintenance.

In response to the feedback from successful projects and failures, industry standards recommend the implementation of specification based on formalisms known as "graphical". The formalism used can either be structured, or a drawing (model)[18] or even a formal modeling. Figure 4.16 shows an example of modeling a railway system.

Industry standards recommend the implementation of graphical environments for managing the formalisms used to write the specification.

4.8.3. *Formal method*

From the beginning of the 1990s, the railway industry has been interested in the implementation of formal models (see, for example, the SACEM[19]) for the verification of software applications. In industry standards such as the CENELEC 50128 standard [CEN 01, CEN 11], formal methods have been introduced as a necessity.

One of the difficulties lies in the fact of having brought forward formal methods as early as the software requirements specification. In our opinion, it is not possible to replace the software requirements specification in natural language by a formal model. The formal model must remain an additional element to verify the requirements (see Boulanger [BOU 06a, BOU 06b]).

As part of Chapter 9 of this volume, we will present the concepts of model, formal method and formal techniques in more detail.

4.9. Considering COTS and reused components

At the level of the software requirements specification, there is no necessity to introduce the need for using Commercial Off The Shelf (COTS) and/or all or part of a preexisting software application.

---

18 Initially, industry standards introduced the notion of semiformal method (method with partial semantics) but many industrials confuse this term with graphical methods. In the latest versions of business standards (for example CENELEC EN 50128:2011 [CEN 11]), the notion of semiformal method is replaced by the notion of modeling, with modeling meaning graphic representation.
19 For Driver Assistance, Operation and Maintenance System.

In the requirements, we could have requirements introducing the need to conform to communication protocols, to a Graphical Unit Interface (GUIs), etc., which might lead to using COTS or preexisting software, but this kind of choice is made at the architecture level of the software application.

In certain projects, we can introduce a requirement to reuse software already in service, but in this case some specific requirement can be introduced and more detail will be introduced at the architecture level of the software application.

4.10. Specification verification

The software requirements specification must be verified. It is necessary to verify that the specification is clear, accurate, consistent, comprehensive and feasible.

The feasibility is based on the preparation work of the overall software requirements testing specification (SwOTS). In fact, if the tester is capable of preparing the SwOTS, it will then be possible to implement a software application that meets the software requirements.

Regarding the other criteria, it is necessary to put in place verification processes. The verification of the software specification stage will be presented in Chapter 7 of this volume.

4.11. Conclusion

This chapter presents the content of a software requirements specification. The software requirements specification is the starting point and increased attention should be given thereto.

In Chapter 10 of Volume 2 [BOU 17], Table 10.1 highlighted that at least 40% of the causes of failure of a software project were related to the requirements (incomplete requirement, requirement unrepresentative of the need, unrealistic need and changing requirements). Our feedback shows that up to 40% of defects discovered throughout the whole of the software implementation are related to a bad specification.

To end this chapter, we recall that we have indicated the criteria defining a *good specification*. We can complete the discussion by recalling that a requirement prescribes a capability or a limitation of the system and that a *consistent* and *comprehensive* set of requirements that can be applied for a system in a given context will be referred to as *specification*.

4.12. Appendix: SwRS template

An SwRS is composed of the following elements:

– a cover page with title, reference, version, author's name, auditor's name and approval;

– an introduction giving a brief description of:

  - the software application in its environment;

  - the characteristics of the application;

  - the restrictions related to this version;

– a section identifying the reference documents being used;

– a section identifying the applicable documents being used;

– a section identifying and defining the vocabulary in the form of a glossary (it is possible to refer to a project glossary);

– a description of the environment of the software application;

– a section making it possible to identify the external interfaces (logical and physical) (external interfaces are comprehensively defined on the basis of the SyRS and all hardware documentations);

– a section making it possible to identify the modes of operation of the software application;

– a section making it possible to identify non-functional requirements such as the safety level, the environmental constraints, the performance requirements, etc.;

– a section aiming to identify and describe general services and associated requirements (requirements will have to be identifiable and may be accompanied by a model);

– a section providing traceability matrices showing:

- that the requirements of input documents (SyRS, SyAD, hardware documentation) are covered;

- that the requirements of the software requirements specification are covered by the requirements of the input documents (SyRS, SyAD, hardware documentation);

- that all untraceable requirements are justified.

5

Modeling

5.1. Introduction

The development of a software application involves several phases ranging from the specification to coding and including all of the test phases. In the specification, architecture and design phases (see [BOU 06a, BOU 06b]), the use of a model is a way to capture the need for and choice of implementation. Finally, it is possible to implement models to perform the verification [BOU 00] but also to select test cases (see [BOU 99]). In the specification phase, modeling is part of requirement elicitation (see Chapter 2 and [BOU 14]).

In the end, modeling is a fundamental means for the different development phases of a software application.

From various experiments [MON 00, BOU 11a, BOU 11b, BOU 12, BOU 13], it can be concluded that modeling is a critical need for the different development stages of a software application and in particular for safety critical software. The main development of recent years lies in the recognition of the need for model development.

New tools, such as STIMULUS[1], will give us the possibility to model the requirement and to simulate the requirement. It is very helpful to play with requirements at very early stages and to identify some discrepancies at the requirement level. These kinds of tools help us to do the elicitation at the software level but also at the system level.

---

1 See http://www.argosim.com for more information.

5.2. Modeling

5.2.1. *Presentation*

In this section, we are going to present the different concepts related to modeling. Modeling can vary from structured to formalized modeling (means used for modeling with formal semantics based on mathematics).

In the present discussion, we will voluntarily remain very general; this discussion can then be instantiated on specific models or specific model elements.

5.2.2. *Model*

5.2.2.1. *Presentation*

A model is an abstract description of a system and/or of a process. Since it is a simplified representation, there is a decrease in complexity, the model is easily manipulated and it allows for reasoning and/or performing a number of verifications. The closer the modeling is, the closer the results will be to those that will be observed from the final system.

A model can be somewhat close to the system under study; this is then referred to as an abstraction. The closer the modeling is, the closer the results will be to those that will be observed from the final system. Another characteristic of models derives from the fact that the supporting language either has a semantics or does not. The presence of a semantics makes it possible to implement reasoning techniques that ensure the correction of the results obtained.

Two complementary models are frequently used with this specification:

– a static model describing the entities constituting the system and states that may be associated thereto;

– a dynamic model describing allowed state changes.

Modeling describes the behavior of the system:

– system states/transitions;

– logical equations.

Modeling has access to data that are:

– controllable (known, fixed, etc.);

– probabilistic.

In summary and overall, modeling consists of translating a physical situation into a symbolic view in a more or less abstract language based on icons (graphic symbols: tables, curves, diagrams, etc.) or having logical mathematical foundations (function, relation, etc.).

This is why the model can be a communication tool between all the parties involved in the project (system designer, software designer, verifier, tester, safety team, customer, authorities, etc.).

A good model must focus on the problem, but in some cases, it may describe a solution and it is then possible to generate all or part of the final code. A model can thus be executable or not (see for examples stimulus tools from Argosim where requirements become executable).

5.2.2.2. Definition

As a first step, we restate the definition of the concept of model introduced in the glossary of the MEMVATEX [MEM 05] project.

DEFINITION 5.1 (Model).– *A model captures a view of a physical system. It is an abstraction following a point of view of a physical system. The point of view enables what should be included in the model to be determined.*

As indicated in Definition 5.1, a model is an abstraction of a physical system according to a particular point of view and with a level of detail suitable for this model.

From a model M, an implementation process is put in place that aims at building different images of this model whose level of detail will become more specific, until obtaining an executable model that will be an implementation of the problem.

More generally, it is possible to have models dedicated to every step in the implementation process of the system; this is then known as a model-based approach (model-based development [MBD]). In France, this is referred to as IdM for "*Ingénierie des Modèles*" (model engineering).

From this discussion, two elements emerge:

– an implementation (C program or...) is an executable practical model;

– an implementation process may be seen as a sequence of phases, where each one produces its models.

In this case, we have mentioned the implementation process intended to produce an executable model, but there is another process that aims to "abstract" models. This process serves to find the properties and/or services described by a model. Such a model can be useful to carry out verification processes or to implement reutilization actions.

DEFINITION 5.2 (Executable Model).– *An executable model is still a model (Definition 5.1). This model is described by a language with a semantics. This semantics enables the description of an interpretation of all the elements used in the executable model.*

The definition of executable model can be applied to a complete model or to a model of which part would be executable

Between two models originating from an implementation process, there is thus a relationship named "model transformation", which is formalized by Definition 5.3.

DEFINITION 5.3. (Model Transformation).– *A model transformation is a manual or tool-based process that takes a model M as input and produces a new model M'.*

Figure 5.1. *Model transformation*

5.2.2.3. *Implementation*

Modeling should be used in addition to the textual description of the requirements; one must be able to express its need to model it. The implementation of a model without textual requirement is tantamount to discovering its need without expressing it; therefrom, the question then arises of how to verify that the model corresponds to the need.

A model is generally composed of two complementary parts:

– a static model (Figure 5.2) describing the entities constituting the system and the states that may be related to them;

– a dynamic model (Figure 5.3) describing state changes allowed.

The static view (Figure 5.2) includes two points of view: the hierarchical point of view that allows viewing the decomposition tree, and the composition point of view that allows viewing communications between modules of the same level; this contributes to the black box perspective of modules.

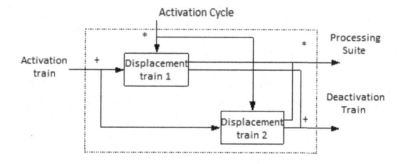

Figure 5.2. *Example of static model introducing different types of communication*

Figure 5.3 shows an example of a dynamic model in the form of a state/transition diagram.

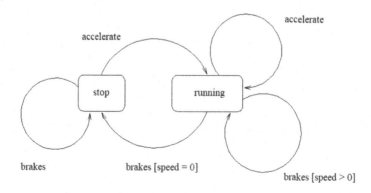

Figure 5.3. *Example of static model introducing different types of communication*

Modeling is often based on a graphical representation of the system, which is described in the form of a tree structure of distinct and autonomous entities that communicate with each other and with the environment of the system. The first models were based on functional system analyses (see the works centered on SADT[2] [LIS 90]).

In summary and overall, modeling consists of translating a physical situation into a symbolic model in a more or less abstract language based on icons (graphic symbols: tables, curves, diagrams, etc.) or having logical mathematical foundations (function, relation, etc.).

5.2.2.4. Summary

The development of a model M is one way to understand and/or apprehend a problem/situation. In general, the specification stage from which the specifications document is derived involves the creation of a model M.

A model can be somewhat close to the system under study; this is then referred to as an abstraction. The closer the modeling is, the closer the results will be to those that will be observed from the final system.

Another characteristic of models derives from the fact that the supporting language either has a semantics or does not.

	SSIL0	SSIL1	SSIL2	SSIL3	SSIL4
Data modeling	R	R	R	HR	HR
Data flow diagram	–	R	R	HR	HR
Control-flow diagram	R	R	R	HR	HR
Finite-state machine or state transition diagrams	–	HR	HR	HR	HR
Time petri nets	–	R	R	HR	HR
Decision truth tables	–	R	R	HR	HR
Formal methods	R	R	R	HR	HR
Sequence diagrams	R	HR	HR	HR	HR

Table 5.1. *New CENELEC 50128:2011 – Table A.17*

2 The acronym SADT means Structured Analysis and Design Technic. This method was developed by the Softech company in the United States. The SADT method is a method of analysis by successive levels of descriptive approaches for any aggregate.

The presence of a semantics makes it possible to implement reasoning techniques (deduction, abstract interpretation, model checking, proof, etc.) that ensure the correction of the results obtained.

The new version of the CENELEC 50128 standard ([CEN 11], Table A.3) recommends, for software that have an impact on safety[3], that the architecture of the software application be based on a structured method (SADT, etc.). However, it is possible to implement a modeling based on the techniques of Table A.17 (see Table 5.1).

These various experiments highlight that modeling is a critical need for the different development stages of a software application. The main development of recent years lies in the recognition of the need for model development. Figure 5.4 shows an example of a SIMULINK model.

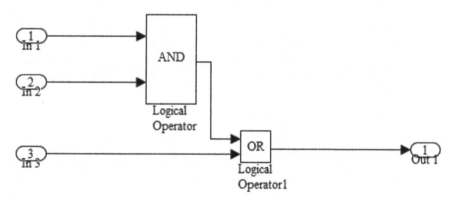

Figure 5.4. *Simulink example*

5.2.3. *Different types of modeling*

Requirements modeling can be performed at different levels and for different purposes. Thus, to each requirement level corresponds a modeling level. We can employ goal or usage models to model user requirements, functional models to model system requirements, and finally performance models to model architecture requirements.

---

3 In the railway, software from SSIL1 to SSIL4 have an impact on safety and SSIL0 have no impact on safety.

We have identified two phases, the analysis phase and the implementation phase. Within the analysis phase, the objective is to identify the need and to better identify it; to this end, a so-called model of the need will be achieved that will allow the various users to express their needs and to make judgments about this need. During the implementation phase, models will be developed that are an image of the software and it will be possible to move forward to the production code.

5.3. Model transformation

5.3.1. *Presentation*

It is important to define the terminology of the notion of "model transformation", because it can be:

– between models or model components (requirements toward diagram): model transformation. The different possible transformations have to be defined: requirement models toward solution models; solution models toward solution models; UML models to Matlab/Simulink models; solution models to verification models;

– from models to text, language or code (Simulink models to C code). The different possible transformations must then be defined.

5.3.2. *Different types of transformation*

Regarding the notion of "transformation", it is stated in [ING 06] that the concept of "transformation" is fundamental to ME, but there is currently no consensus on the corresponding terminology; this concept is very broad and must be specified.

There are three families of model transformations (see Figure 5.5):

– model transformations creating abstractions (section 5.3.3);

– model transformations creating a model (section 5.3.4);

– model transformations known as "code generation" (section 5.3.5).

The difference between the family of creations and the "code generation-oriented" family comes from the fact that code generation is a transformation from an executable model to another executable model.

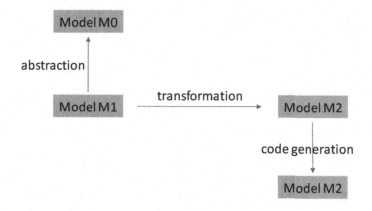

Figure 5.5. *Several types of model transformations*

In addition to the model transformation, the model element transformation can be mentioned. This type of transformation can be carried out within a model in order to produce complementary elements (see Figure 5.6).

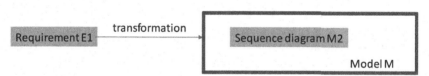

Figure 5.6. *Partial model transformation*

It should be noted that there is another way to characterize model transformations [BOU 07c]. They can be model-to-model transformations or metamodel to metamodel transformations.

DEFINITION 5.4. (Model-to-model transformation).– *A model-to-model transformation is a transformation that is described as the description elements of the model produced are transformed into elements of the target model.*

According to Definition 5.4, such a transformation is described on the real elements of the source model and describes how to generate the target model or its description (file).

DEFINITION 5.5 (Metamodel-to-metamodel transformation).– *A metamodel-to-metamodel transformation is a transformation that describes how elements of the input metamodel are transformed into elements of a target metamodel.*

According to Definition 5.5, a transformation from metamodel to metamodel avoids the reading phase of the source model as well as the file production stage of the target model.

This concerns different types of transformations based on metamodels: endogenous transformations and exogenous transformations. Endogenous transformations mainly focus on working with models following the same metamodel M, whether this is the source model or the target model; exogenous transformations, for their part, concern target and source models associated with different metamodels: the source model respects the metamodel M1 and the target model follows the metamodel M1'.

5.3.3. *Abstraction*

This type of transformation seeks to obtain a more abstract model than the original model. The implementation of an abstraction avoids implementation details making it possible to concentrate on overall behaviors. Behaviors can thus be characterized by requirements.

For example, the model of a railway system will be based on the modeling of the displacement of the train, which will be performed in terms of "x meters per unit of time". An abstraction can be implemented by means of the abstraction "the displacement of trains occurs from area to area".

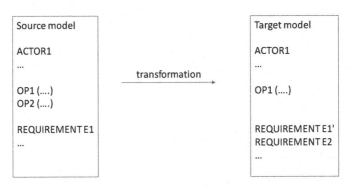

Figure 5.7. *Abstraction*

Abstraction is quite difficult to implement. This difficulty is related to the fact that the practical model may contain a very fine and complex description of the problem being addressed.

The abstraction is generally implemented as part of "re-factoring" processes. Moreover, in order to promote sustainable development (concerning a system with a long lifetime) or to implement component "reuse", it may be necessary to achieve an abstraction to rebuild the specification of the need.

As part of the abstraction, certain services can be removed (for example OP2), requirements can be generalized (for example E1 in E1' in which implementation details have been removed comparing to E1) and requirements characterizing services are added (for example E2).

In order to demonstrate the correction of the transformation, the abstract model AM and the concrete model CM are connected by a so-called "refinement" relationship. The model CM must be a refinement of AM. The refinement relationship is described in section 5.4.

5.3.4. *Implementation*

This type of transformation is intended to materialize a model. Conventionally, this transformation requires the implementation of data and behavior.

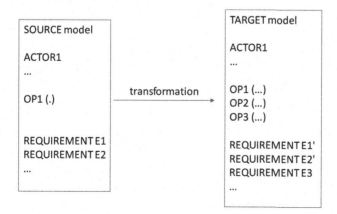

Figure 5.8. *Implementation*

As shown in Figure 5.8, in its simplest form, the implementation is a means to produce a model to be completed that contains the essential and invariable elements to maintain the requirements of the source model.

A source model must define the services and the data and it must characterize the requirements for characterizing the services. The implementation is a transformation that should produce a model that maintains services, data and requirements.

The implementation rules can be based on the notion of "design pattern". Design patterns [COP 95, GAM 95] are diagrams which, based on an existing construct in the source model, enable a systematic implementation.

DEFINITION 5.6 (Design Pattern).– *Design patterns describe standard solutions to address architecture and software design problems.*

In contrast to algorithms whose purpose is to describe in a formal manner how to solve a particular problem, design patterns describe general design procedures.

The advantage of patterns is to decrease the time required for software development and to increase the quality of the result, especially by applying existing solutions to common design problems.

Among design patterns, one should highlight the "Model-View-Controller" (MVC) example, which is a design method for the development of software applications that separates the data model, the user interface and control logic.

In its simplest form, the implementation is a total or partial transformation that produces a target model TM, which includes the same actors, the same data, the same services, the same requirements, etc., and which the designer will have to complete.

For example, the phase for the *generation of C code from a UML model* can be seen as an implementation; the resulting model is incomplete and remains to be finalized by a designer. Unlike the "code generation" introduced in section 5.3.5, we here have a model that is not executable.

In its most complete form, the implementation is a process that makes use of a set of transformations to produce a concrete model. Each usable transformation is formalized and can turn part of the model into more concrete elements.

For example, in the context of the B-method [ABR 96], there is a tool that is used for collection of refinement rules. The application of a rule is chosen by the designer.

In order to demonstrate the correction of the implementation, the source model SM and the target model TM are connected by a "refinement" relationship.

The model CM must be a refinement of the AM. The refinement relationship is described in section 5.4.

5.3.5. *Element transformation*

As part of a model, it is possible to implement transformations that are intended to produce additional information in the model under analysis. The transformations of the elements of the model may enable:

– the specification of existing items: a method for transforming requirements can be brought forward in order to break down certain types of requirements within the same model; this is a means to document (outline) the reasoning implemented;

– the completion of model elements based on existing elements: a requirement may be used to characterize the preconditions and postconditions of an operation;

– the production of information for a complementary activity: production of test cases for V&V stages.

In a UML model, based on some diagrams, it is possible to generate other additional diagrams to analyze other aspects.

For example, from a state/transition diagram, it is possible to generate a collection of unit tests in order to test the whole of the diagram.

During the transformation process of elements, there is no modification or removal of existing elements but there is addition of complementary elements derived from existing elements (in our example, the addition of a use case (Use-Case2) and a sequence diagram can be seen) or modification of existing items (for example, an existing use case Use Case1 is completed by Use-Case1').

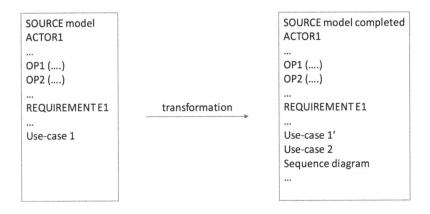

Figure 5.9. *Model element transformation*

The transformation of a portion of model into new elements for this same model implies the demonstration that the whole remains consistent and that no overspecification is introduced. The overspecification is a redundancy of elements that could lead to a misunderstanding of the problem addressed.

The use of transformations based on the requirements or elements as part of the V&V process is an important point. It is thus possible to generate tests related to the different phases (unitary, software/software integration and software/hardware integration, functional validation) based on specific elements of the model. It is worth noting that the generated elements can be complete (fully described tests) or not (description of the need for the test).

5.3.6. *Code generation*

Initially, we will focus on the transformation family known as "code generation". When we have a model M, it is said (see Definition 5.2) that it is executable if there is a semantics S on the entire model M. To this semantic S, it is then possible to associate an interpretation semantic IS. The interpretation semantic IS allows us to characterize the behavior of the model M and therefore to describe the result of an execution.

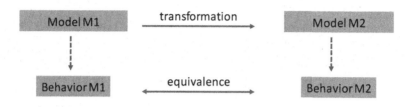

Figure 5.10. *Model equivalence*

In general, the implementation of code generation is done in four steps:

– definition of the scope of the source language;

– definition of the scope of the target language based on the equivalence of models;

– definition of translation processes from the source language to the target language;

– demonstration of the preservation of the semantics by the translation processes.

The correction of code generation is done through the definition of equivalence between the two semantics.

Given an executable model M with the interpretation function IS and the model M' with the interpretation function I'S, then saying that M' is the result of code generation G from M should demonstrate that IS(M) = I'S(M') = I'S(G(M)).

5.3.7. *Summary*

This section presents our thoughts on the different types of transformations and their possible implementations in software development projects.

Transformation	Need	Full model or not	Automation	V&V
Code generation (Example of automatic documentation generation)	Executable model Source language semantics	Yes	Yes	Demonstrate the correction of the transformation on the basis of the knowledge of semantics.
Abstraction	Strong knowledge of the implementation	Yes	No	Demonstrate that the starting model is a refinement of the final model.
Abstraction (specification automatic reconstruction)		Interfaces, services and the main elements are generated	Yes	Verify that both models have the same interfaces. Complete the abstract model with a collection of tests able to characterize the behavior.
Implementation	Make operating modes available for the implementation of the model (delineate the language, practices, etc.)	No	Partially	Demonstrate that the final model is a refinement of the starting model.

Table 5.2. *Synthesis – part 1*

Tables 5.2 and 5.3 are a synthesis proposal of the possibilities of use of model transformation.

Transformation	Need	Full model or not	Automation	V&V
Implementation (model structure generation)		Interfaces, services and the main elements are generated	Yes	Verify that both models have the same interfaces.
Element transformation	Make operating modes available for the implementation of the model (delineate the language, practices, etc.)	No	Application of patterns consistently with the operating modes related to the modeling.	Demonstrate the relevance of patterns and of the coverage of operating modes.
Element transformation	Establish a semantics for a specific element	Yes for elements	Production pattern application	Demonstrate the relevance of the patterns.

Table 5.3. *Synthesis – part 2*

5.4. Model refinement

This section is intended to define what refinement is [MOR 90a, MOR 90 b] and how it can be implemented.

Refinement makes it possible to show that a functional element (function, service, component, hardware, subsystem or system) can be replaced by another. It is therefore possible to apply this verification to a model element or to a model.

DEFINITION 5.7 (Model Refinement).– *A functional element F' is a refinement of another element F if:*

– every service of F exists in F;

– F and F' have compatible signatures (number of inputs, number of outputs and type compatibility);

– the behavior of the services of F' includes those of F.

Given a functional element F providing services {s1(in x1 :X1, out y1 :Y1), s2(in x2 :X2, out y2 :Y2)}. Given a component F' providing services {s1(in x1 :X1', out y1 :Y1'), s2(in x2 :X2', out y2 :Y2'), s3(in x3 :X3)}, it is therefore necessary to show that:

– all services of F are provided by F': for all services belonging to {s1(in x1 :X1, out y1 :Y1),s2(in x2 :X2, out y2 :Y2)} there is a service in {s1(in x1 :X1', out y1 :Y1'),s2(in x2 :X2', out y2 :Y2'), s3(in x3 :X3)};

– for each service s of F', it is necessary to show compatibility between signatures: we have the same number of inputs, the same number of outputs and compatibility between types (X1' contains X1, X2' contains X2, etc.);

– it must be demonstrated that of the behavior of services common to F and F', the services of F' show behaviors compatible with those of F. To demonstrate that the service s' is a refinement of s, it must be shown that s' verifies the same functional requirements as s (using s' instead of s is thus transparent).

It should be noted that F' may provide more services than F and that for a service s' of F', one may have "additional" behavior(s) compared to those of the service s of F.

Much research has been undertaken to study the automation of model refinement. At present, there are solutions that can completely refine a certain type of application. It has been proved that it was more realistic to guide refinement based on a set of rules (this is a situation very similar to design patterns management).

Some languages, such as the formal method named B-method [ABR 96, BOU 13], have taken a different path, integrating refinement verification inside the verification methodology. In other words, the verification conditions of manual refinement are automatically generated.

In this section, we have presented the essential notions related to refinement; readers wishing to learn more can study [MOR 90a]. Refinement is the essential technique to show the correction of a model. This verification is little integrated into the ME process.

5.5. Methods

5.5.1. *Semiformal method*

According to the IEC 61508 standard ([IEC 08], B.2.3), a semiformal method provides a way to develop a description of a system at a development stage (specification, architecture and/or design). The description can be analyzed or animated to verify that the modeled system meets the requirements (actual and/or specified). It is stated that state diagrams (finite automata) and time Petri nets are two semiformal methods.

DEFINITION 5.8 (Semiformal Method).– *A semiformal method is a means to develop a model from the model that can be analyzed or animated.*

We can see that some standards (such as CENELEC 50128 in version 2001 [CEN 01]) give an explicit list of methods for each kind of formalization. This is in general wrong because this list changes with time. For example JSD, SSADM or YOURDON are no longer used and now SDL fulfills the formal method criteria.

	SSIL0	SSIL1	SSIL2	SSIL3	SSIL4
Formal methods comprising for example CCS, CSP, HOL, LOTOS, OBJ, VDM, Z, B	–	R	R	HR	HR
Semiformal methods	R	R	R	HR	HR
Structured methodology including, for example JSD, MASCOT, SADT, SDL, SSADM and YOURDON	R	HR	HR	HR	HR

Table 5.4. *CENELEC 50128:2001 – Table A.2*

The 2001 version of the CENELEC 50128 standard [CEN 01] introduced the notion of semiformal method in Table A.2, which referred to Table A.18.

	SSIL0	SSIL1	SSIL2	SSIL3	SSIL4
Logic/function block diagram	R	R	R	HR	HR
Sequence diagrams	R	R	R	HR	HR
Data flow diagrams	R	R	R	R	R
Finite-state automata/state-transition method	–	R	R	HR	HR
Time Petri nets	–	R	R	HR	HR
Decision/truth tables	R	R	R	HR	HR

Table 5.5. *CENELEC 50128:2001 – Table A.18*

Under the new CENELEC 50128:2011 standard [CEN 11], semiformal methods are no longer present as techniques. This is due to the ambiguity that existed in determining the boundary between formal and semiformal, and some manufacturers considered that the existence of a modeling tool was sufficient to claim the implementation of a semiformal method.

5.5.2. *Structured method*

Structured methods (CENELEC 50128 – B.60) aim to promote software development quality by giving special attention to the first phases of the life cycle. These kinds of methods makes use of specific and intuitive notations (typically computer-assisted) in order to produce and document the requirements and the implantation characteristics of the product.

DEFINITION 5.9 (Structured Method).– *A structured method proposes a guided approach following a principle to achieve a model.*

Structured methods are reflection tools. They are based on an order of logical thinking, a system analysis that takes into account the environment, the production of the documentation of the system, data decomposition, functional decomposition and the elements to be verified and must impose a low intellectual dependency (simple, intuitive and pragmatic method). Among structured methods, SADT [LIS 90], JSD, CORE, real-time Yourdon, MASCOT and OMT can be found.

The structured specification is a technique that aims to bring forward the simplest visible relationships between the partial requirements of the functional specification. The analysis is refined at every step until small clear partial requirements are obtained. The result is then a hierarchical structure of partial requirements that will enable us to specify the full requirements. The method focuses on the interfaces between requirements and makes it possible to avoid interface failures.

5.5.3. Formal method

Section B.30 of the IEC 61508 [IEC 08] standard indicates that a formal method (HOL, CSP, LOTOS, CCS, time logic, VDM[4] [JON 90] and Z[5] [SPI 89]) enables an unambiguous and consistent description of a system at a development stage (specification, architecture and/or design).

DEFINITION 5.10 (Formal Method).– *A formal method includes a syntax and a formal semantics. This formal semantics makes it possible to verify the correction of the model.*

The description assumes a mathematical form and may be subject to mathematical analysis. This mathematical analysis can make use of tools.

In general, a formal method provides a notation, a technique for developing a description in this notation and a verification process to control the correction of requirements.

Bear in mind that the IEC 61508 standard [IEC 08] indicates that it is possible to make changes until "a logic circuit design"[6] is obtained.

Petri nets and state machines (cited within the context of semiformal methods) can be considered as formal methods based on the degree of compliance of their uses to a rigorous mathematical basis.

---

4 In the IEC 61508 standard, references to VDM include VDM++ [DUR 92], which is a real-time and object-oriented extension of VDM. To learn more, visit www.vdmportal.org/.
5 It should be noted that in the IEC 61508 standard, the B-method [ABR 96] is seen as a method associated with Z.
6 These are the terms of the IEC 61508 standard.

5.5.4. *Computer-aided specification tools*

In the IEC 61508 standard [IEC 08] in section B.2.4, it is stated that the implementation of computer-aided specification tools generates a specification in the form of a database that can be automatically inspected to evaluate consistency and completeness. The tool can enable animation.

The application can be done on the various specification, architecture and design stages. For the design phase, the use is recommended from the moment that tools are made available, but it will be necessary to demonstrate the correction of the tool (feedback and/or independent verification of results).

5.5.5. *Summary*

We have quickly presented the different types of methodologies of structured methods for formal methods. In Chapter 6, we will present more comprehensively the environments associated with this type of methodology as well as the verification means associated thereto.

5.6. Conclusion

In this chapter, we have introduced the notion of model, which is essential both for design and verification. We have completed this presentation by introducing the model transformation techniques that are generally put in place to evolve from the design model to the executable model.

The notion of model is usable at any stage of the implementation cycle of the software application both for the construction of the need and for verification. The verification can focus on the consistency but also on the completeness of the need.

In Chapter 6, we will more specifically present the tools to create more or less formal models. The use of models as means for verification and/or as support for verification tools will be presented in more detail in Volume 4 [BOU 19].

6

Formalization

6.1. Introduction

In this chapter, we will introduce concepts such as formalization, formal methods and formal techniques. We will review the advantages of these approaches and techniques to achieve safe software operation.

As we have shown in previous books [BOU 11a, BOU 11b, BOU 12, BOU 13], the railway sector has experienced through practical and complex projects the use of formal methods (Z [SPI 89], B-method [ABR 96] and Safety Critical Application Development Environment (SCADE) [DOR 08]) and formal techniques (proof, model checking and abstract interpretation of programs).

6.2. Approach example

In this section, we have decided to take into account a certain modeling environment. The choice fell on environments known to the authors and the fact that these environments have been used not only to achieve a system (through code generation) but for the implementation of a model that allowed for verification and/or validation.

6.2.1. *Context diagram*

6.2.1.1. *Introduction*

During the definition of the context of the system, the latter must be thought of as a "black box", since the main interest is the system as seen from outside.

The analysis of the needs related to the actors can be done by achieving a model of the environment in which the system evolves by identifying exchanges between parts. The context of a system can be represented in different ways, such as with a context diagram, a data flow diagram (DFD[1]) or a "horned beast" diagram and/or "the octopus" as it is used in the Application to Entreprise Techniques (APTE[2]) method [BRE 00].

These representations aim at identifying the entities exchanged between the system under study and its immediate environment composed of actors. The entities exchanged may be data or matter:

– examples of data: flight information for an airline company;

– examples of matter: a paper receipt for baggage recorded at an airport desk.

6.2.1.2. *APTE method*

The APTE® method [BRE 00] was created by Gilbert Barbey in 1964; it designates a functional analysis and value analysis method for the management of innovation and optimization projects. The purpose of this method is twofold: the concern is both to increase the quality (that is, to obtain a better alignment with user's needs) and to decrease the cost of what is under study. This method can be equally applied for products, manufacturing processes, equipment and organizations.

In order to highlight the purpose of the study, the first tool of the APTE method is the service diagram also called "horned beast" (see Figure 6.1).

---

1 For DFDs, see http://www.idef.com.
2 The APTE method (see section 6.2.1.2) is a functional analysis and value analysis method. This method can be applied equally to products, manufacturing processes, equipment and organizations. To learn more, see http://cabinet-apte.fr.

The first step of the method is to control the validity of the purpose of the study. The study is inserted in a project for achieving strategic business objectives, which can be challenged during this stage. The second step is to develop a set of functional specifications (FS) AFNOR X 50-151 [AFN 91].

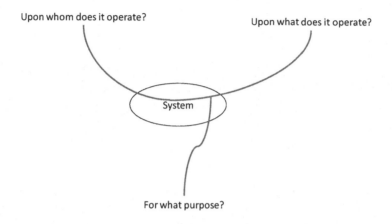

Figure 6.1. *The homed beast*

The purpose of this document is to express services that the system under study must provide to its users. To this end:

– the context of use of the system and other phases or real-life situations have to be listed;

– for each of these contexts, the functions of the system have to be listed and validity checks have to be carried out;

– for each of the functions, one must determine the criteria of value and perform validity checks thereof.

There are two kinds of functions:

– the main functions (MFs), which are the goals of the relationships created by the system between at least two elements of its environment;

– the constrained functions (CF), which are the requirements of a constraining element of the external environment.

Each function is expressed by using a second tool, called "the octopus" and shown in Figure 6.2.

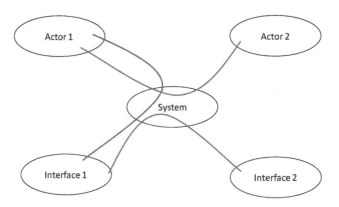

Figure 6.2. *Octopus diagram example*

During each use, the system is in contact with a number of elements of its environment, which constitute its external environment. The system being studied is placed in the center of the octopus surrounded by the elements of the outside environment. The relationships created by the system have then to be described with or between its elements of the external environment.

6.2.1.3. *Horned beast diagram*

As part of a project destined to connect railway system equipment through a global network, a "horned beast" diagram can be constructed that identifies the new system and the actors interacting.

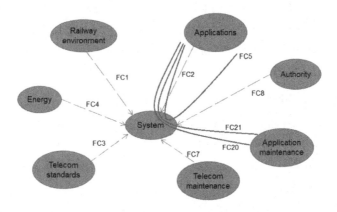

Figure 6.3. *Example: interconnected rail network*

On this basis, it is possible to identify constraint functions (without them, the system cannot work) and the MFs (expected services).

Figure 6.3 formalizes an example of result of a study in the form of an octopus. Three MFs are identified and are complemented by six forced constraint functions. The diagram can be used to verify that no element of the environment is employed. In a systematic approach, it is possible to analyze all the combinations, which allows working on completeness.

6.2.1.4. *Octopus diagram*

The octopus is a diagram that identifies the environment and essential system functions. It is also possible to use a context diagram (see Figure 6.4); the direction of exchanges is represented by an arrow.

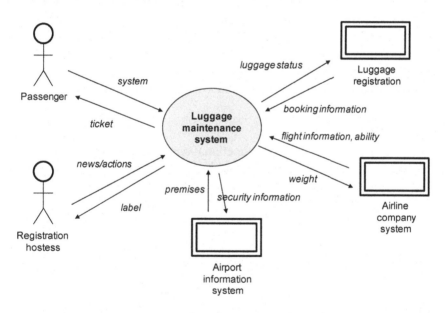

Figure 6.4. *Context diagram*

ADVICE.– In order not to overload the schema, when several objects are exchanged in the same direction between an actor and the system, they are grouped on a single arrow (for example "flight information" and "capacity" between the computer system of the airline company and the system).

6.2.2. *Structured method*

6.2.2.1. *Presentation*

SADT and APTE are so-called structured methods. Structured methods are reflection tools. They are based on an order of logical thinking, a system analysis that takes into account the environment, the production of the system documentation, data decomposition, functional decomposition and the elements to be verified and must impose a low intellectual dependency (simple, intuitive and pragmatic method).

Among structured methods, JSD, CORE, real-time Yourdon, and MASCOT can be found.

Structured specification is a technique that aims to bring forward the simplest visible relationships between the partial requirements of the FS. The analysis is refined at every step until small clear partial requirements are obtained. The result is then a hierarchical structure of partial requirements that will enable us to specify the full requirements. The method focuses on the interfaces between requirements and avoids interface failures.

6.2.2.2. *SADT*

SADT [LIS 90] is a top-down functional approach also known as IDEF0. As shown in Figure 6.5, the analysis set in place ranges from general aspects (black box) to more detailed ones (white box). SADT is a systemic approach to modeling an operating process or a complex system.

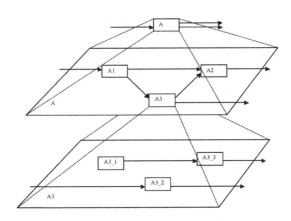

Figure 6.5. *Example of IDEF0 view*

A function is represented by an SADT "box" or "module". A box is placed in its context along with other boxes or modules by means of relationship arrows. These arrows symbolize the constraints of connections between boxes.

The static SADT model can be complemented by a dynamic model of each module in the form of communicating automata (message exchange).

6.2.2.3. *DFD*

Although often used to represent business processes, a DFD can also be used to describe the context of a system.

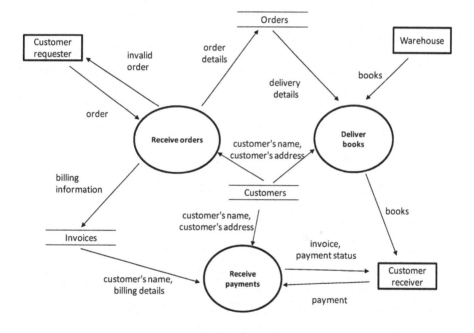

Figure 6.6. *DFD example*

Flow charts answer the question: what does the system do? In this sense, these are working models (that describe system functions). There are two main types of flow charts:

– the context model (CM) where the field of study is seen as a black box. Only flows external to the area are represented;

– the DFD where the activities of the field of study are detailed. The internal flows in the field are also represented.

The DFD is often used directly, which describes both the internal and external exchanges in the field being studied.

The elements composing a DFD are:

– data flows (labeled arrows);

– data transformations (circles);

– data stores (two horizontal parallel lines);

– external entities (rectangles in solid line).

6.2.2.4. Environment

The RATP (www.ratp.fr) and EDF have developed the ASA environment and its updated version the ASA+. These modeling environments are based on an architecture described with SADT [LIS 90] and the implementations in the form of extended communicating (message exchange) automata (using algorithms).

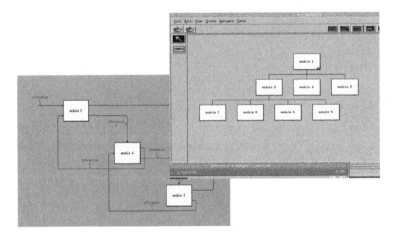

Figure 6.7. *Hierarchical view and communication*

Figure 6.5 shows the hierarchical view of the functional cross-cutting. Figure 6.7 contains several screenshots, in which the hierarchical view of the functions and a view of the data flow can be seen.

The simulation is feasible by means of breaking down the system by the representation of communications and the description of the dynamic behavior.

There are three modes of simulation within the ASA+ environment:

– interactive simulation, based on a manual construction of scenarios and that generates textual and graphical traces;

– automatic simulation, based on a random construction of scenario(s) and that generates statistics and scenarios;

– comprehensive simulation, based on targeted research that allows for a formal verification by exploration of the behavior.

The product ASA was used to validate the design of the SACEM system (1986), which allows controlling the speed of the RER A (French suburban railway). The environment ASA+ was used to validate the safety software of the autopilot system of the SAET-METEOR (1994–1998) and the KCVP (1999), which is part of the control system of the RER B.

6.2.2.5. *SA-RT*

The SA-RT approach is similar to the SADT approach. In the SA-RT model, "data flow" corresponds to any information likely to be transformed by processes and "control flow" corresponds to any event, any change of state, or any condition on the data.

The SA-RT model is broken down into flow charts:

– the first level corresponds to the context diagram, where external interfaces can be seen;

– the following levels are a successive refinement to reach DFDs or control flow diagrams (CFDs);

– a higher refinement (P-Specs: process specifications; C-Specs: control specifications) by means of text or activation tables is achieved for a software specification.

A data dictionary (DD), associated with the model, describes the flows (a flow = a DDE).

The method separates data flows and control flows and represents them by two different graphic symbols:

– solid line arrow for data flow;

– dashed line arrow for control flow.

A DFD is represented graphically by a circle and is described verbatim for a worksheet DFD (P-spec), whereas a CFD is graphically represented by a vertical solid line and described textually (C-spec) or by an activation table (PAT).

A PAT controls the DFD activity at the same level. The terms utilized are as follows:

– v Trigger: the DFD is activated, executes and becomes inactive;,

– v Enable: the DFD becomes active and remains so;

– v Disable: the DFD becomes inactive and remains so.

In the DD, the following notation is used for the description of each flow:

– v * text * = comment describing the flow;

– v [val1 | val2]: the flood can take a value of 1 OR a value of 2;

– v flow1 + flow2: the flow is broken down into flow 1 AND flow 2;

– v <flow1>: the flow is a component of flow 1;

– v <<flow1> flow2>: the flow is a component of flow 1, itself a component of flow 2.

6.2.3. *Modeling*

We have introduced the notion of model in section 5.2.2. In this section, we are going to talk about ways to achieve a model.

6.2.3.1. *UML*

The UML notation [OMG 11, ROQ 07] allows the construction of complex system models through the use of several formalisms (class diagrams, state/transition diagrams, sequence diagrams, use case diagrams, etc.). The UML notation (see Figure 6.8) is one of the most widespread and used to describe functional aspects by use case diagrams and sequence diagrams.

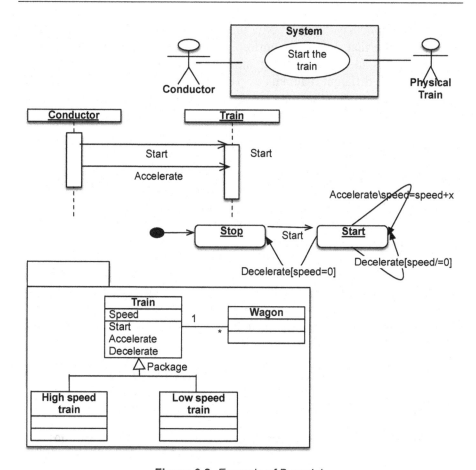

Figure 6.8. *Example of B-model*

Figure 6.8 presents an example of a UML[3] model [OMG 11, ROQ 07] of a railway system implementing different models: use cases, sequence diagram, state/transition diagram and class diagram.

The UML notation is based on a formalization of the metamodel; this formalization has allowed the definition of customizations in the notation that can be achieved through the definition of usage patterns.

---

3 To learn more, see OMG: www.omg.org/.

Note that when using the UML notation, it is necessary to provide a modeling guide that will allow uniform models to be achieved (teams will have common rules for building models), and which will explain the meaning of the different diagrams as well as rules for reading (for example the lifetime bar of an object in a sequence diagram defines the order of the messages exchanged).

6.2.3.2. *UML and/or SysML implementation*

It should be recalled that UML is just a notation and that to turn it into a method, it is necessary to put in place a methodology that will define the elements used, the meaning associated with these elements, the verification points, etc. This methodology must rely on a modeling guide and a training set adapted to each business process.

The use of the UML notation thus raises a number of issues [BOU 07b, OKA 07]. How can a notation with no semantics be employed? How can an application be evaluated based on the UML notation? Several works focus on providing answers to these questions, for example [FED 04a, FED 04b, FED 04c, FED 04d] and [MOT 05].

The UML notation [OMG 11, ROQ 07] is currently not recognized as a formal and/or semiformal method in most standards, despite that many want to completely or partially implement it.

In [BOU 07a, BOU 07b, BOU 09a] and Chapter 19 of [RAM 09], we have showed how the UML notation can be used to build models of critical systems.

In the RT3-TUCS, ANR-SAFECODE, and ANR-RNTL-MEMVATEX projects, we have studied different avenues to introduce UML as a way to model a critical system, see for example [BOU 05, BOU 08, IDA 07a, IDA 07b, OKA 07, RAS 08].

In recent years, several works have contributed to proposing a formalization of the UML notation through a transformation toward formal languages, for example [IDA 06, IDA 09, LED 02, MAM 02, MAR 01, MAR 04]; works such as [MOT 05] that have contributed to propose additional rules to verify UML models should also be mentioned.

6.2.3.3. *SysML*

SysML can be seen as a usage profile. Moreover, SysML [SYS 12, ROQ 13] includes (see Figure 6.9) part of UML 2.0 and provides supplements associated with system aspects and requirement processing.

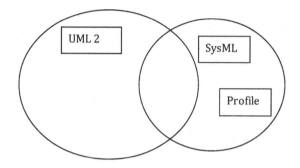

Figure 6.9. *UML model example*

SysML takes into account requirement processing [HAU 05] by including two new diagrams called the requirement diagram and parameter diagram.

SysML offers two interesting concepts for the requirement management aspect, the notion of requirement and the notion of test case. It is then possible to make the connection with four links: composition, derivation, satisfaction and verification.

The requirement stereotype is associated with attributes by default: the identifier, the source, the text description, the type of requirement, risk and the verification method.

SysML is thus a means to describe the requirements within a UML model and to describe the result of the derivation process, as shown in Figure 6.10 taken from [BOU 07c].

The requirements diagram enables modeling requirements, test cases and all the links (refinement, trace, verification, etc.). Requirements can then be linked to the elements of other diagrams through "callout" links.

As already indicated in Chapter 2, a requirement consists of at least three properties: name, identifier and the requirement text.

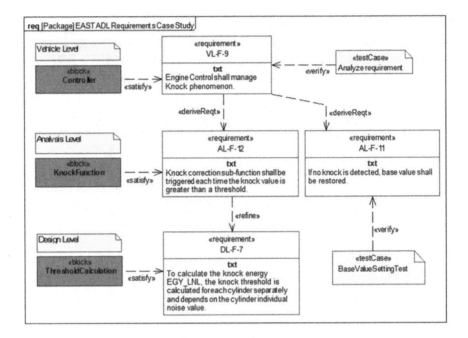

Figure 6.10. *Example of requirement model in SysML*

There are links that allow connections to be established between requirements:

– containment: a requirement is broken down into several requirements;

– copy: the requirement of the provider is identical to the requirement of the customer;

– DeriveReqt: indicates that the requirement is developed from a more general requirement;

– verify: indicates the link between a requirement and a test case;

– satisfy: indicates that a requirement is taken into account by an element of the model;

– refine: a requirement is specified by another;

– trace: there is a traceability link (other than those listed above) between two requirements.

For the links DeriveReqt, Satisfy, Verify and Trace, there is an internal link to the requirement diagram and a link onto an external element (suffix Callout).

By default, there are seven additional attributes that are inherited from the relationships between requirements: satisfiedBy, verifiedBy, tracedTo, derived, derivedFrom, refinedBy and master.

Regarding the links, the notion of "constraints" makes it possible to model a constraint between one and several model elements in the various diagrams. This constraint can be modeled in the form of a mathematical condition or logical expression.

It is possible to identify constraints (properties) and parameters within "Block Definition" diagrams. The parameter diagram makes it possible to establish links between the different constraints.

6.2.3.4. Modeling actors

The UML notation [OMG 11, ROQ 07] proposes several formalisms. These formalisms introduce elements such as actors. The notion of actor is important because it can formally identify users and elements in interaction with the element being modeled.

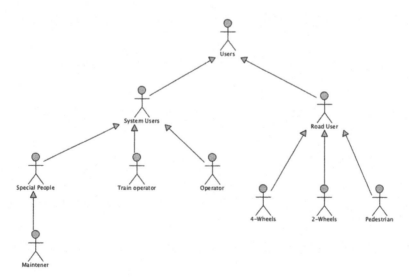

Figure 6.11. *Example of actor tree structure*

Figure 6.11 represents the hierarchy of the users of a level crossing management system.

6.2.3.5. Use case modeling

The UML notation [OMG 11, ROQ 07] proposes several formalisms and among them, the use case diagram can be found for example. This diagram is used to model system lifetime phases and relationships between actors and the system. Use cases can structure users' needs and the corresponding objectives of a system: they provide a user view.

A use case will describe all of the possible uses of the element under study (system, subsystem, hardware, software application) allowing an actor to achieve a major goal. For example, in the case of an ATM system, the goal "Withdraw cash" is a use case for the actor "Card holder".

Use case = {main actor, major goal}

A use case may involve several actors; in this case, there will be a lead actor and one or several secondary actors, the main actor being the initiating actor of the use case.

User

Figure 6.12. *Example of use case*

The use case diagram shows the scope of the element analyzed. It allows the interactions between a component and its environment to be described. It thus describes the features of the system as seen from the outside (stimuli toward the system and system responses).

The outside world is represented by one or more actors (physical person: user, maintenance technician, etc., or an entity considered as external: peripheral device, interfacing system, etc.), which can be modeled as a tree of actors (see Figure 6.11).

Use cases do not completely describe all the users' needs. They enable the description of functional requirements, but they are not suited to the description of non-functional requirements.

The scenario (of a use case) is a concrete description of the satisfaction (or failure of satisfaction) of a goal (or a set of goals). A scenario typically defines a sequence of interaction steps performed to satisfy the goal, and connects these interaction steps with the system context.

The scenarios are particularly very effective to:

– clarify the problem and solution requirements;

– develop test cases;

– communicate with clients/users.

This modeling practice resorting to use cases and scenarios is largely widespread, regardless of the type of system being considered, namely information system (IS) or embedded system. This is due to the fact that the different components communicate their requirements more easily in the form of usage examples rather than conceptual goals.

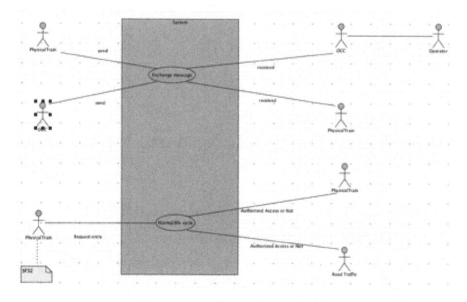

Figure 6.13. *Modeling the behavior of the level crossing*

Figure 6.13 presents a use case diagram that helps to formalize the behavior of the level crossing (manage message exchanges, authorize the movement of vehicles) and Figure 6.14 is a formalization of the requirement related to the avoidance of collision between trains and cars.

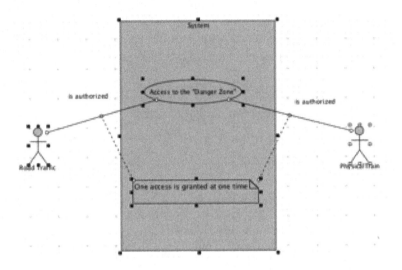

Figure 6.14. *Modeling of the no collision property between train and car*

6.2.3.6. *Modeling scenarios*

A scenario is described in text form. It includes at least the following information, which must be documented:

– scenario: the name of the scenario;

– actor(s): person(s) or system(s) that interact with the system. A scenario;

– roles: specific classes of actors;

– goal(s): each scenario illustrates the satisfaction of goals;

– precondition(s): necessary conditions before executing the scenario;

– postcondition(s): definition of the conditions in the system or the system context after execution of the scenario;

– course: sequence of interaction steps between actors and system;

– special cases: variations and extensions of the scenario.

Use case: Make a leave request

Nominal scenario: Make a leave request

Actor(s): Contributor, IS Management

Role(s): User, remote system

Goal(s): Register an application for leave in order to submit it later

Precondition(s): Contributor authorized to use the management tool

Postcondition(s): The leave application is registered in the system

Course:

1) The contributor identifies herself in the system by entering her identifier and her password
2) The contributor enters the information to apply for leave: leave type, start date, end date, number of days requested
3) The system queries the IS management about the number of days allowed
4) The IS management provides the number of days allowed
5) The contributor registers the leave application in the system
6) End of the scenario

Special cases (variations/extensions):

1a) The contributor has entered the wrong identifier, the system prompts her/him to re-enter a new identifier. Return to step 1.
1b) The contributor has entered the wrong password, the system prompts her/him to re-enter a new password. Return to step 1.
2a) The system detects an inconsistency between the start date, the end date and the number of days requested, the system suggests a new input to the contributor. Return to step 2.
4a) The IS management provides a number of authorized days smaller than the number of days requested, the system informs the contributor that the number of days requested exceeds the number of authorized days and requests the contributor to type a new input. Return to step 2.

Box 6.1. *Example of use case*

In Box 6.1, you will find an example of a textual scenario for the use case "Make a leave request" of an application for the management of leave vacation for an IS.

In this regard, we can only recommend the reading of Alister Cockburn's work on writing text scenarios [COC 00].

6.2.3.7. *Modeling sequence diagrams*

The sequence diagram is a diagram that makes it possible to characterize a snapshot of the system and to formalize a sequence of exchanges. Sequence diagrams are a graphical representation of the interactions between the actors and the system.

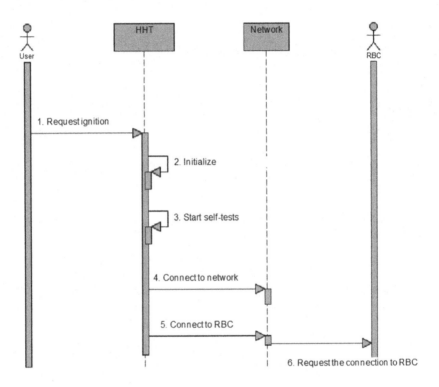

Figure 6.15. *Modeling of the no collision property between train and car*

The sequence diagram is used to describe the interactions between the different interlocutors. As shown in Figure 6.15, the interactions between the driver and subsystems (HHT, RBC, Trigger system) are described according to a dynamic view; time is represented by lifelines (vertical lines) connected to the interlocutors.

Sequence diagrams can be used to illustrate a use case.

6.2.3.8. *UML class diagram*

The class diagram is a diagram used in software engineering to present data used by systems as well as the different relationships between them.

It presents a set of static models, their content (internal structure) and their relationships to other components.

The main elements represented in a class diagram are classes, packages, inheritances and dependencies.

A class is an entity composed of a name, attributes and operations. Attributes characterize the class. Operations are processes that can be implemented onto the class.

Classes have links between them, these links are called associations. An association describes a set of similar links. On each association, it is possible to indicate cardinalities that specify how many objects can be linked to a source object. Cardinalities are constants and one can indicate a minimal cardinality and a maximal cardinality: Cmin and Cmax.

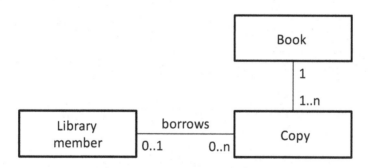

Figure 6.16. *Example of a class diagram*

An example of a class diagram with three classes and two associations is presented in Figure 6.16.

More complex associations can be achieved between classes; we shall mention:

– recursion;

– generalization/specialization;

– aggregation;

– composition;

– constraints.

For further information on UML class models, we recommend reading the book by Pascal Roques *UML 2 par la pratique* [ROQ 06].

6.2.3.9. *Entity-relationship diagrams*

The entity-relationship model is widely used for designing databases and can also be used to describe the data of a system and their structure.

As for the class diagram, the entity-relationship diagram is easy to use and powerful enough to represent relational structures. It is mainly based on a graphical representation that facilitates its understanding.

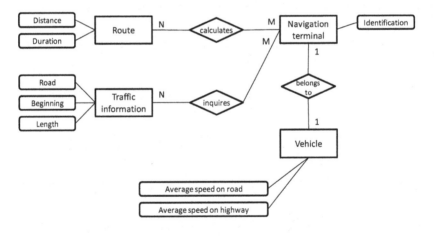

Figure 6.17. *Example of a class diagram*

The concepts used are:

– entity-types: a set of entities that share data characteristics (e.g. "student", "courses", "university");

– relationship-types: a set of relationships between entity-types (e.g. "study", "teach", "is registered with");

– attributes: a property of an entity-type or a relationship-type;

– cardinality (of a relationship): the number of relationship instances to which an entity can participate.

6.2.3.10. *UML activity diagrams*

The UML activity diagram is used to model a process (workflow) in one or more use cases. It allows the description of the sequence of activities and the control flow between activities

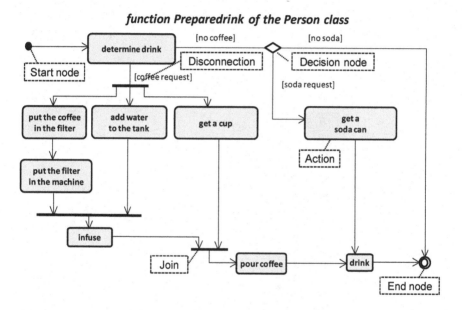

Figure 6.18. *Example of an activity diagram*

There are two types of representation of an activity diagram:

– in sequence;

– in swim lanes.

The area of responsibility of an actor can be identified by the swim lane representation.

6.2.3.11. *State transition diagrams*

State transition UML diagrams describe the internal behavior of an object using a finite state automaton.

They present the possible sequences of states and actions that a class instance can address during its life cycle in response to discrete events (such as signals or method invocations).

In practice, a state transition diagram is a graph that represents a finite-state automaton; in other words, a machine whose behavior on output depends not only on the state of its inputs, but also on a past solicitations history.

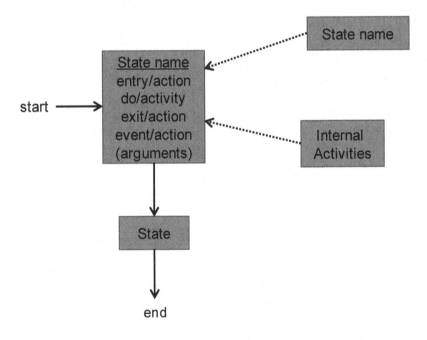

Figure 6.19. *Example of state-transition diagram*

6.2.4. *Formal method and/or technique*

6.2.4.1. *Introduction*

A formal method (HOL, CSP, LOTOS, CCS, Temporal logic, VDM [JON 90] and Z [SPI 89]) is a means to implement an unambiguous and consistent description of a system at different development stages (specification, architecture and/or design).

The description assumes a mathematical form and may be subjected to mathematical analysis. This mathematical analysis can be assisted by tools.

In general, a formal method provides a notation, a technique for developing a description in this notation and a verification process to control the correction of requirements.

Petri networks and state machines can be considered as formal methods if they are associated with a rigorous mathematical basis (more non-determinism, etc.).

6.2.4.2. *Formal technique*

Formal techniques (simulation, model-checking, abstract interpretation, proof, etc.) are not new. As matter of fact, the first papers that deal with the topic date back to the early 1970s (see, for example, [COU 77, DIJ 76, HOA 69]). However, the implementation of formal methods dates from the 1980s [HAL 91, JON 90, SPI 89] with industrial uses in the 1990s [BEH 93, OFT 97].

In [BOW 95] and [OFT 97], we can find the first feedback opinions from the industry concerning formal techniques, and in particular feedback about the B-method [ABR 96], the LUSTRE language [OBS 97, HAL 91] and SAO+ the ancestor of SCADE[4]. Other books, such as [HAD 06, MON 00] provide a panorama of formal methods from a more scientific point of view.

---

4 It should be noted that initially SCADE was a development environment based on the LUSTRE language and that since version 6, SCADE has become a full-fledged language (in version 6, the code generator actually takes on input a SCADE model and not a LUSTRE code).

6.2.4.3. *Formal method*

The purpose of a formal specification is to express, in a rigorous and consistent manner, the document of software specifications in order to generate error-free code. If we consider the example of Z [SPI 89] or B [ABR 96], formal specifications make use of mathematical tools borrowed from set theory (Bourbaki) and from the principles of first-order logic, containing quantifiers and functionals (but no functional quantifier).

The approach consists of writing a simple and abstract model of the problem and then in adding, as it proceeds through the so-called refinement stages [MOR 90a], more practical and more complex elements while proving the consistency of the new models created.

The final step is free of the original abstract data types that became programmable structures such as tables or files. Subprogram preconditions, simultaneity and the non-determinism that were present in the abstract model have been eliminated, and programming control structures such as sequencing and the loop have been introduced.

It is at this stage that automatic conversion to Ada or C code or even assembly code can take place for some tools, simply because it is clear that it is impossible to make a formal specification "stick" directly to a conventional programming language, since they use opposed ways of thinking.

The advantages of formal methods are as follows:

– the code generated complies with formal specifications since we have actually verified it. It is then possible to consider removing unit tests;

– the resulting code is consistent (no unnecessary variable, not typing problem, no sections of inefficient code, no test unvisited, no infinite loop, no side effect, etc.);

– the process is rigorous and of quality.

6.2.4.4. *Objectives of formal methods*

The purpose of formal methods is to eliminate ambiguities, misunderstandings and misinterpretations that may arise in the description in natural language.

The term "formal method" designates:

– languages:

  - having a vocabulary and syntax formally defined;

  - whose semantics is defined mathematically;

– processing and verification techniques based on mathematical proof.

The formal specification always provides a description of what the software should achieve and not how it should do it.

It is worth noting that in critical applications, at least two formal methods make use of recognized and commonly employed design environments covering part of the implementation process from the specification to the code, while integrating one or more verification process, namely the B-method [ABR 96, BOU 13] and the LUSTRE language [HAL 91, OFT 97] and its graphical version named SCADE [DOR 08]. The B-method and the SCADE environment are associated with industrial tools that have proven their possibilities.

The interest of formal methods lies in the fact that verifications of properties such as proving properties (through proof activities, comprehensive simulation [BAI 08], etc.) can be implemented as early as possible in the development cycle. The underlying idea is to obtain safe software by construction.

6.2.4.5. *From Z to the B-method*

One of the first applications of formal methods was made *a posteriori* in the SACEM[5] [GUI 90]. Within the framework of the SACEM [GEO 90], the RATP[6] has performed a Hoare proof [HOA 69] to demonstrate that the requirements were taken into account (for more information, see [GUI 90]). The Hoare proof is a method that from a program P and a set of preconditions C can bring forward the set of post-conditions.

---

5 The SACEM (Driver Assistance, Operation and Maintenance System), which was installed in 1988, makes it possible by means of a screen installed on trains to provide drivers with indications about the speed at which the train must be conducted (side signaling indication inside the cab) in order to assist the operation.
6 See www.ratp.fr.

Hoare's proof, which was performed within the framework of the SACEM, has enabled a number of properties of the code to be identified, but it was not possible to make the connection with safety-related requirements (non-collision requirement for example).

Faced with this situation, it was decided to achieve a formal model in Z [SPI 89]. This formal model has contributed to breaking down the properties and to establishing links between requirements and the code. Around 20 significant abnormalities have then been identified by the expert team in charge of the re-specification in Z.

As a result of the difficulties that have been encountered with the implementation of the SACEM (manual processing, introduction of errors, complexity of obtained properties, difficulty in achieving the proofs, traceability problems, etc.), the industrialist in charge of the development of the SAET-METEOR [LEC 96, MAT 98] was asked to use a formal process that integrated formal proof and was assisted by tools. It was in this context that the B-method was chosen.

```
_ FileSys _____
  fsys: NAME ⇸ FILE
  open: ℙ NAME
 _____
  open ⊆ dom fsys
```

Figure 6.20. *Example of Z process*[7]

This is the reason why in the French railway sector, the use of formal methods, and in particular the use of the B-method, is increasingly more common within the framework of the development of critical systems. The software of these safety critical systems (railway signaling, automatic operation) must meet very strict quality, reliability and robustness criteria.

---

7 This Z process represents a file management system, in which the state is represented by a function mapping between file names and their content and a group of files opened for reading.

6.2.4.6. *B-method*

6.2.4.6.1. Presentation

The B-method [ABR 96, BOU 13] was developed by Jean-Raymond Abrial. It is a model-oriented formal method like Z [SPI 89] and VDM [JON 90] but which allows for incremental development of the specification up to the code, through the notion of refinement [MOR 90a, MOR 90b], and this is as part of a unique formalism, the language of abstract machines. At each stage of the B development, proof obligations are generated in order to ensure the validity of the refinement and the consistency of the abstract machine. The B-method is therefore based on the notion of proof.

Similarly to Z, the B-method is based on set theory and first-order predicate logic. Unlike Z, the B-method has a *development* nuance in the way the operations are specified. Furthermore, operations are not specified in terms of pre- and post-conditions, but by means of generalized substitutions.

Some most recent projects such as the CTDC, KVS, SAET-METEOR[8] [BEH 93, BEH 96, BOU 06a], the VAL (Light Automatic Vehicle)[9] of the Charles de Gaulle airport and line 1 of the Paris metro all use the B-method throughout the whole development process (from specifications up to the code) (see Figure 6.21).

It should be noted that the B-method has an industrial environment. The atelier B is marketed by the company CLEARSY[10]. This tool entirely covers the development cycle proposed by the B-method (specification, refinement, code generation and proof).

---

8 The SAET-METEOR [MAT 98] team, since October 1998, line 14 of the Paris metro. The computer architecture of the SAET-METEOR (Train Operation Automation System – East-West Fast Metro) is presented in Chapter 2 of [IDA 09] and the software safety development, V&V and demonstration processes are presented in Chapter 2 of [BOU 11c].

9 The first VAL was inaugurated in Lille in 1983. It is nowadays active in the cities of Taipei and Toulouse, Rennes and Turin (since January 2006). Regarding the deployment of the VAL, there are at least 119 km of line that are deployed around the world and more than 830 cars are in operation or under construction. The VAL CDG combines the technology of the VAL and complementary digital hardware based on the B-method.

10 See http://www.clearsy.com.

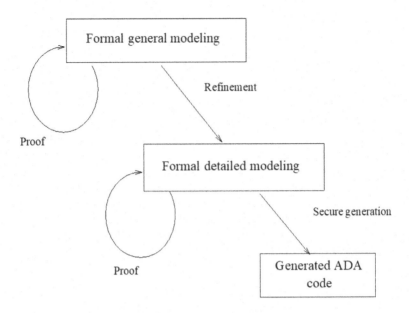

Figure 6.21. *B-development cycle*

In the example of Figure 6.22, we introduce the specification of the program *HelloWorld* and its implementation *HelloWorld_n*.

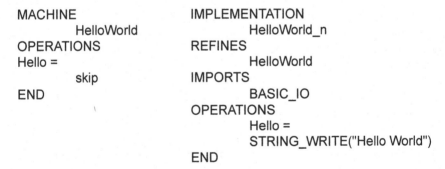

Figure 6.22. *The program "Hello" in B*

Collection IC2 [BOU 13] is dedicated to the B-method and presents various implementation examples.

```
MACHINE
   Exemple
SETS
      TRAIN ; POSITION
VARIABLES
      Domaine
INVARIANT
      Domaine : TRAIN - - >POW(POSITION)
    &    !(t1,t2). ((t1,t2: TRAIN*TRAIN) => ((Domaine(t1) ∧ Domaine(t2) = {}) & (t1/=t2)))
INITIALISATION
      Domaine :( Domaine : TRAIN - - >POW(POSITION)
                & !(t1,t2). ((t1,t2: TRAIN*TRAIN) => ((Domaine(t1) ∧ Domaine(t2) = {}) & (t1/=t2)))
            )
END
```

Figure 6.23. *Second example of B*

Figure 6.23 is a formalization example of property P1

P1: "there should not be any risk of collision"

which is formalized in first-order set logic by $\forall\ \{t_1,t_2\} \in [T]$, *then* $D_{t_1} \cap D_{t_2} = \phi$, *si* $t_1 \neq t_2$ with D_{t_i}, which is the operating perimeter of the train i and $[T]$, which is the set of trains.

6.2.4.6.2. From machines to implementations

6.2.4.6.2.1. Principle

The abstract machines used to describe the specification employ non-deterministic constructions and all the power of set language and first-order logic. However, at the abstract machine level, algorithmic constructions (sequences, loops) are prohibited.

In order to progress toward an executable application, it is necessary to introduce a process known as *refinement*, which allows the data set structures to be gradually replaced by structures close to those of programming languages; the non-determinism is thus lifted and generalized substitutions similar to sequences and loops (WHILE) are introduced.

All these *refinement* stages are subject to proofs of conservation of invariants and of conformity of refined machines with respect to the more abstract machines.

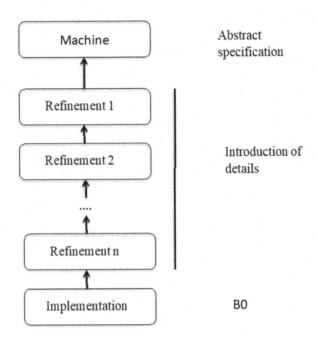

Figure 6.24. *From the description of need to the implantation*

6.2.4.6.2.2. Refinement

As shown in Figure 6.24, the refinement process (see [MOR 90a, MOR 90b]) is conventionally represented as a series of independent steps to which verifications are associated. A component $i + 1$ (refinement or implementation) refines a component i (machine or refinement).

The refinement process begins with the definition of a machine that contains the abstract description of the need. Refinements are a means to implement the need and to avoid deterministic and non-sequential elements. The implementation is a B-component, which uses a subset of the B language named the B0.

The sublanguage B0 is a language close to conventional languages (C, ADA, etc.). As a result, B0 is easily translatable toward programming languages.

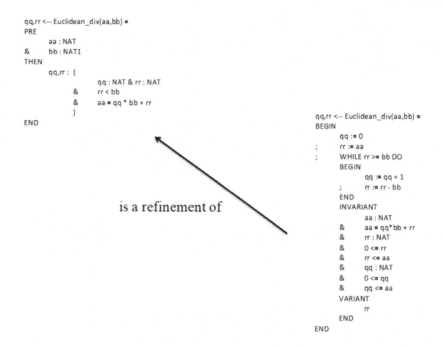

```
qq,rr <-- Euclidean_div(aa,bb) =
PRE
        aa : NAT
&       bb : NAT1
THEN
        qq,rr : (
                qq : NAT & rr : NAT
            &   rr < bb
            &   aa = qq * bb + rr
                )
END
```

```
qq,rr <-- Euclidean_div(aa,bb) =
BEGIN
        qq := 0
;       rr := aa
;       WHILE rr >= bb DO
        BEGIN
                qq := qq + 1
        ;       rr := rr - bb
        END
        INVARIANT
                aa : NAT
        &       aa = qq*bb + rr
        &       rr : NAT
        &       0 <= rr
        &       rr <= aa
        &       qq : NAT
        &       0 <= qq
        &       qq <= aa
        VARIANT
                rr
        END
END
```

is a refinement of

Figure 6.25. *Refinement example*

Figure 6.25 presents an example of refinement (for more on refinement processes, see [MOR 90a, MOR 90b]). The specification states that the need is to find two numbers **q** and **r** such that **a = q*b + r** and that **r < b**. It can be seen that the mathematical specification of the Euclidean division can be replaced (within the meaning of refinement) by an algorithm performing the computation through successive subtractions.

The proposed algorithm makes use of a WHILE ... DO END statement. The B language integrates the notions of INVARIANT and VARIANT. The VARIANT is used to demonstrate the termination of the loop and the INVARIANT makes it possible to verify the proper behavior of the loop.

6.2.4.6.2.3. Process

Figure 6.26 introduces the conventional process that is focused on searching for defaults within the software application. The search for default is based on the notion of program execution. The goal of this approach is to demonstrate that the software is correct.

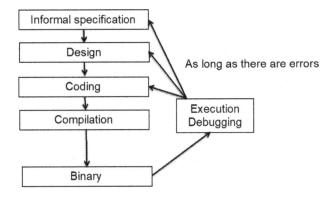

Figure 6.26. *Cycle development with the B-method*

As part of the implementation of formal methods, the process is based on a different observation: "the software is correct by construction". That is why the process is different: it focuses on need analysis and the demonstration that certain properties are true during all executions (see Figure 6.27).

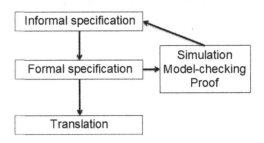

Figure 6.27. *Formal process*

As shown in Figure 6.28, the approach consists of writing a simple and abstract model of the problem, and then in adding, during the course of the so-called refinement steps [MOR 90a, MOR 90b], more concrete and more complex elements proving at the same time the consistency of the new models being created.

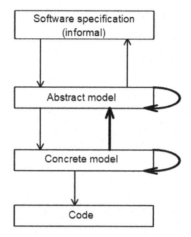

Figure 6.28. *Development cycle with the B-method*

The implantation, which is the final step, is exempt from the original abstract data types that have turned into programmable structures such as tables or files. The subprogram preconditions, simultaneity and non-determinism, which were present in the abstract model, have been eliminated, and programming control structures such as sequencing and loops have been introduced.

It is at this stage that automatic conversion to Ada or C code, or assembler code for some tools, can take place because it is clear that wanting to "stick" a formal specification directly to a conventional programming language is impossible, since their ways of thinking are contradictory.

The notion of proof (represented in Figure 6.28 in bold arrows) is intimately linked to B-development and the specification is written based on these future obligations. The proof occurs at all abstraction levels. After outlining a machine, proof of its internal coherence is performed. If it succeeds, then development may progress.

Proof is thus obtained after every abstraction level, verifying its internal coherence and its compliance with the abstraction level that is above.

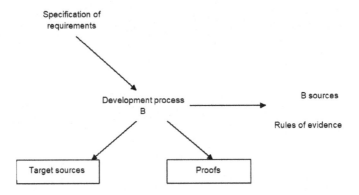

Figure 6.29. *B-process*

Figure 6.29 shows a summary of the implementation process of a B-model. On input, need specifications can be found and on output we encounter the sources of the B-model, the rules added, the Burden of Proof (BoP), proofs and the source code.

6.2.4.6.3. Atelier B

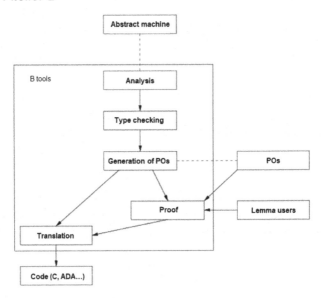

Figure 6.30. *Architecture of a B-tool*

6.2.4.6.4. Verification by the proof

The notion of proof is intimately linked to B-development and the specification is written based on these future obligations. The proof occurs at all abstraction levels. After outlining a machine, proof of its internal consistence is performed. If it succeeds, then the development may progress. Proof is thus obtained after each abstraction level, verifying its internal consistency and its compliance with the abstraction level that is above.

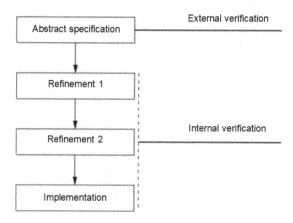

Figure 6.31. *Verification*

Burdens of proof are represented by a purpose to be achieved provided that a number of assumptions are present. These are established based on the preconditions and the definitions contained in the refined component, but also based on the information read in the visualized or imported machines.

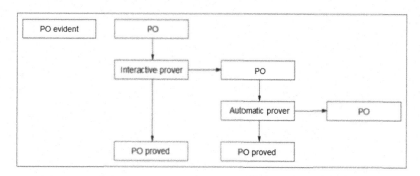

Figure 6.32. *Proof implementation*

The automatic prover then applies its rule sets to each of the requirements, rewriting the goal and assumptions until they coincide. The major drawback of these new writings is that the atelier does not keep any trace of the former goal, which sometimes results in failures that should not happen. On the other hand, a number of additional rules are available, but these are applied only if the user wishes so when she/he launches the interactive proof option.

The prover may fail when demonstrating burdens of proof for two reasons. Either the burden of proof is false (goal searched for: $100 < 50$), which indicates a flaw in the design, or the burden of proof is correct but the set of rules is not enough to be able to establish it.

Since the automatic prover of the atelier does not have a set of rules able to solve any problem, it is sometimes necessary to add rules. The user has a choice between several possibilities. First of all, it can resort to the rules defined in the atelier. These rules are not consistently applied because they considerably slow down the resolution time. If adding these rules is not enough, users can then write their own rules. Particular care must be taken when defining these rules because there is nothing to validate them and it is then possible to write a rule that could even enable a false burden to be solved.

In most cases, the addition of the tactics identified in the atelier was enough to prove all of the burdens.

6.2.4.7. *SCADE*

6.2.4.7.1. From LUSTRE to SCADE

Following the observation that conventional computer languages were inadequate to achieve real-time automatic applications, the LUSTRE language was developed within the VERIMAG[11] laboratory in the 1980s [BEN 03, HAL 91, HAL 05].

From LUSTRE, we moved on to SCADE[12] through different phases and reconciliations (SAGA with Merlin Gérin, SAO[13] with AIRBUS). It is worth noting that two main features could be identified in SAO:

---

11 To learn more, see site www.verimag.fr.
12 SCADE is distributed by the company ANSYS, see https://www.ansys.com.
13 SAO (Computer Assisted Specification) is an "in-house" formalism developed by AIRBUS, which revisits the concepts of analog block diagrams, thus making it possible to propose specification and code generation tools.

– code generation based on automatic models allowed the number of errors to be reduced;

– the graphic language close to the culture of aerospace engineers facilitates communication within AIRBUS. As a result, there is an acceleration of the development and a capitalization of know-how; SAO is one of the key factors of success of the A320.

Halbwachs [HAL 05] explores LUSTRE and SCADE history in detail more as well as the differences that may exist.

6.2.4.7.2. SCADE environment

The SCADE environment implements an extension of the LUSTRE language (textual). This extension maintains the properties of the LUSTRE language and enables modeling based on the concepts of blocks functional diagrams and data flow. The LUSTRE language is part of "formal methods", in the sense that it is based on a specific syntax and semantics. The LUSTRE language is a textual language.

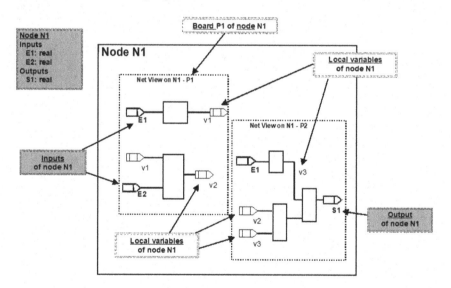

Figure 6.33. *Board example*

The SCADE environment makes it possible to model an application in graphical form by means of components (box, state/transition graph, etc.), which are grouped onto a "board" (see Figure 6.33).

SCADE is a language and a development environment that is used in areas such as avionics (AIRBUS, Eurocopter), the nuclear industry (Schneider Electrics, ECA), the railway sector (Ansaldo STS, AREVA, THALES, RATP) and recently the automobile industry. Chapter 6 presents more detailed usage examples.

SCADE is meant to be compatible with the recommendations of the various business standards (DO-178, CEI/IEC 61508, EN 50128 and IEC/IEC 60880).

Figure 6.34 shows the tools of the SCADE environment in the V-model. Whether the SCADE environment is used in specification or design phases, there is always an initial document, which is here referred to as "Specification". This document can either be a textual specification or a formal specification (SART), which can be at the system level or software level, etc.

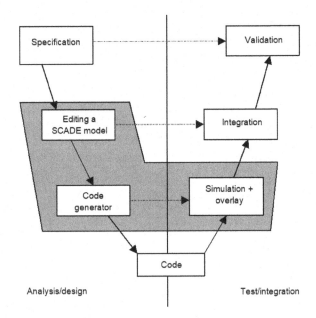

Figure 6.34. *SCADE as design environment*

The SCADE environment can be used to manage:

– the design through:

- the editing of the model. The model is broken down into several models that are then considered as libraries;

- automatic generation of a "certifiable" target code;

– the verification through:

- a semantic verification phase (typing, clock, etc.);

- a verification phase of the design rules;

- a simulation phase of all or part of the model;

– validation through proving properties.

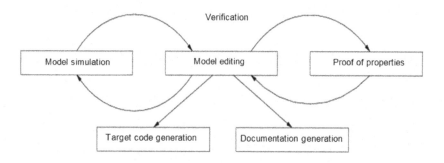

Figure 6.35. *SCADE link between activities*

At the global level, it is interesting to implement a model that describes the software functional architecture. The system to be modeled is then broken down according to needs that will correspond to SCADE models. This decomposition allows us:

– to distribute the global specification onto several SCADE models (a model per need function);

– to independently develop each SCADE model;

– to produce the corresponding interface document.

The diagram in Figure 6.36 details the models used to manage SCADE nodes as well as the relationships that govern them.

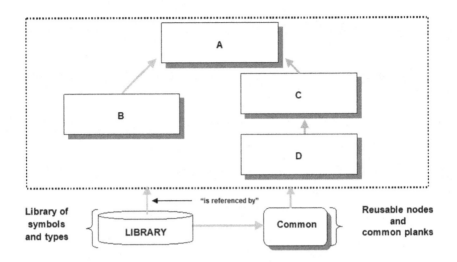

Figure 6.36. *The SCADE model architecture*

Decomposition must satisfy the synchronous assumption and preserve the data flow. Compliance with the time constraints of the network nodes is enough to ensure that the constraints of the father node are satisfied.

The logic behind the decomposition should be the separation of the data flow. A SCADE component can be materialized either:

– by a board (behavior composition already defined);

– by a state/transition diagram;

– by importing code as discussed in the following section.

Chapter 6 of [BOU 12] is dedicated to the presentation of SCADE and examples of industrial uses are presented.

6.2.4.7.3. SCADE modeling including integration of external code

The reuse of external code (C or ADA) can be done by directly (the code is described within the model) or indirectly importing the code (access to files).

The obvious goal is to enjoy the experience acquired from other projects.

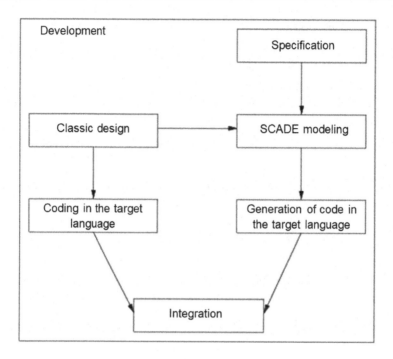

Figure 6.37. *SCADE/target language*

6.2.4.7.4. Verification process

The controls carried out on the SCADE specification are intended to verify:

– the consistency of the clocks of the different functions (for the sequencer and/or for each model);

– the coherence of data flows (typing, etc.);

– syntactic and semantic controls;

– methodological controls (development verification rules, test quality verification, etc.).

The SCADE environment includes a simulator of all or part of the model. The results of the review stage of the SCADE model must therefore include:

– the verification of the traceability of the requirements with the model;

– the verification of the model fitness.

As part of an application combining SCADE and external code (C or ADA):

– a review phase should show that the code reused executes its function as expected (specification analysis) and that useful documents (specification, design, test) do exist. The UTs and ITs associated with the code imported must be available in order to show that it reacts properly;

– within the SCADE model, it is necessary to verify that the code fits the SCADE model (interface);

– it will then be possible to test the overall behavior (SCADE + imported code) using the simulator.

6.2.4.7.5. Validation process

The SCADE environment includes a property verifier. In order to verify a property P on the model M, a specific board P has to be developed that instantiates the model M and the observer O associated with property P.

This board P can be achieved inside a specific model MO, which will see model M as a library.

The verification of property P can show that a requirement is verified in the entire model. This validation phase by proof is expected to reduce the number of test to be performed.

The application validation process will thus be based on two activities:

– formal proof of properties originating from the requirements of the upper level and for safety studies;

– functional tests based on the specification of the next level.

The formal proof, with the Design Verifier (DV) toolkit, contributes to the detection of errors in the specification and modeling in the early phases of the development cycle. This minimizes the risk of detection of these errors during the final validation phases and contributes to the decrease in the functional validation effort. Proof of compliance of the model with respect to safety requirements results in increased software reliability.

The proof with the DV toolkit facilitates the various phases of the software development process:

– requirement specification: formal methods are highly recommended (see the CENELEC EN 50128 standard, for example) for the requirement specification, particularly for the software SSIL4. The DV toolkit uses the SCADE notation for the formal requirement specification;

– modular testing: the presence of strong typing, formal verification and a certified code generator considerably reduces the scope of tests, allowing for the verification of the fitness between the modules and the safety requirements. The DV toolkit is capable of the verification of safety properties related to the analysis of limit values;

– modular testing: the presence of strong typing, formal verification and a certified code generator considerably reduces the scope of the tests allowing for the verification of the fitness between the modules and the safety requirements.

Concerning the model comprising imported external code (C or ADA), for the implementation of the property formal proof, we are faced with the lack of property in this code.

Several cases may appear:

– the lack of property in the imported code does not hamper the proof process of the model: this means that the model does not expect any specific property and that in all cases the application will run;

– this particular case can be seen as an anomaly in the sense that regardless of the service provided by the imported function, it has no impact on the property;

– in the event of failure of proof due to the lack of information, it is then possible to isolate the component and to introduce assertions characterizing the imported component;

– once the proof has been achieved, it will then be required to show that the imported code actually verifies the assertions (complementary testing);

– failure of proof: it may happen that the imported component does not provide adequate operation.

6.2.4.7.6. Code generation

Through the use of a "certified" generator (in addition to the proof), it is possible to avoid unit and integration testing given that the SCADE model has been verified.

The software engineering atelier SCADE includes the C code generator "KCG". Based on the formal modeling language, KCG is able to automatically generate the C code corresponding to the data flow, to the state machines, while respecting the synchronous dynamic performance of the model.

These source code files are then compiled and assembled to produce an executable for the update. Compilers are either validated (internally) or certified.

The code generation process can generate the code of the SCADE model and take into account the imported code. It is necessary to put in place an integration testing process to verify the impact of the imported code on the generated code.

6.2.5. *Synthesis*

Previous books [BOU 11a, BOU 11b, BOU 12, BOU 13] have given us the opportunity to present examples from an industrial environment enabling the implementation of formal methods. Although to this day there are numerous environments and a large number of applications, it should be noted that a significant change has occurred; as a matter of fact, we moved on from a "shy" implementation of formal techniques toward an industrial implementation as we will explain in the following.

However, this change does not happen without raising a number of difficulties. The development of a software application having an impact on safety is a rather difficult issue, which is oriented towards "quality control"[14]. Moreover, the only effective technique to achieve safety software is to avoid the introduction of defects and/or to detect the maximum number of defects; for this purpose, quality control is required. Quality control involves the definition of process and a substantial documentary production.

14 "Quality control" in the sense of the application of a process that satisfies a standard related to quality control, for example the ISO 9001:2015 [ISO 15].

The introduction of formal methods in the process makes us shift from a quality control approach to a "model-centric" approach, which can give the impression that the documentation becomes unnecessary and that makes the safety level of the application software dependent on the safety level of the tools implemented.

6.3. Model verification

It should be noted that formal techniques were originally used by manufacturers to verify that a specification, an architecture, design principles and/or code complied with certain properties.

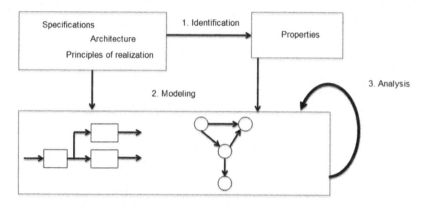

Figure 6.38. *Identification, modeling and analysis*

As shown in Figure 6.38, the verification work previously consisted of:

– identifying properties: an analysis of input elements (specification, architecture, implementation principles, code, etc.) was intended to identify properties. Properties can be classified into two families: safety properties and liveliness properties;

– modeling: after having chosen a technology (technique + tools), it is then necessary to achieve a model M that can be interpreted by tools and which will carry out the implementation of the chosen verification technique (model checking, proof, simulation, etc.);

– analyzing: the third phase consists of performing the verification itself.

For example, Chapter 2 of [BOU 11b] shows how the approach in Figure 9.9 has been implemented by the RATP[15] to validate the specification of the safety functions of the SAET-METEOR[16].

6.4. Setting up of formal methods

Two different approaches have been presented in the various chapters:

– the first type of approach consists of creating a formal model based on a specification (see Figure 6.39) and performing verifications on this model;

– the second type consists of performing formal analyses on code conventionally achieved (in C, ADA or C++, for example) based on a specification (see Figure 9.4).

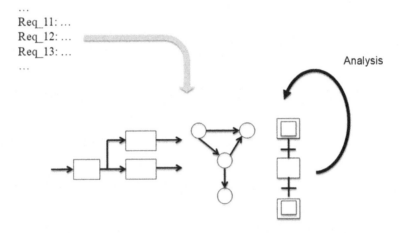

Figure 6.39. *Model implementation*

In [BOU 11a], we presented several implementation examples of the static analyzer of the "abstract interpretation" family (see [BOU 11a, Chapter 3; COU 77; COU 00]). We have thus presented examples of the use of FramaC, Polyspace, Astrée and CodePeer.

---

15 For more information, see www.ratp.fr/.
16 The system [MAT 98] that equips, since October 1998, line 14 of the Parisian metro, is called SAET-METEOR (Train Operation Automation System-East-West Fast Metro).

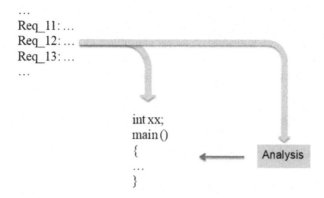

Figure 6.40. *Formal analysis of a code*

Taking formal methods into account requires a development of the implementation process that must take into account the modeling phase, as shown in Figure 6.41.

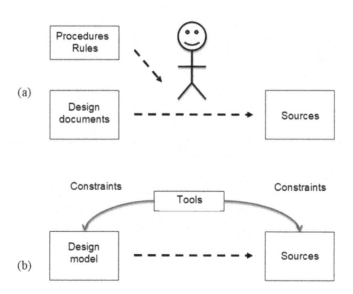

Figure 6.41. *Formal analysis of a code*

Conventionally (Figure 6.41(a)), the code has to be produced from design documents (specification, architecture, design, etc.) as well as from business processes. The fact of including a modeling phase (Figure 6.40(b)) increases the significance of the notion of tool and the need to qualify the tools according to their impact on the software application.

6.5. Implementation of formal methods

6.5.1. *Conventional processes*

The implementation of a software application is broken down into stages (specification, design, coding, testing, etc.). This is referred to as lifecycle. The lifecycle is needed to describe dependencies and sequences between activities.

This lifecycle makes it possible to identify phases and for each phase, to identify the inputs, outputs, activities to be performed, the people involved and the verification means implemented.

Figure 1.3 shows that in a conventional V-model, the cycle is decomposed into two phases, the descending phase and the ascending phase[17]. There are different testing phases: unit testing (focused on lowest level components), integration testing (focused on software and/or hardware interfaces) and functional testing (sometimes called validation testing) for the purpose of demonstrating that the product satisfies its specification. The activities of the ascending phase (execution of UT/IT and VT) are prepared during the descending phase.

Regarding the operation/maintenance phase, it concerns the operational lifetime and the management of possible developments. The maintenance of the software application remains the most sensitive activity. In fact, following a development, it is necessary to maintain a safety level while controlling the development cost and by minimizing the impact on a system in service.

---

17 It should be noted that there is a horizontal correspondence (dotted arrow) between specification, design and testing activities.

6.5.2. Process taking formal methods into account

In general, the implementation process of a software application goes through various phases requiring the execution of the software application. As shown in Figure 6.42, the notion of execution is then fundamental to demonstrate that the software application works correctly.

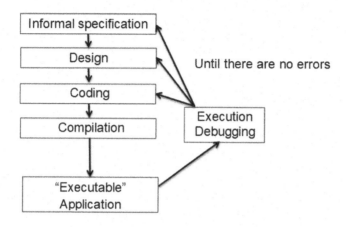

Figure 6.42. *Conventional processes*

Inserted within a development framework based on the concept of modeling (Figure 9.9), the process does not rely on the execution of the application to demonstrate the proper functioning of the application but on the implementation process. Consequently, the software application is then considered to be correct following the process that has been implemented. The correction is thus intrinsic to the product implementation.

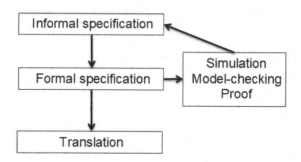

Figure 6.43. *Formal process from the specification onwards*

Figure 6.43 provides an example in which a model is achieved starting from the specification, and in this case the model is a complement to an informal specification, which may contain the requirements. However, the model can also be introduced at the design level (Figure 6.44).

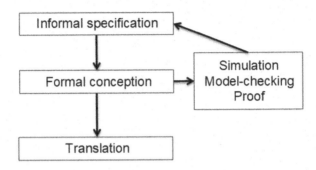

Figure 6.44. *Formal process starting at the design level*

In Figure 6.44, the specification is indicated as being non-formal, but it is possible to obtain a first model (formal or at least structured) whose purpose is to structure requirements and to help in identifying inconsistencies and incompleteness. This model can then, during the design phase, become associated with a formal design model.

Included in the development of the SAET-METEOR (see Chapter 3 of [BOU 11c]), we have shown how the B-method [ABR 96] has been implemented for the design of safety software. The process of the SAET-METEOR is thus a process similar to Figure 6.44.

In the area of applications for the railway sector, software specifications are generally associated with a structured model based on SADT[18] [LIS 90] and/or SA-RT.

It is worth noting that as part of the development of software for a new CBTC[19], a manufacturer of the railway industry is in the process of

18 The acronym SADT stands for Structured Analysis and Design Technique. This method was developed by the Softech company in the United States. The SADT method is an analysis method that makes use of successive levels of descriptive approaches destined for any aggregate.
19 Communication Based Train Control: this is a system for operating and driving trains and subways and demonstrating their safety. The CBTC is a system composed of embedded

implementing a software application where the specification is modeled using SA-RT and where the design combines SCADE and the B-method.

6.5.3. *Issues*

The introduction of techniques and formal methods as part of the implementation of software applications reveals new processes that are no longer consistent with the V-model recommended by standards. The formal methods implementation cycle shifts verification activities toward the descending phase and concentrates the whole of the information in the model (Figure 6.45).

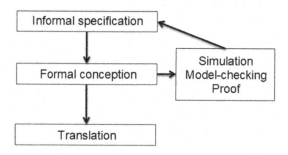

Figure 6.45. *Process taking models into account*

Given the concentration of information inside the model, we can say that this is not a "model-oriented" approach but a "model-centric" approach, which is different. Furthermore, in a "model-centric" approach, the model becomes the medium conveying all activities, or even becomes the container of the activities (in Figure 9.16, dotted lines correspond to verification activities).

Quality control standards (ISO 9001:2015 [ISO 15], for example) recommend that processes, activities and deliverables be identified. Business standards such as the CENELEC EN 50128 standard [CEN 01] identify a minimal list of documents to be produced.

---

devices on trains and of interconnected stationary equipment (usually by radio). A standard is dedicated to the CBTC [IEE 04].

In a model-centric process, UTs and ITs can be replaced by simulations and/or proof of property. However, these verification elements are then part of the model in addition to elements such as:

– metrics computation;

– model consistency verification;

– verification of compliance with rules of coding.

This kind of "model-centric" approach is interesting but it removes several document elements that then become "unnecessary" since they can be produced on demand. We have here a potential "non-compliance" with "objective"-oriented standards such as IEC 61508 [IEC 10], the ISO 26262 [ISO 09] and the CENELEC EN 50128 [CEN 01, CEN 11].

The strength of the "model-centric" approach lies in its capability to help business convergence, as we have shown in [BOU 99, BOU 06a]. As a matter of fact, the various teams (software and hardware, design, V&V and RAMS) can share information concerning their activities, which allows us to better understand the difficulties. In general, the team in charge of safety, which employs its own functional models and methods, may have a somewhat different view from that of the design team and differences can have a strong impact on costs and deadlines. The use of a common model allows us to make as soon as possible safety-related recommendations and requirements available and it is possible to link these elements to portions of model.

The "model-centric" approach will[20] unveil four difficulties:

– the use of modeling at all levels and of any kind. The difficulty concerning this topic lies in the lack of semantics of modeling tools (UML notation, SIMULINK or MATLAB models, etc.);

– the lack of documents will not lead to repeating the design in the event of obsolescence of tools;

– the tools become the central point of the process; it is then necessary to show that tools can be used for the safety level applicable for the software application to be achieved. This qualification should apply both to the code generators and verification tools;

---

20 We use the future because there has been no model-centric application that is in service long enough to cause any problems, but it does not mean that it will never happen.

– the complexity of the techniques implemented (see, for example, abstract interpretation tools [BOU 11A]) imposes a high level of competence for the people in charge of the activities.

6.6. Software application maintenance

The maintenance of the software application remains the most sensitive activity. In fact, following a development stage, it is necessary to maintain a safety level while controlling the development cost and by minimizing the impact on a system in service.

Software application maintenance is subject to a difficulty: the life expectancy of the software application. In effect, in the railway sector, the lifetime is 40–50 years, for the aeronautics industry it is 40 years, 50 years for the nuclear sector and 15 years for the automobile sector.

In view of these lifetimes, it is therefore important to take measures to ensure the maintenance of the service and maintenance of the software application. These measures must take into account the type of machine used for development, as well as the tools implemented, and the documentation to be produced to carry out maintenance and recovery if needed.

The SACEM (Driver Assistance, Operation and Maintenance System) is a system that was implemented in 1986 and which is regularly updated. The choice of a language such as ADA [ISO 95] or C [ISO 99] enables us to prevent hardware, tool and operating system obsolescence problems.

Nonetheless, what will happen to formal development environments such as the Atelier B and/or SCADE? Will it be possible to port the model from one tool to another? Will it be possible to redevelop a tool?

6.7. Conclusion

Formal techniques and formal methods are now being used successfully in an industrial manner in projects of various sizes. The tools associated have reached their maturity, making it possible to take into account the complexity of such applications. It should be noted that the complexity of industrial applications very often has an impact on processing time[21].

Accounting for technical and formal methods has an impact on the process being implemented and it is therefore necessary to build a new frame of reference that meets quality standards in use. The construction of this frame of reference should take into account the fact that the model is able to replace documents which were originally to be produced but considering the lifetime of the system and associated maintenance objectives. Moreover, if the tool is no longer maintained and the formalism is proprietary, it may be difficult, if not impossible, to update the application in the absence of a model.

Another difficulty of model-centric approaches placing the safety level of the software application at the same safety level of the tools being used. It is difficult to show that a C compiler is SSIL4, inasmuch as it will be even harder to demonstrate that a prover is SSIL4. With regard to compilers, it was possible to implement redundancy and diversity-based strategies, both for specific tools such as provers, model-checking tools and/or abstract interpretation tools; it is difficult to have two tools of similar effectiveness in the same area.[22] It is then necessary to implement records for the qualification of the tools.

The various standards (ISO 26262, IEC 61508, DO-178, CENELEC EN 50128) are or will bring up the notion of "qualification record". The qualification of a tool depends on its impact on the final product.

The situation is not reduced to a single vision. The main quality of the B-method [ABR 96] and SCADE 6 [DOR 08] is to propose an approach that starts from the software specification until the coding phase (involving architecture and design stages). The code generator of the Atelier B is considered for some versions as qualified by the utilization and the code generator of SCADE 6 includes a certificate.

With regard to formal techniques and formal methods, the issue of the qualification of tools is therefore of paramount importance, because the

---

21 Concerning the SAET-METEOR, the analysis of the 100,000 lines of ADA code took more than 1 week in 1998 using the program Polyspace (see Chapter 8 for more information), while at the moment it would take 1 or 2 h.

22 It should be remembered that for many of the tools currently in use, algorithms are not public and are not even copyrighted.

complexity of the technologies implemented (prover, model-checking, etc.), the confidentiality aspect (algorithm under license, etc.), the innovation aspect (new technology, few users, etc.) and the maturity aspect (product resulting from research, product implemented under "free" license, etc.) do not contribute to easily establishing a trust bond.

	SSIL0	SSIL1	SSIL2	SSIL3	SSIL4
Formal methods comprising for example CCS, CSP, HOL, LOTOS, OBJ, VDM, Z, B	–	R	R	HR	HR
Semiformal methods	R	R	R	HR	HR
Structured methodology including JSD, MASCOT, SADT, SDL, SSADM and YOURDON	R	HR	HR	HR	HR

Table 6.1. *CENELEC EN 50128 [CEN 01] – Table A.2*

It is worth noting that one of the difficulties in the implementation of formal techniques is due to the lack of recognition of these techniques within current standards. In fact, certain standards (see Table 6.1 taken from the CENELEC EN 50128 standard [CEN 01], for example) advocate the implementation of formal methods but they do not mention the concept of abstract interpretation (or of derived methods).

Software Specification Verification Stage

7.1. Introduction

As presented in Figure 1.3, the implementation of a software application goes through the establishment of a development cycle (for example a V-model) consisting of several phases.

The first phase of this cycle is the specification phase of the software application, which is composed of two activities: the software requirement specification (SwRS) and the software requirement testing specification (SwOTS). In Chapter 4, the development process of the SwRS has been described and the development of the SwOTS is described in Volume 4 [BOU 19].

The purpose of this chapter is to present verification activities to be put in place in the context of the software specification phase. A similar chapter will be dedicated to each phase of the implementation cycle (specification, architecture, design, component testing, integration testing and overall testing) in order to properly identify the necessary verifications to be implemented.

The various verification techniques have been presented in Chapter 11 of Volume 2 [BOU 17].

7.2. Verification

7.2.1. *Presentation*

As presented as part of Chapter 11 of Volume 2 [BOU 17], the verification can be done through static analysis and/or dynamic analysis. Since the intent here is to verify the requirement specification of a software application, static methods are more suitable.

7.2.2. *Verifications of the software requirement specification*

7.2.2.1. *Methodology*

The software requirements specification is produced based on system requirements and safety-related requirements. The verification of the software requirement specification can be carried out by means of several activities:

– through a more or less formal design review (reviewing, by using control lists, etc.) (see sections 7.2.2.2 and 7.2.2.3);

– through the implementation of a model and/or a prototype (see section 7.2.2.5);

– through the preparation of the testing specification (see section 7.2.2.6).

As indicated in Chapter 4 of Volume 2 [BOU 17], the verification activities are performed by a dedicated team. This team must be independent of the design team. The verification team includes testers (TST), integrators (INT) and verifiers (VER).

However, the verification team is not the only one to participate; in fact, it is necessary to verify that the software requirements specification meets the quality criteria (under the responsibilities of the QUA). Bearing in mind that the main topic here is a verification that the system need is properly taken into account, it is therefore necessary that this verification work is also achieved by members of the system team.

Similarly, the SwRS must be verified by the RAMS[1] team (RAMS team cover RAM and Safety) in order to verify that safety-related requirements are properly taken into account at the software application level.

---

1 RAMS refers to Reliability, Availability, Maintainability and Safety.

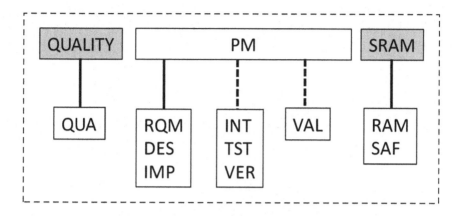

Figure 7.1. *Organization*

7.2.2.2. *Design review*

The verification of a phase requires the verification of the implementation of quality requirements (procedure application, format compliance, etc.), the application of processes (compliance with plans, compliance with the organization, etc.), the correction of activities and that RAMS[2] requirements be properly taken into account.

7.2.2.2.1. Documentation review

The documentation review is then conducted through a quick reading (*walkthrough*) or a design review (*formal design review*).

The document review (see Figure 7.2) is a verification that follows a multistep process. Figure 7.2 highlights several types of development requests: corrections (2), change requests (3) and process improvement requests (4).

This verification must have a goal. This goal may be formalized in the form of a control list (checklist). Control lists are essential for improving the

---

2 For software applications, RAMS requirements are generally limited to safety and increasingly to security. For maintenance requirements, the introduction of performance requirements is requested (memory consumption, processor loading, time limit, etc.) and software maintainability is, in general, related to complexity.

quality (process distribution, implementation of a preestablished and systematic process) and the effectiveness of verification activities (there is a goal).

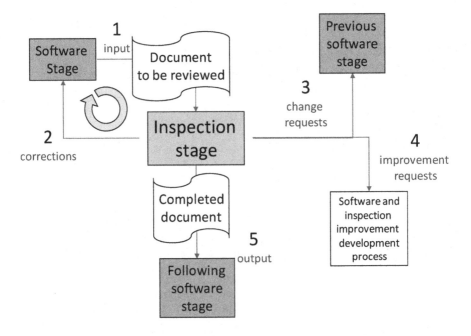

Figure 7.2. *Documentation review*

7.2.2.2.2. Quality activity

The quality team (QUA) will be in charge of the verifications related to the quality requirements and part of the application of the processes. The quality team will participate in design reviews and will be able to implement specific verifications. Table 7.1 defines a typical job form for the quality team in charge of quality control.

For design reviews, the quality team will make use of a checklist (see Table 7.2, for example).

Verifications (see Chapter 15 of Volume 2 [BOU 17]) can be planned audits in order to verify the management and the application of the quality standard or of specific audits. Specific audits can be customer audits or internal audits.

Role: Quality Manager: QUA

Responsibilities are as follows:
 	
   – shall keep the quality standard alive;
 	
   – shall transmit the knowledge of the quality standard;
 	
   – shall verify the correct application of the quality standard;
 	
   – shall perform quality controls.

Main skills are as follows:
 	
   – shall know the quality standards (ISO 9001 [ISO 15], ISO 90003 [ISO 04], SPICE[3], CMMi[4], IRIS, etc.) applicable to the company;
 	
   – shall know the quality standard of the company;
 	
   – shall have good interpersonal skills;
 	
   – shall be able to take into account the needs of the projects;
 	
   – shall be able to contribute to projects;
 	
   – shall be able to bring change;
 	
   – shall be able to make a critical judgement on an activity or a document.

Table 7.1. *Quality manager skills*

Therefore, for the specification phase, a configuration audit (are all elements properly archived, see Chapter 7 of Volume 2 [BOU 17]) or a process audit (verification that plans and/or procedures are correctly applied, see Chapter 2 of Volume 2 [BOU 17]) is necessary.

In addition, QUA can verify that all people involved in this phase have the correct competencies (see Chapter 5 of Volume 2 [BOU 17]).

---

3 Software Process Improvement and Capability Determination (see [ISO 04a]).
4 Capability Maturity Model for integration (see www.sei.cmu.edu/cmmi).

Item	Rule	Status OK/KO	Comment
Q_1	Document meets the company template and/or the project template.		
Q_2	The reference, the version and the page numbering (x/y) appear on every page of the document.		
Q_3	For each reference document and each applicable document, the title, the reference and the version are correct.		
Q_4	All the figures and all the tables are numbered.		
Q_5	There are no references such as "see figure above" or "see figure below".		
Q_6	Are quality plans, procedures and other applicable documents cited as applicable documents?		
Q_7	Are quality plans, procedures and other applicable documents applied?		
Q_8	If some part of the quality plans, procedures and other applicable documents are not applied, a derogation is formalized.		
Q_9	Is the revision table present and does it contain relevant and correct information (date consistency)?		
Q_10	All references used in the document are defined in applicable section or reference document.		
Q_11			
Q_12	...		

Table 7.2. *Example of checklists for quality control*

7.2.2.2.3. Verifier

As already stated, the verification of the software requirements specification must be made by a verifier (see Figure 7.1 concerning the organization). The verifier must verify the technical content of the document.

Role: Verifier: VER
Responsibilities are as follows: – shall develop a Software Verification Plan (which may include issues related to quality) mentioning the elements that should require verification and what type of process (for example review, analyses, etc.) and testing is required as proof; – shall verify the adequacy (completeness, relevance and traceability) of documented proofs based on reviews, integration and tests including verification goals that must be specified; – shall identify anomalies, evaluate them in terms of risk (impact); report and communicate them to the department responsible for change management in view of the evaluation and decision making; – shall manage the verification process (review, integration and tests) and ensure the independence of activities according to needs; – shall develop and maintain records on verification activities; – shall prepare a verification report indicating the result of verification activities.
Main skills are as follows: – shall be proficient in the field where the verification is performed, for example requirements concerning software, data, code, etc.; – shall be proficient in various verification approaches/methodologies and be able to identify the method or combination of methods most suitable in a given context; – shall be able to deduce the types of verification of given specifications; – shall have skills for analytical thinking and a good sense of observation; – shall understand applicable standards; – shall understand the legislation applicable (if necessary).

Table 7.3. *Role definition: verifier[5]*

For a project with a low safety level[6] (unsafe, SSIL0), it is possible to ask a designer to carry out the software requirements specification verification, but as soon as the security level moves to higher levels (2, 3 and 4), it is necessary that the verifier become more competent. He/she must be able to detect errors in the specifications.

---

5 This description of the role of the VER (Verifier) is extracted from the CENELEC 50128:2011 [CEN 11] standard.

6 Domain standards define safety levels. For the IEC 61508 standard [IEC 15] and children standards (such as for example the CENELEC 50128:2011 standard [CEN 15]), the SIL (Safety Integrity Level) is used for the system as well as the SSIL (SIL Software). The SIL may take several non-SIL values, SSIL0 to SSIL4.

Table 7.3 defined the role (responsibility and skill) of the verifier. The verifier's activity for the software requirements specification is defined in sections 7.2.2.2.4 and 7.2.2.2.5.

7.2.2.2.4. Requirement specification verification

As indicated, a software requirements specification must define:

– the boundaries of the software application through the identification of the external software/software and software/hardware interfaces;

– the states of the software application;

– the parametrization data;

– the requirements to assume.

On this basis, it is possible to set up several verifications of the software requirements specification:

– verify that all the external interfaces are identified in the system architecture document;

– verify that all external interfaces show up at least once in a requirement. If an external interface were not included, then it would not be used;

– verify that all the software states are related to states identified in the system architecture document or in the system specification;

– verify that all software states show up at least once in a requirement. If a software state were not included, then it would not be used;

– verify that all software parametrizing data are at least included once in a requirement. If a software data element were not included, then it would not be used;

– verify that all the requirements utilize external interfaces as inputs, otherwise the requirement is not observable;

– verify that all requirements identify the states in which they are applicable. If not, there would be a possible ambiguity.

This is an initial set of verifications that ought to be completed by your feedback. It is very important to put in place a REX-based (Return of Experience) approach, when certain defects are not detected at early stages. It is very important to verify whether it is possible to improve the verification and the checklist used during verification.

7.2.2.2.5. Verification of requirement complexity

The clarity of the requirements depends on the vocabulary being used (hence the need for a project glossary); uniqueness is intended to avoid duplication and atomicity is used to avoid a situation where requirements become too complex. Requirement complexity is an important criterion that can be analyzed through traceability.

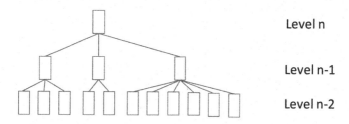

Figure 7.3. *Example of traceability between requirements*

From a situation that can be considered to be normal where a requirement at a level n is refined into a reasonable number of requirements of level $n-1$ (see Figure 7.3), several scenarios may occur. Figure 7.3 shows that the level $n-2$ may again be broken down, which corresponds to the normal case (requirements are broken down progressively). However, it appears that the existing requirement at level $n-1$ to the right can be decomposed into six requirements, which is more complex than for the other 2. It is necessary to verify that this is acceptable.

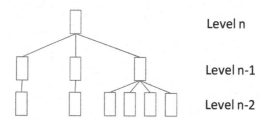

Figure 7.4. *Example of traceability between requirements*

Figure 7.4 shows that at level $n-2$, certain requirements are copied from level $n-1$ to level $n-2$. This is an abnormal situation.

7.2.2.2.6. Verification of requirement traceability

In order to cover the needs for completeness and consistency for each phase of the implementation process, it will be necessary to put in place a requirement verification phase that has three objectives:

– that the initial need was taken into account: traceability between the requirements of the higher level and the requirements of this level must be implemented. This traceability should be verified: there are existing links and they are justified;

– that the set of requirements forms a correct whole: it must be demonstrated that the requirements are understandable, unambiguous, verifiable, feasible, etc. It must be demonstrated that the set of requirements is comprehensive and coherent (no conflict);

– that no non-traceable element has been introduced: the purpose of this verification is to control that all requirements in the process of definition are traceable with a need of the upper level. Very often, requirements can be seen to emerge that are said to be design and/or architectural requirements and which have no connection with the upper level. An analysis of these requirements shows that, most of the time, they are unsaid and very rarely design requirements. Furthermore, what constitutes a design and/or architecture requirement should be defined.

SyRS	SwRS
SyRS _EX_1	SwRS _EX_11, SwRS _EX_12, SwRS _EX_13
SyRS _EX_2	
SyRS _EX_3	SwRS _EX_11

Table 7.4. *Example of traceability table between the SyRS and SwRS*

In the first and third point, the traceability study (analysis of each line of traceability matrices) should show that all requirements have been implemented (in Table 7.4, the requirement SyRS_EX_2 is not implemented) but it should also be able to show that everything that has been implemented is required (in Table 7.5, the requirement SwRS_EX_14 has no parent requirement).

SwRS	SyRS
SwRS_EX_11	SyRS_EX_1, SyRS EX_3
SwRS_EX_12	SyRS_EX _1
SwRS_EX_13	SyRS_EX_1
SwRS_EX_14	

Table 7.5. *Example of traceability table between the SwRS and SyRS*

7.2.2.2.7. Checklist for requirement verification

Requirement verification can be done with a checklist. This checklist (for example, see Table 7.6) must define control points. These are related to the knowledge of the types of errors that can be introduced during the activity that produced the documents to be verified.

Point	Rule	Status OK/KO	Comment
R_1	All parent requirements must be drawn or a justification must be given		
R_2	All document requirements must be drawn with at least a parent requirement or a justification must be given		
R_3	All identified interfaces are involved in at least one requirement		
R_4	All system states are involved in at least one requirement		
R_5	Is every requirement readable?		
R_6	Is every requirement simple (not too long, no complex traceability, etc.)		
R_7	Is every requirement atomic (no need to read a set of requirements to understand the need)?		
R_8	Is every requirement verifiable?		
R_9	All requirements described a need and no solution.		
R_10	If a requirement identified a specific choice, a specific marker is used. It is possible to identify a hypothesis exported to the system.		
R_11	....		

Table 7.6. *Example of checklist related to requirements*

7.2.2.3. *Implementation of a model/prototype/mockup*

7.2.2.3.1. Presentation

The implementation of a model can be a way to verify the specification of a software application. A model can be somewhat close to the system under study; this is then referred to as an abstraction. The closer the modeling is, the closer the results will be to those that will be observed in the final system.

The implementation of a model can help us to understand the need during the need identification phase. Another characteristic of models derives from whether or not the supporting language has a semantic. The presence of a semantic makes it possible to implement reasoning techniques that ensure the correction of the results obtained.

7.2.2.3.2. Prototyping

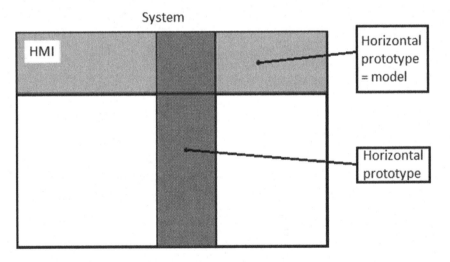

Figure 7.5. *Prototyping and mockup*

Nielsen [NIE 93] distinguishes between two prototyping degrees according to the level of interaction provided by the prototype (see Figure 7.5):

– the horizontal prototype (or model) corresponds to the development of the graphical part of the human–machine interface (HMI); this is sometimes a simple paper drawing;

– the vertical prototype implements certain features of the application so that the user can fully complete a typical scenario for using the software.

A mockup (horizontal prototype) is a first very simplified model of the problem. The mockup is intended to model some aspects of the problem to be solved in a more or less accurate way.

A prototype (vertical prototype) can be static. The goal is to model interactions between different elements, including actors, but it can be dynamic and simplified behaviors will be modeled; it will then be possible to run scenarios.

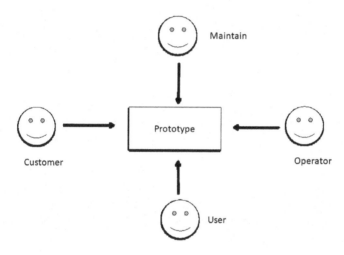

Figure 7.6. *Prototype and expression of need*

The model and the prototype are means for confronting the vision of the different parties involved and expected behaviors (see Figure 7.6).

The implementation of a prototype (horizontal or vertical) is a good way to facilitate understanding of the need, but there are costs associated with the creation of prototypes and there is often a temptation to consider that the prototype is part of the solution.

It should be noted that prototypes are increasingly employed to validate a concept (website, etc.). The main difficulty with a prototype is to keep in mind that it is a prototype (which can be extremely well achieved) and that it is not the design of the final product.

To conclude, a prototype is a good aid for requirement elicitation, but do not forget that is just a prototype. It is not possible to use the prototype code directly in the safety-critical application. Generally, a prototype is a design without consideration of certain processes and without documentation.

7.2.2.4. Preparation of the overall software application tests

7.2.2.4.1. Tester

The selection of test cases is carried out by a different person to the one who wrote the SwRS. This person is named TESTER (TST). Table 7.7 describes the role of the TST by introducing the responsibilities and skills expected.

Role: TESTER: TST
Responsibilities are as follows: – shall ensure that testing activities are planned; – shall develop the testing specifications (objectives and scenarios); – shall ensure the traceability of testing objectives with respect to the specified requirements related to the software and that of testing scenarios according to the specified testing objectives; – shall ensure that planned tests are achieved and specified tests carried out; – shall identify deviations from expected results and report them in testing reports; – shall communicate differences with the organization responsible for change management in view of the evaluation and decision making; – shall record the results in reports; – shall choose the software testing equipment.
Main skills are as follows: – shall be proficient in the field where testing is performed, for example: requirements concerning software, data, code, etc. – shall be proficient in various testing and verification approaches/methodologies and be able to identify the most appropriate method in a given context; – shall be able to infer testing scenarios based on given specifications; – shall have skills for analytical thinking and a good sense of observation; – shall understand applicable standards; – shall understand the legislation applicable (if necessary).

Table 7.7. *Skills and responsibilities of the TESTER*

7.2.2.4.2. Principles

Requirement verification of the requirement specification involves the development of an overall testing specification for the software application. This is one of the most important verifications.

As shown in Figure 7.7, based on requirements, test cases (TC_x) are identified, namely the test cases describing a situation to achieve, this situation being linked to an equivalence class. From the test cases, it is possible to prepare testing scenarios (TS_x) describing a situation. A test case may therefore be involved in several scenarios.

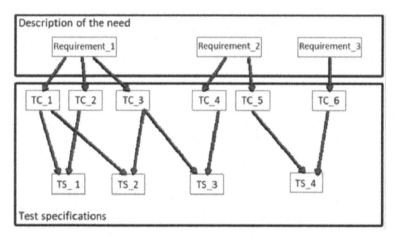

Figure 7.7. *Link between testing and requirements*

Since at this level, the only input element is the software requirement specification; we are actually specifying black box testing (without knowledge of the implementation).

Some requirements are not testable, and in this case we need to introduce a verification. For example, a requirement that requests that the software be SSIL2 is not testable, we need to introduce a verification that the safety team must confirm that the software is effectively SSIL2.

If, for every requirement, it is possible to produce test cases, then the SwOTS will make it possible to demonstrate that the SwRS is implementable (SwRS feasibility). If some non-functional requirements are not tested but verified, we need to verify that this is justified and acceptable.

7.2.2.4.3. Verification example

Figure 7.8 (case 1) shows that a requirement gave rise to numerous test cases, which shows that the requirement is complex (or even too complex). If this requirement comes to evolve, there will be a strong impact on the software application and on revalidation.

Figure 7.8 (case 2) shows that a set of requirements gave rise to a test case, which shows that the requirements are not atomic. In fact, it is necessary to read several requirements to achieve a test case, which will be similar for implementing the associated code.

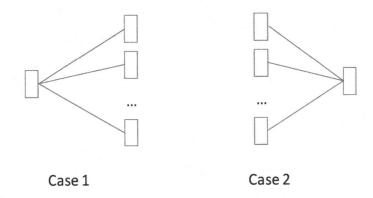

Case 1   Case 2

Figure 7.8. *Example of traceability between requirement and testing*

7.2.3. *Overview*

The phase of the requirement specification of the software application requires the implementation of different skills:

– requirement management through the RQM;

– management of testing techniques through the TST;

– verification control through the VER;

– standard and process management through the QUA and the VAL.

Therefore, it will be necessary to ensure that the people involved satisfy the skills requirements (see Chapters 4 and 5 of Volume 2 [BOU 17]).

When the verification activity is finalized, it is necessary to produce a verification report RS_VR (Requirement Specification–Verification Report):

– which identifies the stage inputs and outputs;

– which identifies the means being used (people, tools, etc.);

– which describes the activities carried out, the results of these activities, the anomalies detected and the remaining open topics;

– which concludes on the possibility to move on to the next phase.

This report is generally written by the VER and the QUA and verified by the VAL, under the approval of the project manager (PM).

7.3. Conclusion

This chapter has enabled us to present ways to verify the requirement specification of a software application. This is an important phase. The verification will be achieved in the form of static analysis such as the SwRS review, the analysis of requirements traceability and traceability analysis with the tests.

One of the fundamental verifications of the SwRS is related to the production of the SwOTS. If it is possible to produce overall software application test cases, then it will be possible to implement the SwRS in the form of software.

8

Component Versus Module

8.1. Introduction

As shown in Figure 8.1, a software application uses, in general, an abstraction of the hardware architecture and its operating system (OS) by means of a lower layer called "basic software".

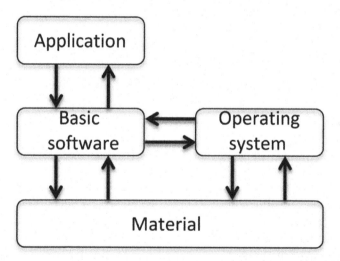

Figure 8.1. *A software application in its environment*

The basic software is generally written in low-level languages such as assembler and/or C language [KER 88]. It makes it possible to encapsulate the OS and these utilities services, but it also allows for varying levels of direct access to hardware resources.

If the software application is associated with a high safety level, then the lower layers (basic software, utility and OS) are also associated with safety goals. The safety goal of the lower layers of the software application will be dependent on the hardware architecture implemented (single processor, architecture 2 out of 2 [2oo2], architecture 2 out of 3 [2oo3], architecture n out of m [NooM][1], etc.) and the safety concepts implemented.

In [BOU 09a, BOU 11c], we presented real examples of safe operation architectures. As part of this series, we will assume that safety analyses have been performed and that a safety level has been allocated for all software applications (including the low layer).

As has already been indicated, every software application is composed of a set of so-called functional services. The implementation of a functional service is provided by a set of compilation units. There are two types of compilation unit, either it is a set of structured files called a module or an autonomous file set, which is then referred to as a component. Component is now a recommended approach in certain domains such as for railways where we want to manage reusability and the low level of impact in case of change.

8.2. Reusability, maintainability and continuity of service

The software application architecture is an important point that needs to be looked into at a very early stage. Various topics regularly keep reemerging, such as reusability (implementation of elements previously developed on new projects), maintainability (possibility to change over time) and service continuity (despite changes and obsolescence).

Reusability is essential when trying to manage development costs. It is necessary that the adherence of code elements (service, module, class, component, library, etc.) remains restricted to the reference product and to external elements (software, drivers, hardware, library, etc.). Figure 8.2 shows the dependencies that may exist between a software element and its environment (OS, library, hardware support and interacting software).

---

1 nOOm for *n out of m*. A redundant architecture n among m achieves m computations and considers the result as being correct if n results are identical (see [BOU 09a], Chapter 1).

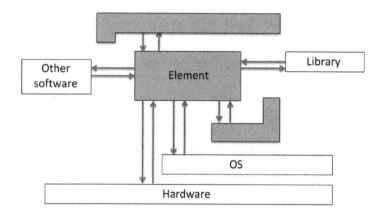

Figure 8.2. *Adherence*

Once the notion of adherence is defined (Definition 4.2), it is possible to make the connection with the notion of reusability. The stronger adherence is, the more difficult it is to reuse the element without adaptation.

Reusability is a misunderstood concept. In fact, a number of developers consider that a reusable component is a software element proposing numerous features – a broad spectrum of possible applications is thus implemented but not used – whereas a reusable component is a component providing minimum functionality, which is however fully documented and tested when properly developed. A reusable element is therefore adaptable.

Software maintainability is related to the ability to develop the software application for a given period (from a few days to several decades). It is closely connected to the establishment of an implementation process and change management. It is necessary to control complexity. Maintainability will be covered in more detail in the following chapters.

Service continuity of a software application is generally not addressed, but it becomes an issue for safety critical systems (transport, energy, services, etc.).

One must be able to ensure that the software application will be functional over a period of time despite:

– changes in the software application: correction of defects, addition of new features;

– obsolescence of the hardware platform: processor, memory, hard drive, USB drive, firewire, etc.;

– obsolescence of the software platform: OS^2, libraries, drivers.

In the end, conventional applications are hardly maintainable and reusable because they strongly depend on hardware and software platforms. This is the reason why several projects propose to make the software application independent of these platforms. These architectures are called *modular architectures*.

8.3. Module and component

8.3.1. *Presentation*

It proves important to consider a software application as a set of elements that interact to achieve the processing of an information set. At this point in time, we are talking about elements; as a matter of fact, we have shifted from the notion of monolithic software to the concept of structured software, seen as an aggregate of elements.

8.3.2. *Module*

It is interesting to note that standards (CENELEC 50128, IEC 61508, DO-178, etc.) in their *late 1990s* versions introduced the notion of module and that updated versions in 2011 referred to components.

DEFINITION 8.1 (Module).– *A module is part of the software program, deemed indivisible during the implementation. It performs a sufficiently explicit process so that it can be the subject of a direct transcription in a programming language.*

A module is identified as:

– having an input point and an output point;

– having a limited number of parameters;

---

2 For example, when Windows XP was discontinued, users were forced to move to Windows 7, and in the same year, they were informed that Windows 7 would no longer be maintained and that they had to move to Windows 8 or even Windows 10.

– having a completely defined interface;

– having a low complexity.

This modular approach somewhat reminds us of procedures, functions or files that contain a set of functions and, in a more advanced form, a class in an object-oriented language. It thus appears that the notion of module is vague enough so that the different languages and the level of granularity desired in a project can be covered. It is therefore straightforward to make the connection between an ADA package, a C file and/or a C++ class and a module.

It should be noted that in the 2001 version of the CENELEC 50128 standard [CEN 01], there is a mixture of the notion of subprogram and module.

The notion of module is not adequate to describe an architecture; it would be desirable to be able to identify an element by a scope in order to be able to replace it (like a mechanical element) and reuse it.

As can be seen in Figure 8.3, a module may be dependent on other modules (in C, the module STDIO.H will likely be utilized by many other modules), which results in a major difficulty for reuse. Moreover, in the event a module is reused, the latter is not compilable (it depends on other modules) and some modules may be dependent on the compiler (module linked to an implementation) and/or the hardware platform.

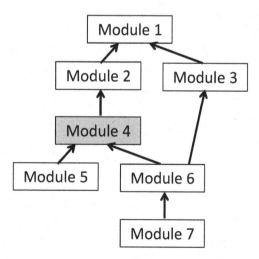

Figure 8.3. *Example of module tree structure*

Figure 8.3 shows a tree of modules. Each module is managed in the configuration. The reuse of module 4 in another project requires the associated subtree to be recovered and if module 7 is a module linked to the compiler, the tests will have to be repeated.

If the purpose is to replace and reuse, the basic element of the architecture must be defined by means of a functional scope and a set of interfaces. The functional scope is characterized by a set of requirements and a set of functions. In addition, reusability involves the management of the configuration of the element.

Another difficulty concerns the identification of input points in the module, *what features are available*? And *what do they do*? Given that the set of services of a module is accessible, it is located at the same level in the source code.

For each module, one will seek to implement a so-called modular testing strategy. The purpose of this testing strategy is to show that the module services correctly implement their processing. Some services may be internal (intended to be called by others without having any specified functionality), partial (a global service was broken down into several pieces and one piece does not implement a need) or non-significant (a processing factorization was conducted without specified functionality). It will be difficult to demonstrate their proper operation and the use of testers would not make sense.

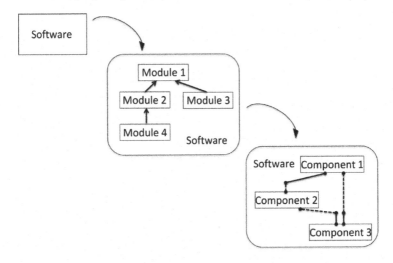

Figure 8.4. *Software application structure development*

In view of the difficulties associated with the concept of module, the concept of component was introduced (see Figure 8.4) with the idea that the component is an autonomous entity (compilable) with clearly identified interfaces.

8.3.3. *Component*

The 2011 version of the CENELEC 50128 standard [CEN 11] introduces the notion of component software that we characterize by Definition 8.2

DEFINITION 8.2 (Component).– *A component is a software element performing a set of well-defined services; these services satisfy a well-identified set of requirements; it has well-defined interfaces and it is managed in the configuration as an element on its own.*

A component is characterized by:

– a set of fully defined external interfaces (see section 9.4.5.3);

– a set of requirements assumed by this component;

– a version associated with this component, this component is managed in the configuration as a standalone element.

Two reasons explain the popularity of this new paradigm: by using it, it becomes possible to develop applications faster and to reduce development costs. In effect, to build an application is tantamount to laying out software components analogously to electronic components. More precisely, this involves:

– designing and developing systems based on prefabricated, predesigned and pretested components;

– reusing these components in other applications;

– facilitating their maintenance and their development;

– enhancing their adaptability and their configurability to produce new functionalities and new characteristics.

Subsequently, the basic element is thus the component. We will then talk of component integration and component testing (instead of unit testing or modular testing); to learn more, refer to Chapter 2 of Volume 1 [BOU 16].

Definition 8.2 introduces the notion of requirement. At this point, it is necessary to recall that a requirement characterizes a need [BOU 14]. Chapter 10 of Volume 1 [BOU 16] is dedicated to the presentation of requirement management.

In view of Definition 8.2, a component may thus be a software application, a library, a commercial component (Commercial Off The Shelf software [COTS]), etc. The main point of this definition is the autonomous aspect of the component. This way, reusability and maintenance of the software application are therefore ensured. In effect, when a component becomes obsolete (evolution of the OS, hardware obsolescence, etc.), it is possible to replace the software component with another, provided that interfaces and requirements are satisfied. A component is self-contained and contains all the elements guaranteeing its proper operation. That is why, considering Figure 8.5, if component 2 is reused in a new project, it will be necessary to verify the assumptions for use of component 2 and then to achieve the software/software integration.

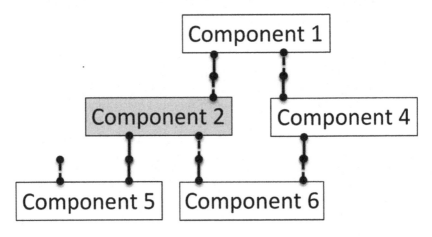

Figure 8.5. *Software application component-based architecture*

Another situation occurs, in Figure 8.5, if there is a change in hardware platform and *component 6* is dedicated to the management of interfaces with the platform, it will be necessary to rerun software/software integration tests between *components 2 and 6* but not to retest the behavior of *component 2*.

If changes occur, regression activities can be restricted through component management to component boundaries. Another advantage of component management lies in the granularity of the test; regarding component testing, it is necessary to test the services provided by the component that thereby becomes fully specified.

8.3.4. *Data encapsulation versus information hiding*

In the 2011 version of the CENELEC 50128 standard [CEN 11], Table A.20 (component definition) and Table A.3 (architecture requirements) indicate that it is necessary (HR) that information encapsulation be employed and that hiding is not recommended. Furthermore, information hiding raises a problem at the level of the observability of the software application behavior and this therefore has an impact on testability and maintenance. The curative maintenance of a software application requires an analysis of the behavior on the target in its real environment (the system in service), it is thus necessary to have access to the internal states of the software application.

Encapsulation consists of introducing access services to data, which has various advantages:

– there is no longer direct access to the data, thus providing data protection;

– it is no longer necessary to know the data representation to access them which facilitates maintenance and reusability.

Hiding and encapsulation can be manually managed or be proposed as a language facility (C++, ADA, etc.).

In configuration management, the files of a service are grouped in a directory having its name.

8.4. Conclusion

When speaking of architecture, one mainly refers to elements connected by means of interfaces. The notion of interface has been described in Definition 8.1 as a way of managing exchanges between different software entities. We still had to define what these software entities are.

Throughout this chapter, we have introduced the notion of module and component, as shown in Figure 8.4; we went from a set of files called module to a set of requirements known as component. The component is an autonomous entity that assumes a requirement set, making it possible to ensure maintenance and reusability.

In so-called safety systems, the lifetime ranges from 15 to 50 years (even 80), which raises a large number of issues, the most important ones being obsolescence and maintainability (capability to develop the software application).

The software component allows for the complexity control of the software application.

9

Software Application Architecture

9.1. Introduction

Chapter 4 presented the notion of software specification and the implementation process of the specification of a software application. Based on a software requirement specification (SwRS), it is necessary to design a software architecture for this software application.

The architecture of a software application must take into account the interfaces with the hardware and the different software and propose an organization based on the services (functions, operations, etc.) that the software application has to provide.

This organization must ensure independence (in the sense of low coupling) between components, component testability, component management (reuse of previously developed components, inclusion of COTS[1], etc.) as well as the software application maintainability in time.

The implementation of the software application architecture is an important step because it must identify the elements to be developed, the elements being reused and the commercial elements (COTS) as well as the interfaces between these elements and the interfaces with hardware resources (memory, specific address, input/output ports, CAN, IP, etc.).

In this chapter, we are going to present the notion of architecture and the architecture implementation process in the context of software applications.

---

1 Commercial off-the-shelf.

9.2. Objective of the architecture phase of a software application

The objective of the architecture phase of a software application is to decompose a software application into a set of components, while following several criteria such as independence, coupling, complexity, testability and/or maintainability.

These software components will include a set of interfaces and will have to provide a service set. Components could be specifically implemented components, standard components or reused components.

Regarding these primary objectives, we see certain concepts coming forward, such as architecture and components, which will be defined in section 9.3.

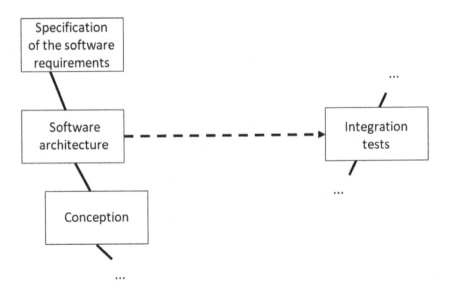

Figure 9.1. *Positioning of the software architecture phase*

Figure 9.1 allows us to position the software application architecture phase in the implementation of the V-model. The architecture phase can be found after the specification phase. It should be noted that this phase is essential for achieving software/hardware integration tests and that these productions are an input to design phases (preliminary and/or detailed).

Figure 9.2 shows the contents of the software application architecture phase.

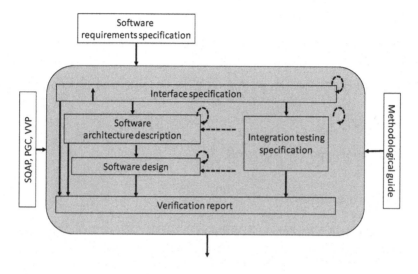

Figure 9.2. *Software application architecture phase*

For the software application specification stage, the inputs are as follows:

– Plans:

- Software Quality Assurance Plan (SQAP);

- Software Verification and Validation Plan (SVVP);

- Software Configuration Management Plan (SCMP).

– Project documents:

- Software Requirements Specification (SwRS) Document;

- Glossary (GL);

– Methodological guides:

- SwAD writing guide;

- SwCD writing guide;

- STIS writing guide (S/S and S/H integration);

- Modeling guide.

The outputs of the software application architecture stage are as follows:

– Software Architecture Description Document (SwAD);

– Software Component Design Document (SwCD);

– Software/Software Integration Testing Specification Document (S/S SITS);

– Software/Hardware Integration Testing Specification Document (S/H SITS);

– Glossary[2] (GL);

– Verification report (ARCH_VR).

9.3. Software architect

As indicated in Chapter 4 of Volume 2 [BOU 17], software application architecture- and design-related activities are carried out by the Designer (whom we will call DES). The DES is part of the design team along with RQM (Requirement Manager) and IMP (Implementer).

Role: Designer (DES)
Responsibilities are as follows: – transform the specified software-related requirements into acceptable solutions; – posses architecture and top-down design solutions; – define or select design methods and tools; – apply appropriate principles and standards of safety design; – develop component specifications, if applicable; – maintain traceability to and from specified software-related requirements; – develop and maintain design documentation; – ensure that design documents are taken into account by change and configuration management.

2 The project glossary is to be updated throughout the software application implementation. New concepts could emerge at every level.

Main skills are as follows:

   – proficient in the appropriate engineering of the application domain;

   – proficient in terms of safety design principles;

   – proficient in design analysis and design testing methodologies;

   – able to work within the limits of design constraints in a given environment;

   – competent enough to understand the scope of the problem;

   – understands all of the constraints imposed by the hardware platform, the operating system and interfacing systems;

   – understands the requirements of the business standards applicable to the project and/or the company.

Table 9.1. *Software application designer[3]*

Table 9.1 brings up the DES responsibilities as well as her/his skills.

9.4. Software architecture description document

9.4.1. *Introduction*

The software architecture description document (SwAD) remains the main document that enables the connection between the specification and the design to be made and that ensures the control of the software development. In this section, we will present the description and formalization principles of the software application architecture.

9.4.2. *Constraint on the methodology*

A so-called critical software application is associated with a safety level. This safety level requires that a number of constraints be taken into account.

One of these constraints serves to avoid the introduction of faults; to this end, it is important to preserve the formalism introduced in the SwRS within the software application architecture. This means that if the SwRS introduces

---

3 This description of the DES's (Designer) role is taken from the CENELEC 50128:2011 [CEN 11] standard.

state machines or an object-based approach, it would be preferable to use a similar formalism in the architecture.

A second constraint concerns error detection; it is important to detect errors as soon as possible and as a result, it would be desirable to have an approach that enables error detection at the earliest stages. Structured methods of the SADT/SART types or model-based approaches such as SCADE or MATLAB/SIMULINK are mechanisms for building an architecture as well as for verifying the connection of all of the interfaces or even conducting semantic tests on the data exchanged. A graphical tool-based approach (for example, VISIO or UML) does not allow for detecting errors.

9.4.3. Description of the interfaces with the environment

In Chapter 4, we reported that the specification of a software application should present the interfaces (known as external) with its environment. The software application environment is composed of hardware resources (memory, specific address, inputs/outputs, watchdog, etc.), software applications (basic software, related applications, etc.) and/or the operating system.

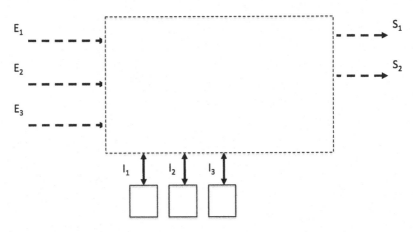

Figure 9.3. *Software application environment*

This software application environment can be defined through external interfaces that it has to manage.

Furthermore, the external interfaces are of two types: logical interfaces (software–software interface) and physical interfaces (software–hardware interface).

Figure 9.3 depicts a software application environment that consists of three input interfaces (E_i), two output interfaces (S_j) and three physical interfaces (I_k) along with hardware resources (for example, access to a specific memory address).

9.4.4. *Typical architecture*

Very often, the people responsible for the implementation of a software application think that it is not necessary to put in place a software application architecture, arguing that it is only a single application and that considering its size this architecture is not necessary.

It is worth noting that in the railway sector, the size of software applications varies from a few thousand lines to 400,000 lines for high-level safety applications (SSIL[4]3-SSIL4), but for little critical (SSIL2, SSIL1) or non-critical (non-SIL or SSIL0) software applications the number of lines can reach one million lines.

The example in Figure 9.4 shows a so-called layered architecture, each layer of the software application having a different purpose. The operating system layer is intended to manage the application execution and resource allocation aspects; the middleware layer is designed to manage communications between the different software applications of the system; the generic application layer is intended to implement the specific services of our application; the parametrization layer gives access to instantiated data for a specific application and the common service layer is designed to provide all of the services common to the other layers.

---

4 SSIL is short for Software SIL. SIL, short for Safety Integrity Level, is the requested/ expected safety integrity level. It is used for E/E/EP systems and in the railway industry. Non-SIL means no impact on safety, SSIL0 means very low impact, SSIL1 and SSIL2 mean medium impact (serious injury), SSIL3 and SSIL4 mean strong impact (death of people). We could have chosen the ASIL (Automotive SIL) or the DAL (Design Assurance Level) (see [ARI 11]).

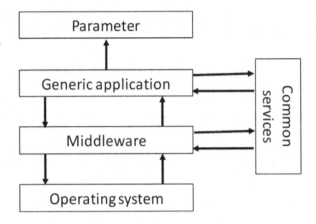

Figure 9.4. *Example of software application architecture*

The architecture of a software application is thus a code unit composition (see Figure 9.5). The main question is knowing what the code unit is. As already indicated in Chapter 2 of Volume 1 [BOU 16], the code unit can range from the module to the component going through the software and/or library layer. Figure 9.4 is rather library or software layer-oriented.

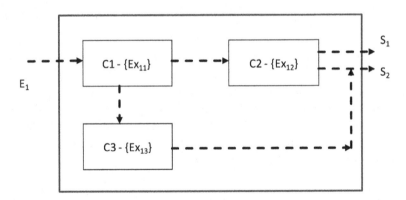

Figure 9.5. *Example of component-based architecture*

The component approach (see Definition 8.2) allows for easy maintainability and reusability (see Chapter 8).

However, one of the fundamental points of the software architecture is that it must be formalized through a structured method and/or a model.

9.4.5. *Component, module and interface*

In order to be able to build a software application architecture, it is important to identify the basic elements of this architecture. Concerning the content of the software application architecture, it is composed of modules or components. In Chapter 8, we compared modular- and component-based approaches.

9.4.5.1. *Modules*

In Definition 8.1, we introduced the notion of module and recalled that a module is identified as having:

– an input point and an output point;

– a limited number of parameters;

– a completely defined interface;

– a low complexity.

The notion of module does not allow us to have an autonomous element, one that is easily replaceable and reusable; this is the reason why it is replaced by the notion of component.

9.4.5.2. *Components*

The architecture consists of a set of components (see Definition 8.2) and software interfaces (see Definition 4.3), which can be external or internal.

Figure 9.6 presents an example of a component. In gray the services connected to the interfaces are represented and in blue the internal services are represented.

A component is characterized by:

– a set of fully defined external interfaces (see section 9.3.4.3);

– a set of requirements assumed by this component;

– a version associated with this component this component is managed in configuration as a standalone element.

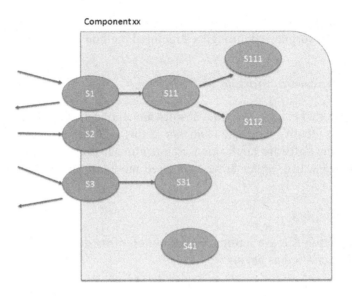

Figure 9.6. *A component. For a color version of this figure,*
see www.iste.co.uk/boulanger/applications3.zip

9.4.5.3. *Interfaces*

The notion of software interface was introduced in Definition 4.3. Therefore, for an interface I, we have to describe at least:

– the list of data exchanged and for each data element:

- the name;

- the family and/or the type;

- units (if necessary);

- the range of acceptable values;

- values representing an error;

– real-time characteristics (time constraint, protocol, etc.);

– error handling:

- Is the interface capable of detecting errors during exchanges?

- If yes, what are the associated behaviors?

- Is there exception handling management?

– memory management:

  - Is there memory allocation?

  - Is there a buffer? If yes, what happens when it is full?

  - If there is no memorization mechanism, what happens if several data elements are received at the same time?

9.4.6. *Architecture principle*

9.4.6.1. *Presentation*

With regard to certifiable software applications, it is necessary to keep in mind that there are several objectives that must be achieved such as testability, maintainability and the ability to perform analyses to implement the demonstration of the safety of the software application.

Maintainability requires that modules be low coupled (section 9.4.6.4). The loosely coupled nature is linked to the fact that every component depends on a limited number of components. The notion of dependency is related to the notion of interface and especially to the number of components connected to this component through the interfaces.

Testability (section 9.3.4.6) requires that behaviors be observable. The observation of a behavior is possible only if it is not hidden by another behavior.

The architecture of the software application being made up of different components, it is possible that some components (maintenance management, for example) do not have an impact on the safety of the system in the case of failure. There are then two possibilities: either we introduce a partitioning of the software application (section 9.3.4.5) or we develop the whole at the highest safety level.

To finish with the good properties of architecture, the notion of complexity has to be introduced. The architecture complexity is characterized by the number of components, the number of interfaces, the number of dependencies between components, etc.

9.4.6.2. *Abstraction*

A component should not reveal the details of its implementation; for this purpose, abstraction and encapsulation mechanisms have to be put in place. Components must then be used in the form of a black box.

Figure 9.7 shows three specific services named F1, F111 and F122. These services allow other components to have access to the internal services of the component.

Figure 9.7. *Abstraction*

9.4.6.3. *Protected data versus encapsulation*

9.4.6.3.1. Global variable and local variable

In computing, the notion of storing information by using variables is a fundamental point (although functional languages do not consider them). Data memorization can be done through global or local variables.

The concept of global variables is to be avoided[5]; in effect, all parts of the software application can access these data during a read and/or a write. This introduces several issues, such as:

– the use of an obsolete datum (refresh problem);

– the use of an incorrect datum (hardware failure, service failure, etc.);

– every function rewrites the same variable (difficulty in analyzing the behavior at the end of the cycle, in other words an observability problem).

It is possible to implement protection mechanisms for global variables, for example by means of encapsulation and/or directories for controlling users of global variables, but in practice these techniques are difficult to put in place.

5 In the 2011 version of the CENELEC 50128 standard, the number of global variables is required to be limited. This recommendation means that in the case where a global variable is used, we should explain how the proper use of data is ensured.

Regarding data protection, a protection code (CRC[6], Hamming code) can be implemented and/or data redundancy may be implemented (two identical data or two different data).

In the end, the best approach consists of avoiding global variables and using local variables that must be protected. There are two approaches to protecting local variables and these are called encapsulation and data protection.

9.4.6.3.2. Variables management

Figure 9.8 shows the way in which a component can be put in place of which the role is to create a variable xx and to manage read and write accesses to this component. This component will provide at least three services (create, set and get). If implemented, this mechanism must be used for global variables and local variables.

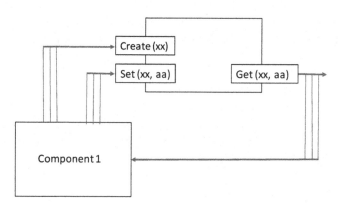

Figure 9.8. *Component responsible for data*

Since its function is to create a variable, it will be able to implement all means necessary to manage random faults (such as memory problems). These means include the implementation of a protection code or memory redundancy.

This component could also implement a directory to manage permissions for accessing stored data.

---

6 The CRC (Cyclic Redundancy Code), Hamming codes and/or checksums are mechanisms to protect one or more data elements (for more information, see [BOU 09a, BOU 11c]).

The component responsible for the management of variables must be able to allocate memory to a datum according to its type, which is not advisable for a safety-critical application, but given that the list of variables and their types can be easily obtained, it is possible to statically evaluate the necessary location and statically allocate the necessary location at the beginning of a cycle.

The implementation of such a mechanism within the architecture will create an access node. Any component that needs variables will be granted access to this component, which introduces strong coupling (see section 9.4.4.4); however, the safety level is increased through data protection.

9.4.6.3.3. Protected data

Data protection (*hiding variables*) is a technique supported by programming languages through the use of *private* and/or *protected* instructions. Although it is useful, this approach has a direct impact on observability. The datum no longer being observable, there will be problems during testing and especially during defect analysis phases that could appear during operation.

It should be noted that in the rail sector, the 2011 version of the CENELEC EN 50128 standard [CEN 11] requires that data hiding is not used.

Data protection should not be used in the context of so-called critical software applications; it must be replaced by *data encapsulation*.

9.4.6.3.4. Data encapsulation

Data encapsulation has still to be addressed. Data encapsulation is similar to data protection, but to the latter, we add *set* and *get* services for read (get) and write (set) accesses. An example of encapsulation of the variable xx is provided in Figure 9.9.

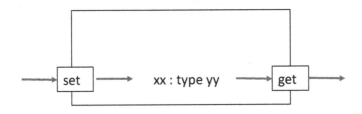

Figure 9.9. *Encapsulation*

Data encapsulation requires at least the read function (get), which could be used by the maintenance tool to access internal data in the event of operating issues.

9.4.6.4. *Low coupling*

A component should not make its implementation dependent on the implementation of another component. We must be able to develop the implementation of a component without having to modify the components that utilize it.

Figure 9.10 shows that the component C3 is dependent on at least four components, which is challenging for maintenance. The use of global variables is a situation that creates strong coupling.

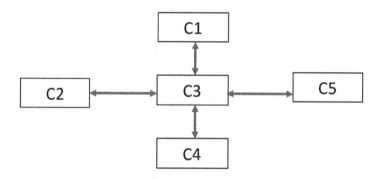

Figure 9.10. *Example of coupling*

The notion of coupling appears as soon as we use so-called service components. Service components can be employed to encapsulate hardware and/or to manage low-level services (for example for the management of software application error messages). It is worth noting that object-oriented languages naturally introduce coupling between classes.

9.4.6.5. *Partitioning*

Figure 9.11 shows four components that interact with one another. Components in gray are safety-impacting components and white components have no impact on safety.

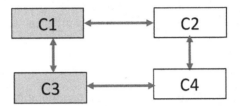

Figure 9.11. *Example of software application architecture*

There are then two possibilities: either everything is developed at the highest safety level, which has an impact on costs, or partitioning is put in place. Figure 9.12 presents partitioning. The partitioning mechanism makes it possible to ensure that non-safety components will have no impact on safety components. The partitioning mechanism will have the same safety level as safety components.

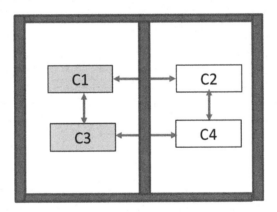

Figure 9.12. *Partitioning*

The partitioning mechanism needs to ensure that:

– the processor will correctly execute the safety component (it must be ensured that non-safety critical components cannot control the processor);

– memory areas associated with safety components are protected against potential changes due to non-safety components;

– the clock and the interrupt handler cannot be manipulated by non-safety components;

– common resources such as network managers may not remain as the responsibility of non-safety components.

From the 1990s, it was easier to develop the entire application at the highest safety level, but with the advent of virtualization and hypervisors, new solutions emerged that contributed to the introduction of rather simple partitioning. For an example, the case of PikeOs[7] may be of interest.

9.4.6.6. *Parameter management*

Regardless of the field, the notion of parameter is fundamental. For the automotive and rail sectors, the notion of parametrization appears implicitly within the applicable standard (ISO 26262 or CENELEC 50128). Concerning the railway industry, it is even more accurate, because the CENELEC 50128 standard includes a specific chapter related to the preparation of parameters.

As has been identified in Chapter 4, the parameters of the software application must be identified during the specification phase.

At the architecture level, it is necessary to identify the parameters and the place where they are managed. Figure 9.13 shows the development of parameter management at the software application level. Initially, parameters were seen as constants scattered throughout the software application. They were then grouped inside a component (for example a library) that was linked with the rest of the application. In modern systems, parameters can be found outside of the software application.

Figure 9.13. *Parameter positioning. For a color version of this figure, see www.iste.co.uk/boulanger/applications3.zip*

---

7 To learn more about PikeOs, see https://www.sysgo.com/products/pikeos-hypervisor/.

Figure 9.14 introduces two examples of parameter management. In the first architecture (a), parameters are located in a different memory area of the software application and the purpose of the *parametrization* component is to make the set of parameters available to other components.

The second architecture (b) highlights that the parameters are received in the form of a bit stream, which will be transformed by the *parametrization* component into a set of parameters that it will make available to the other components. The bit stream may be received during the system startup or on the fly. The on-the-fly reception raises two concerns: the first is linked to the time it is received and when they have to be taken into account, and the second is related to their validity from the safety-integrity point of view (security).

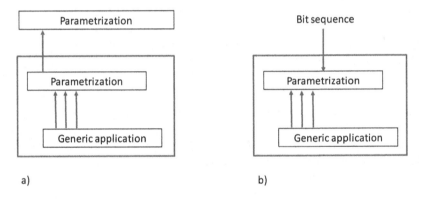

Figure 9.14. *Parameter-managing architectures*

Since parametrization data are stored in memory, there is a risk that an external disturbance (EMC, particle, etc.) or a hardware defect may cause their corruption. Thereby, it is also important to consider and put in place a protection mechanism such as a checksum[8], which will be periodically verified.

9.4.6.7. *Testability*

Testability requires that behaviors be observable. The observation of a behavior is only possible if it is not hidden by another behavior.

---

8 The checksum is a way to protect one or more data elements; for more information, see [BOU 09a, BOU 11c].

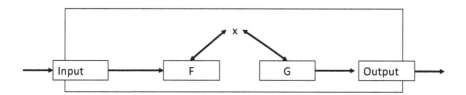

Figure 9.15. *Global variable management*

If the behaviors of functions F and G result in developing the variable X (see Figure 9.15), then the execution of the statement "F; G" is not observable, because the effect of function F on variable X is not visible since the value of X is overwritten by the execution of G.

Testability requires a clear decomposition and well-defined interfaces but it is important to avoid having hidden links between components. Hidden links make their appearance not only along with global variables, but also when passing parameters in pointer form which allows links to be established between two remote variables.

Observability can be introduced through the addition of an observable (by adding access functions) or though the management of a trace file, which can be accessed (directly or indirectly by means of a maintenance tool, for instance).

9.4.6.8. Complexity

At the architecture level, complexity is an important topic. Complexity may surge through the number of components (see Figure 9.16), as well as through the number of interfaces.

Regarding the number of components, it is paramount to keep in mind that we have to be able to produce a document. That is why the number of boxes is generally limited to seven per screen page (printable figure).

Figure 9.16. *Example of software application architecture*

Figure 9.17 illustrates the fact that a component is connected to several other components; in the case of failure of C2, several components will be impacted.

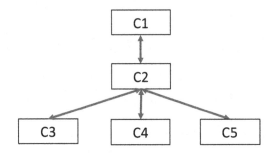

Figure 9.17. *Example of software application architecture*

Regarding the number of interfaces for a component, it is similar to the number of boxes per page, which is around seven.

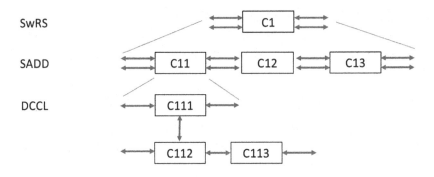

Figure 9.18. *Documentation hierarchy*

Complexity control in terms of numbers of components can be done through a multilevel hierarchical vision (see Figure 9.18) and for the management of the complexity of interfaces, it is possible to use data aggregation which allows us to combine several data elements through an interface.

9.4.6.9. *Hierarchical view*

The hierarchical aspect of components is managed through a documentation tree. The System Architecture Description Document (SADD) describes the architecture of the first level and for each component a Software Component Design Document (SCDD) can be produced.

The content of the SADD and SCDD is identical (see section 9.4.5): the architecture component (the software application is a component), the external interfaces of the component, the components implementing the component and the internal interfaces are described therein. The requirements will be identified for each component.

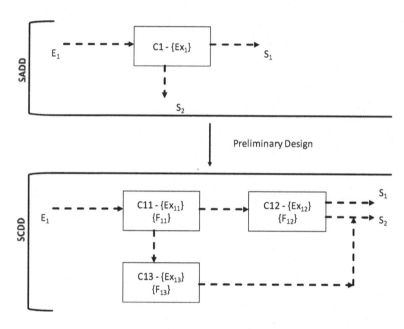

Figure 9.19. *Architecture decomposition*

Figure 9.19 shows how the component C1 is broken down into three subcomponents (C11, C12, C13). The hierarchical vision makes it possible to break the complexity but if properly used, it also contributes to facilitating reuse and maintainability. The SCDD must therefore identify the components C_{ij} and describe for each C_{ij} the services and requirements to be achieved. The SCDD must show that all components identified at the architecture level of the software application (SADD) are correctly taken into account and that there is traceability between the requirements of the SADD and those of the SCDD.

9.4.7. Description of the software application architecture

9.4.7.1. Content of the document

In the SADD and SCDD, it is necessary to identify:

– the external interfaces of the software application;

– the internal interfaces for each component;

– how components are involved in the operation modes of the software application: initialization phase, normal phase, maintenance phase, etc.;

– the functionalities of each component: functionalities can be defined through a list of requirements (see section 9.4.5.2), a model and/or a text description;

– non-functional characteristics such as performance and/or scaling;

– data local to each variable (a high-level component could have local data shared among several subcomponents);

– parametrization data used by each component;

– performance goals for each component: these goals can be related to the memory footprint of the software application and/or of these data, CPU load, numbers of messages, etc;

– safety goals associated with each component: it is required to identify safety functions and the levels associated with them.

9.4.7.2. Allocation versus requirement refinement

SwRS has made it possible to identify applicable requirements and the software application architecture (SADD) identifies the components; it may seem natural to implement the allocation of requirements. Requirement allocation is intended to create a link between a requirement and at least one component (see Figure 9.20).

Requirement allocation is an approach that does not contribute to ensuring testability and maintainability. For example, as shown in Figure 9.20, the requirement Ex1 is allocated to two components (C1 and C3), but how can we know what part of requirement Ex1 is allocated to each component during the preparation of test cases? In the event the requirement Ex1 changes, how do we know which component is impacted, and conversely, if a component changes how do we know if the requirement is affected? Generally, requirement allocation requires implementing a mechanism for traceability at the requirement level, as shown in Figure 9.21. This process remains manual and difficult to maintain.

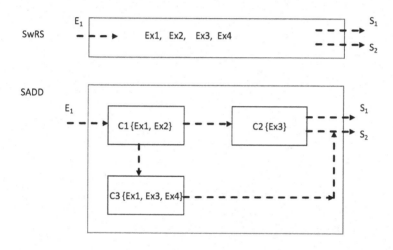

Figure 9.20. *Allocation*

Ex1: The level crossing is equipped with gates and traffic lights. There are two traffic lights associated with a level crossing, one red and one amber. When the amber light is on, it means that road users (cars, cyclists, pedestrians, drivers etc.) must stop at the limit of the crossing if possible. The red light indicates that the crossing is closed to road traffic and that it is forbidden to move forward.

Figure 9.21. *Example of manual allocation management. For a color version of this figure, see www.iste.co.uk/boulanger/applications3.zip*

This is the reason why it is preferable to implement the notion of requirement refinement. Requirement refinement means that for each documentation level, there are requirements and traceability links.

An example of requirement refinement management is provided in Figure 9.22. For example, requirement Ex1 was broken down into two requirements Ex11 and Ex12. The requirements Ex11 and Ex12 are clearly defined and identified.

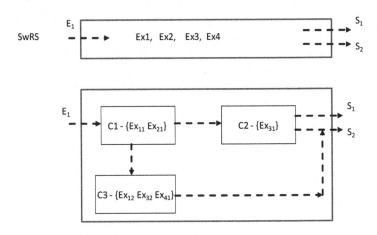

Figure 9.22. *Example of requirement refinement*

The requirement refinement-based approach provides a means to ensure not only maintainability and testability, but also reusability because the documentation of the component C3 is autonomous.

9.4.7.3. *Requirement traceability*

Table 9.2 shows an example of traceability between the DAL and DCP. The purpose of this traceability is to demonstrate that all top-level requirements have been taken into account.

SADD	SCDD
SADD_EX_1	SCDD_EX_11, SCDD_EX_12, SCDD_EX_13
SADD_EX_2	
SADD_EX_3	SCDD_EX_11

Table 9.2. *Example of SADD/SCDD traceability*

In this example, there is a requirement which has not been included; it is necessary to add an explanation that justifies the fact that requirement SADD_EX_2 is taken into account fully during the software application architecture phase and was not taken into account during the design stage.

As a general rule, a requirement associated with a component at the architecture level must be covered by requirements at the detailed design level.

Table 9.3 shows an example of traceability between the SCDD and SADD. The purpose of this traceability is to demonstrate that there is no untraceable design element with a need.

SCDD	SADD
SCDD_EX_11	SADD_EX_1, SADD_EX_3
SCDD_EX_11	SADD_EX_1
SCDD_EX_13	SADD_EX_1
SCDD_EX_14	

Table 9.3. *Example of SCDD/SADD traceability*

In the example, the requirement SCDD_EX_14 is not traceable with the architecture requirements of the software application. We must then identify the need associated with this requirement:

– This may be a requirement related to methodological processes (quality control, tool qualification, use of a language, etc.) and a requirement should exist at the architecture level that indicates the safety level (hence quality control or language choice needs), the quality level (at least the application of the ISO 9001:2015 standard), standards to be satisfied and business processes.

– This may be a so-called "design" requirement; it would be a design choice. A design choice (decomposition, redundancy, etc.) allows us to address either a safety goal, for example code segregation avoids the propagation of defects or a functional purpose, for instance reusing components can be a means to address the functional need. In general, this type of requirement makes it possible to establish the connection between different design requirements to implement an architecture requirement as shown in Figure 9.23.

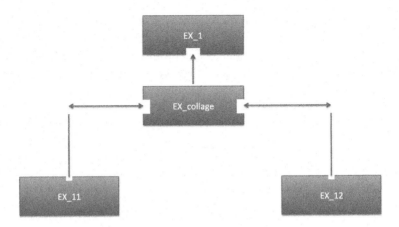

Figure 9.23. *Detailed design phase*

9.5. Verification of the software application architecture

The SADD and SCDD must be verified. It is necessary to verify that the architecture is not too complex, that it is balanced, that it is testable and that it enables us to assume the requirements identified in the SwRS.

The preparation of software/software integration tests (S/S IT) and software/hardware integration tests (S/H IT) based on the SADD and SCDD will make it possible to identify problems of observability and complexity as early as possible.

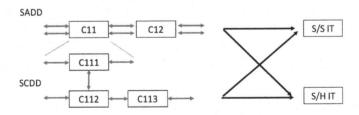

Figure 9.24. *Relationships between the SADD and SCDD and the IT*

As shown in Figure 9.24, the SADD and SCDD are inputs of the S/S IT. In fact, a S/S integration strategy has to be defined that goes from low-level components to the full software application. Concerning the S/H IT, the strategy is different: the right level has to be found to test the interaction between the software and the hardware. The easiest is at the lowest level but requires code to be developed to manage exchanges. The preparation of integration tests is described in Volume 4 [BOU 19].

The verification of the architecture stage of a software specification will be presented in Chapter 10.

9.6. Consideration of COTS and reused components

9.6.1. *Introduction*

In the SADD and SCDD, and after having identified the need, it is possible to make the link with preexisting components and/or commercial components (COTS). As shown in Figure 9.25, it has to be demonstrated that the component CC can actually be used instead of C13.

The notion of reusability is related not only to the notion of preexisting component and/or COTS, but also to the notion of reusable component. Preexisting components are related to the fact that there have been previous developments and that there is confidence in these developments.

Some components may have been provided by a third party and in this context, these will be referred to as COTS. With COTS, it is sometimes difficult to obtain a documentation describing the algorithms and the verifications that have been effectively implemented.

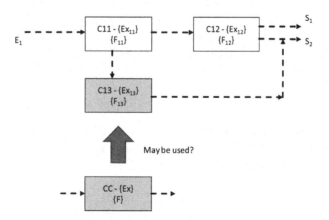

Figure 9.25. *Use of a reusable component. For a color version of this figure, see www.iste.co.uk/boulanger/applications3.zip*

9.6.2. *Preexisting component*

As indicated in Definition 8.2, all components must be characterized by a set of interfaces (see section 9.3.4.3) and a set of requirements that can characterize their behavior.

A preexisting component will at least have to provide these elements (set of interfaces and set of requirements), but it must also be defined through a version and a set of assumptions for use.

The component version enables us to make the link between the constituents of the component and all the proofs of proper operation (type of process put in place for the implementation and for the V&V, list of standards applied, documents, verification elements and testing results).

Assumptions for use must ensure the proper operation of this component within the whole. These assumptions should describe:

– hardware-related constraints (memory size, cache size, number representation, addressing, CPU load, etc.);

– real-time constraints.

– safety-related constraints (safety level, safety requirement, etc.).

As has been stated, it is necessary to have elements that are able to demonstrate that the component assumes the requirements associated with it. Items of proof can be in the form of documentation but feedback can also be of interest. Feedback should then be formalized (project list, project type, security level, scope of use, number of operating hours, distance traveled, etc.) and demonstrate that the component has incurred no defect.

9.6.3. *COTS*

A COTS is a black box provided by a third party, which means that there is little documentation available and that there are doubts about implementation and V&V processes.

Generally, feedback is not formalized and we thus obtain things such as "Windows XP is used by several million people therefore...". Furthermore, in the presence of a COTS, it will be necessary to limit the functions being used, but it will also be necessary to achieve a safety study that will analyze all of the potential failures and their impact on the software application. Failure detection and/or protection mechanisms will then have to be put in place.

In general, the encapsulation of the COTS is implemented (see Figure 9.26), which limits the usable functions but also limits the effects of the defects of the COTS.

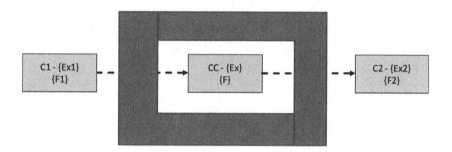

Figure 9.26. *COTS encapsulation. For a color version of this figure, see www.iste.co.uk/boulanger/applications3.zip*

In addition to the encapsulation of the COTS, the interfaces will have to be identified (internal services function call) as well as the requirements for describing the behavior. In order to ensure the good behavior of the component for the functions being used, a validation strategy will have to be developed based on the component tests (usually, there is no access to the COTS code).

Regarding the development process of a COTS, there is little hope that it follows any recognized standard. If (and the chances are good) the COTS is written in C, it is most likely that the code makes use of pointers and memory allocation or even code that does not satisfy the ANSI C standard. If the code does not meet the ANSI C standards, this means that it uses features that are not supported by all compilers; it is thus not compliant with the MISRA-C [MIS 12].

If the version of the COTS changes, special attention will have to be given concerning the impacts of these changes. For example, in the transition from Windows XP to Windows 7, we identified that some functions of the basic libraries had disappeared.

9.6.4. *Reusability*

Reusability is a concept that is sometimes misinterpreted by the people in charge of implementing a software application. In effect, they have a tendency during the designing of a component to implement all of the features that could one day be used.

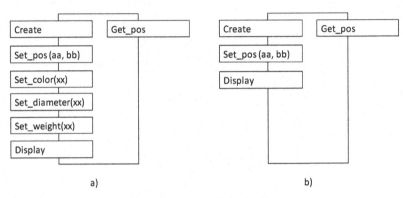

a)   b)

Figure 9.27. *Two examples of component*

Figure 9.27 describes the "billiard ball" component. Version a) is that of students who think it necessary to implement all of the services that can be used someday. Version b) is that which should be implemented, knowing that a billiard ball cannot change color, weight and especially diameter. This example shows that the development effort is almost doubled as is the V&V effort.

Reusability is the property of a software element that ensures that this element will be reused in the future. This only implies that what has been done has been properly done and mainly that it is well documented. This is why the various standards require the production of enough documentation during the implementation of a software application.

9.7. Model approach

The architecture of a software application is a model (see Figures 9.4 and 9.5, for example) that is at least structured (see the notion of structured method, Chapters 5 and 6). In fact, we have a vision of the components and relationships between these components.

The description of the architecture can be based on a more complex model, which will use another formalism such as the UML (see Figure 9.28).

The implementation of a model must be accompanied by a guide that will serve two functions: to explain how to achieve the model and how to interpret it.

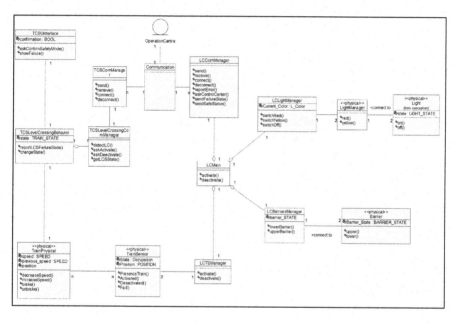

Figure 9.28. *Example of software application architecture modeled with UML*[9]

In effect, it should be explained how to implement the model because a notation such as UML is rather broad and it is not sufficient to refer to the document of the OMG[10] [OMG 07] or to the associated literature; it is necessary to define the constructions that can be employed in the company's projects. As a result, we limit the construction to be used.

The limitation of the constructions is not enough; it is also important to clearly explain how the model can be interpreted. For example, in

---

9 Figure 9.4 shows an example of a model for a level crossing. To learn more about this example, see [BON 03, BOU 04, BOU 07b].
10 To learn more, visit: http://www.omg.org/.

Figure 9.24, aggregation relationships are seen as a flow of communication between two classes, and each class is seen as a software component.

The use of the UML notation is not without raising some questions [BOU 07b, OSS 07]: how can a notation with no semantics be used? How can an application based on the UML notation be evaluated? etc. Several works are dedicated to providing answers to these questions (see, for instance, [FED 04a, FED 04b, FED 04c, FED 04d] and [MOT 05]).

9.8. Conclusion

This chapter has allowed us to present the elements used for describing the architecture of a software application. Several goals have to be taken into account in order to ensure maintainability: abstraction, composability, low coupling and testability.

We also put forward that it was necessary to have a methodology and especially a guide that explains how to achieve the architecture model and how to interpret it.

We have broadly discussed requirement management and the need to put in place a requirement refinement and traceability process over all architecture levels.

Software Application Architecture Verification

10.1. Introduction

The second phase of the V-model in Figure 1.3 concerns the implementation of the architecture of the software application.

The second phase of the V-model is the software application architecture phase that consists of two activities: the software architecture (SADD and SCDD) and the integration testing specification (S/S Integration Test Specification (ITS) and S/H ITS). In Chapter 9, we described the developing process of the SwAD and SwCD; the development of the S/S ITS and S/H ITS is described in Volume 4 [BOU 19].

The purpose of this chapter is to present verification activities to be implemented as part of the architecture stage of the software application. A similar chapter will be dedicated to each phase of the development cycle (specification, design, components, integration tests and overall tests) in order to identify the necessary verifications to be implemented during each phase. The various verification techniques were presented in Chapter 11 of Volume 2 [BOU 17].

10.2. Verification

10.2.1. *Reminder*

As was presented in Chapter 11 of Volume 2 [BOU 17], the verification can be done by means of static analysis and/or dynamic analysis. Since the object here is to verify the architecture of a software application, static methods are more suitable.

10.2.2. *Software application architecture verifications*

10.2.2.1. *Context*

In the software requirement specification (SwRS), software is a component. The software application architecture (SwAD) and the design documents of software components (SwCD) describe compositions of components. These documents provide at least a graphic view of architecture that constitutes more or less structured models. Effectively, the models at least contain boxes (components) and links (interfaces).

10.2.2.2. *Methodology*

The verification of the SwAD and/or a SwCD may be achieved through several activities:

– a more or less formal design review (proofreading, use of checklists, etc.) (see sections 10.2.2.3 and 10.2.2.4);

– the preparation of the testing specifications (see section 10.2.2.5).

As indicated in Chapter 4 of Volume 2 [BOU 17], verification processes are carried out by a dedicated team. This team must be independent from the production team (see Figure 7.1). The verification team includes testers (TST), integrators (INT) and verifiers (VER).

However, the verification team is not the only one involved as a matter of fact; it is necessary to verify that the SwAD and the SwCD meet quality criteria (which will be the function of the QUA). In the same way, the architecture must be verified by the safety team (SAF).

10.2.2.3. *Design review*

The verification of a phase requires that the implementation of quality requirements is verified (procedures application, respect of formats, etc.), the application of the process (compliance with plans, respect for the organization, etc.), correction of activities and that safety requirements are properly taken into account.

Concerning the architecture phase, methodological guides related to modeling and architecture principles will be part of input documents, therefore, there will be additional verifications.

The modeling rules include:

– naming conventions for all objects (constant, global variables, interfaces, local variables, software parameters, function parameter, functions, module, etc.);

– rules related to documentation;

– rules related to designing;

– decomposition rules.

10.2.2.3.1. Documentation review

The documentation review is then conducted through a quick (informal) reading (walkthrough) or a design review (formal design review). The documentation review has been presented in detail in section 7.2.2.2.1.

This verification must have a goal. This goal may be formalized in the form of a checklist (control list).

10.2.2.3.2. Quality activity

This activity was presented in section 7.2.2.2.2.

10.2.2.3.3. Verifier

As already stated, software application architecture verification (SwAD and SwCD) must be performed by a verifier (see Figure 7.1 for the organization). The verifier (see Table 7.3) shall verify the technical content of the document (see section 7.2.2.2.3 for more information).

10.2.2.3.4. Software application architecture verification

As already previously indicated, a description of the architecture of a software application should define:

– the boundaries of the software application through the identification of the external software/software and software/hardware interfaces; this information has been introduced in the case of the SwRS; it can be resumed and/or completed;

– stored data (global variables) and access mechanisms;

– the parametrization data management principles; parametrization data have been introduced in the SwRS but in the SwAD, the component(s) dedicated to their management must be identified;

– components and internal interfaces of the software application;

– for each component, one should identify the requirements to be assumed as well as their traceability with the SwRS requirements.

On this basis, it is possible to set up several verifications of the software requirements specification:

– verify that all the external interfaces are connected. There is at least an internal component that consumes information circulating through each external interface;

– verify that all internal interfaces are correctly defined;

– verify that all the external interfaces are connected. There is at least one internal component that consumes information circulating through each internal interface;

– verify that all the internal interfaces are connected. There is at least one internal component that consumes information circulating through each internal interface;

– verify that the use of global variables is justified;

– verify that the use of global variables is protected[1].

---

1 In order to protect the global variables, it is possible to implement a directory which will be responsible for verifying that only authorized components have access to global variables.

And for each component:

– verify that all internal interfaces are included at least once in a requirement. If an internal interface is not included, then it will not be used;

– verify that all the states that have been identified in the components requirements are connected to states identified in the SwRS;

– verify that all software parametrizing data are included at least once as part of a component requirement. If a parametrization data element is not included, then it will not be used;

– verify that all requirements are traceable with the SwRS;

– verify that all the requirements utilize internal interfaces as input, otherwise the requirement is not observable.

– verify that all requirements identify the states in which they are applicable. Otherwise, there will be a possible ambiguity;

– verify that all local variables of a component are correctly identified and justified.

This is a first verification set that ought to be completed by your feedback. It is very important to put in place a REX (Return of Experience) approach when some defects are not detected at early stages. It is also required to verify if it is not possible to improve the verification and the checklist used during verification.

10.2.2.3.5. Software components design verification

As has been stated, the description of the design of a software component must define:

– the boundaries of the software application through the identification of the external interfaces (software/software and software/hardware);

– stored data (global variables) and access means;

– the principles for the management of parametrization data; parametrization data have been introduced in the SwRS and SwAD, but in the SwCD, the interfaces allowing access to parameters must be identified;

– components and interfaces internal to this component;

– for each component internal to this component, the requirements to be assumed and their traceability with the SwRS requirements have to be identified.

On this basis, it is possible to put in place several verifications of the SwCD:

– verify that all the external interfaces are connected. There is at least one internal component that makes use of the information circulating through each external interface;

– verify that all internal interfaces are correctly defined;

– verify that all the internal interfaces are connected. There is at least one internal component that consumes information circulating through each internal interface;

– verify that all the internal interfaces are connected. There is at least one internal component that consumes information circulating through each internal interface;

– verify that the use of global variables is justified;

– verify that the use of global variables is protected[2].

And for each component:

– verify that all internal interfaces are included at least once in a requirement. If an internal interface is not included, it will then not be used;

– verify that all the states that have been identified in the components requirements are connected to states identified in the SwRS and/or in the SwAD;

– verify that all software parametrizing data are included at least once as part of a component requirement. If a parametrization data element is not included, then it will not be used;

– verify that all the requirements utilize internal interfaces as input, otherwise the requirement is not observable;

---

2 In order to protect the global variables, it is possible to implement a directory which will be responsible for verifying that only authorized components have access to global variables.

– verify that all requirements identify the states in which they are applicable. Otherwise, there will be a possible ambiguity;

– verify that all requirements are traceable with the SwAD;

– verify that all local variables of a component are properly identified and justified.

This is a first verification set that ought to be completed by your feedback.

10.2.2.3.6. Verification of architecture complexity

In section 7.2.2.2.5, we mentioned the verification of the complexity of the requirements in terms of decomposition. At the architecture level, the complexity is related to the distribution of requirements.

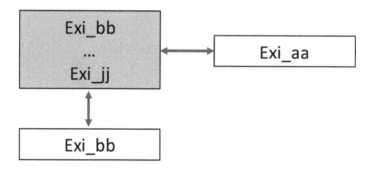

Figure 10.1. *Complex component requirement*

The complexity of a software architecture can be analyzed through several topics:

– analysis of the distribution of requirements per component: Figure 10.1 shows that the component in gray supports more requirements than the others. It is necessary to check if this is normal. It is preferable to have a balanced distribution of requirements within the architecture;

– analysis of the number of components: each architecture level should be analyzable and printable. It is thus necessary to limit the number of components of a level. The number 7 reappears fairly regularly as the maximum number of boxes on a screen or on a page;

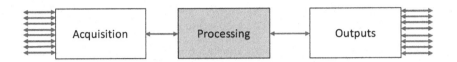

Figure 10.2. *Example of architecture*

– analysis of interface distribution: as for the requirements, it is necessary to verify that the interfaces are evenly distributed onto all of the components. In the context of acquisition/processing/output architectures (see Figure 10.2), it is possible to justify that interfacing components have many interfaces.

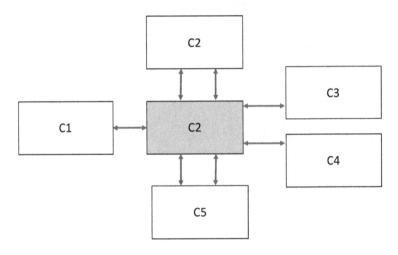

Figure 10.3. *Example of strong coupling*

– coupling analysis: it is necessary to verify that there is no strong coupling in the point architecture. Coupling for a component is characterized by the number of components in direct relationship. One should therefore measure the coupling of each component and look for critical points. Strong coupling is similar to a plate of spaghetti and introduces difficulties in executing the integration tests. This type of software architecture can appear when implementing a component for the management of error messages or messages from the software application.

10.2.2.3.7. Verification of requirement traceability

In order to cover the needs for requirement completeness and consistency, it is necessary to put in place a requirement verification phase for each phase of the implementation process, as defined in section 7.2.2.2.6.

10.2.2.3.8. Checklists for architecture verification

Requirement verification can be achieved using a checklist. This checklist (for example, see Table 10.1) will have to define control points. These latter are related to the knowledge of the types of errors that can be introduced during the activity that has produced the documents to be verified.

Point	Rule	Status OK/KO	Comment
R_1	The requirements of the SwRS must be laid out with the SwAD or a justification must be given		
R_1_1	If a requirement of the SwRS is not traced, a judgment on the justification will have to be provided		
R_2	All the requirements of the SwAD must be laid out with the SwRS or a justification must be given		
R_2_1	If a requirement of the SwAD is not traced, a judgment on the justification will have to be provided		
R_3	All external interfaces introduced in the SwRS are included in the SwAD		
R_3_1	If an external interface is not used (no connection), a justification and a control mechanism must be present		
R_4	All the parameters introduced in the SwRS are inserted in the SwAD		

Table 10.1. *Example of a checklist concerning an architecture*

10.2.2.4. *Model implementation*

The architecture of a software application is a model that is at least *structured* (see the notion of structured method, Chapters 5 and 6). As mentioned in Chapter 9, it is required that a modeling guide be created that explains how a model can be implemented and how it can be read.

At the architecture level, it will be necessary to verify that the type of modeling implemented is consistent with the type of problem. As an example, a railway signaling system can be seen as a set of state machines, thereby a model in the form of an automaton would allow us to avoid the introduction of biases during the implementation, the bias being introduced during the change in formalism.

It will be important to put in place an activity for verifying that the model is consistent with this modeling guide.

10.2.2.5. *Explicit and implicit interfaces*

During the verification of the SwAD and SwCD, it is necessary to verify that all interfaces are explicit. It may happen that some data are not exchanged through interfaces but directly: access to global variables, access to pointers, etc. Implicit interfaces make maintenance, testability and reusability more difficult.

10.2.2.6. *Safety level associated with the data exchanged*

During the architecture verification (SwAD and SwCD), the consistency of safety levels will have to be looked into. As shown in Figure 10.4, the component C2 was assessed as being SSIL2[3]. It makes use of two data elements: one was produced by a SSIL0 component and the other by a SSIL2 component.

For this example, it is necessary to introduce an element of defensive programming whose objective will be to verify the validity of the SSIL0 data before using it. As an example, in a train the request for opening a door (latch locking) is SSIL0 (anyone can request the door to open at any time),

---

3 In order to characterize a safety level, we employ the notion of SIL (Safety Integrity Level) ranging from 0 (no safety impact) to 4 (death of several people). Concerning software, we will use the acronym SSIL for Software SIL.

however the software component responsible for controlling the door opening makes a correlation with the speed of the train, which is SSIL4.

A Software Error Effect Analysis (SEEA) may be carried out on the architecture in order to verify if there are weaknesses at the architecture level. The SEEA (see the discussion in [BLA 18]) is then a means of justifying the defensive programming elements that are to be implemented.

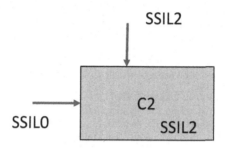

Figure 10.4. *SSIL2 component using data of a different safety level*

The SEEA must allow the verification of the proper use of the data at the architecture level. One of the issues concerns the notion of functional area. A datum is defined on a computing type, which may be broader than the functional area (see Figure 10.5); it is then necessary to add defensive programming elements.

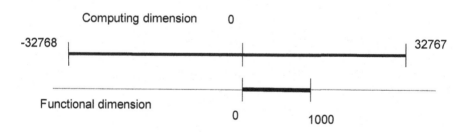

Figure 10.5. *Computing field versus functional area*

10.2.2.7. *Preparation of integration tests*

10.2.2.7.1. Integrator

The selection of integration test cases is performed by someone who is not the person who wrote the SwAD and SwCD. This person is called the *Integrator* (INT). Table 10.2 describes the role of the INT by introducing the responsibilities and skills expected.

Role: INTEGRATOR: INT
Responsibilities are as follows: – shall manage the integration process using the software base line;   – shall develop the Software and Software/Hardware Integration Testing Specification for software components based on the specifications and architecture of the designer's components, indicating which are the necessary input components, the sequence of integration activities and resulting integrated components;   – shall develop and maintain records on verification activities;   – shall identify integration anomalies, record and communicate them to the body responsible for change management in light of the evaluation and the decision-making process;   – shall write a component and overall system integration report indicating the result of the integration.
Main skills are as follows: – shall be proficient in the field where component integration is performed; for example, the relevant programming languages, software interfaces, operating systems, data, platforms, codes, etc.;   – shall be proficient in various testing and verification approaches/methodologies and be able to identify the most appropriate method in a given context;   – shall be competent in understanding the design and functionality required at various intermediate levels;   – shall be able to deduce the types of integration tests from a set of integrated functions;   – shall be capable of analytical thinking and have a good sense of observation that allow understanding the system as a whole;   – shall understand applicable standards;   – shall understand the legislation applicable (if necessary).

Table 10.2. *Skills and responsibilities of the INT*

10.2.2.7.2. Principles

We generally call it integration testing but it would be preferable to refer to as interface testing. In fact, the purpose of integration testing is to test the set of interfaces of the software application. In order to test the interfaces, it is therefore necessary to have a description of the set of interfaces included in the architecture documents (SwAD and SwCD).

An interface is not only defined by its name and its type but, as has already been stated, we will have to describe at least:

– the list of data exchanged and for each data element:

- the name;

- the family and/or the type;

- the units (if necessary);

- the range of acceptable values;

- the values representing an error;

– real-time characteristics (time constraint, protocol, etc.);

– error management:

- Is the interface capable of detecting errors during exchanges?

- If yes, what are the associated behaviors?

- Is there exception handling management?

– memory management:

- Is there memory allocation?

- Is there a buffer? If yes, what happens when it is full?

- If there is no memorization mechanism, what happens if several data elements are received at the same time?

The name integration testing means that once all the basic components have been verified, it is possible to perform their integration in order to obtain the final application. The integration of a software application can be achieved through two approaches:

– the so-called "big bang" approach: the whole of the software application is integrated once. Basically, if the software application compiles, it is integrated. This approach is not without risks especially when using the C language. It may happen that parameters are reversed but that they are of similar types, therefore the compilation succeeds;

– the so-called "progressive integration" approach: based on the architecture documents (SwAD and SwCD), an integrated strategy is implemented which allows building the components of the upper levels gradually until the application software is obtained. This approach allows for detecting interface defects at the earliest. Figure 10.6 reveals two possibilities for connecting the two components and according to the architecture one of the configurations is erroneous.

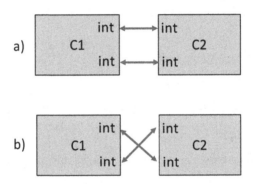

Figure 10.6. *Example of interface defects*

The objective of progressive integration is to look for defects in interfaces; we are in the piping system of the software application and analogously to a plumber, leaks and bad connections should be discovered. This is maybe what makes this activity less enjoyable among developers.

The interfaces of a component are of two types, logical interfaces (software/software interface) and physical interfaces (software/hardware interface). Consequently, there are two families of integration tests to implement: S/S integration tests and S/H integration tests.

S/S integration tests can be carried out on the development machine but S/H integration tests will be carried out on actual hardware (final target). For

S/H integrations tests, they can be executed at different levels but at lower architecture levels; it will be easier to test all the behaviors induced by the physical interface.

The implementation of a component integration strategy as part of a process for verifying logical and physical interfaces can lead to identifying errors at the definition level (incompatibility, value never used, etc.) of the interfaces and/or of their uses (too many messages, lack of exception handling, etc.).

10.2.2.7.3. Reminder

As already explained, based on the interfaces definition and on the SwAD and SwCD, test cases are identified (TC_x); these are test cases describing a situation to achieve, this situation being linked to an equivalence class. From the test cases, it is possible to prepare testing scenarios (TS_x), a test scenario describing a situation. A test case may therefore be included in several scenarios.

Since, at this level, the only input elements are the SwAD and SwCD, we are actually in the process of specifying black box tests (without knowledge of the implementation).

10.2.2.7.4. Verification example

The first verification consists of asserting that all interfaces are associated with at least an integration test, or more specifically, it is important to verify that all of the interface description (all portable data types, etc.) is at least associated with one test.

Similarly, as in section 7.2.2.5.2, we must verify that a requirement does not result in too many tests and that a test does not require too many requirements; it is necessary to verify that there is a balance at the interface level.

The number of tests allocated to each interface should be similar. If an interface appears to be more complex than the others (too many tests associated), one should verify whether this situation is acceptable (risk of non-maintainability).

Conversely, if a test requires a large number of interfaces, it is necessary to verify whether this is acceptable, because it seems that there is strong coupling between these interfaces and therefore a risk for non-maintainability.

10.2.3. *Synthesis*

The requirement specification phase of the software application requires the implementation of different skills:

– the management of the architecture by the DES;

– the management of integration techniques by the INT;

– verification management by the VER;

– standard and process control by the QUA and the VAL;

– safety management done by the SAF.

This is the reason why it will be necessary to ensure that the people involved clearly satisfy the skills requirements (see Chapter 4 of Volume 2 [BOU 17]).

When the verification activity is finalized, it is necessary to produce a verification report ARCH_VR (architecture–verification report):

– which identifies the stage inputs and outputs;

– which identifies the means being used (people, tools, etc.);

– which describes the activities carried out, the results of these activities, the anomalies detected, the remaining open topics;

– which concludes on the possibility of moving on to the next phase.

This report is generally written by the VER and the QUA and verified by the VAL under the approval of the project manager (PM).

10.3. Conclusion

Verification is a topic that is not always easy, and the purpose of these chapters is to provide verification objectives for each phase of the software application implementation lifecycle.

In this chapter, we have thus provided the elements that make it possible to verify that an architecture is correct.

11

Software Application Design

11.1. Introduction

The software application architecture phase (Chapter 9) allowed us to identify components, interfaces between these components and interfaces with the environment. As we have explained, the architecture phase could be built upon at least two levels (SwAD and SwCD), but if needed more decomposition levels should be employed. It is now necessary to define the content of each component. This stage involves the identification of the services performed by these components and the definition of the associated algorithms.

The safety implementation principles (information encoding, data redundancy, etc.) for a software application must be taken into account within the context of the design.

In order to prepare the coding phase, the design phase considers the type of programming language that will be used. For example, when using the C++ language, an object-oriented-based design must be implemented so as to avoid inconsistencies or issues during coding.

11.2. Component

The notion of software application has been mentioned in Definition 1.1; on the basis of this, it is possible to define what a software component is (see Definition 11.1).

DEFINITION 11.1 (Software Component).– *Entirety of the source code, processes, requirements, proper operation and documentation proofs, relating to the functioning of a component.*

As indicated in Definition 11.1, the component is not a file but an entity managed by configuration that contains the code, documentation, as well as all traces and verification results.

This allows for reusability. Furthermore, a C file is not easily reusable (problems with includes) and code without its documentation is not very useful. Most projects are considered as monolithic blocks (documentation is not broken down) and in a new project it proves difficult to reuse some of the documentation without having to perform unlucky cuts and pastes.

In the component approach, as for electronic components, the documentation is attached to the smallest element that assumes requirements.

11.3. Purpose of the design phase

Based on a software application architecture that describes components, the interactions between the components and interactions with the environment, it is important to define the behavior of each component. Component behavior is related to the services that they perform and these services rely on data that have to be identified and defined. Therefore, the inputs of the design phase are the set of elements produced by the software application architecture phase (see Chapter 9), as shown in Figure 11.1.

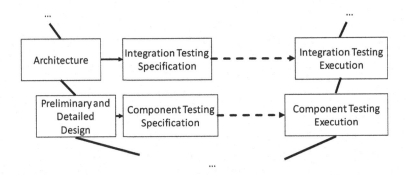

Figure 11.1. *Positioning of a component design phase*

Based on the description of the components, carried out during the design, it will be possible to identify tests for every component. Figure 11.2 shows the contents of a component design phase.

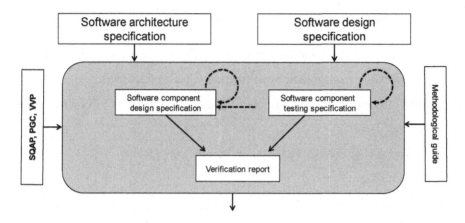

Figure 11.2. *Software component design phase*

A module-based approach considers references to module testing (MT) and unit testing (UT). A component-based approach will mainly refer to software component testing (SwCT).

For the component design phase, the inputs are:

– the plans:

   - Software Quality Assurance Plan (SQAP);

   - Software Verification and Validation Plan (SVVP);

   - Software Configuration Management Plan (SCMP);

– project documents:

   - Software Component Design (SwCD) document;

   - Glossary (GL);

– methodological guides:

  - SwCS writing guide;

  - SwCTS writing guide;

  - modeling guide.

The outputs of the software application architecture stage are as follows:

– the Software Component Specification (SwCS) document;

– the Software Component Testing Specification (SwCTS) document;

– Glossary[1] (GL);

– Software Component Verification report (SC_VR).

11.4. Designer

As indicated in Chapter 4 of Volume 2 [BOU 17], the activities related to the design of software components are carried out by the designer (whom we refer to as DES).

The DES is part of the design team. Table 9.1 specifies responsibilities and the main skills of the DES.

11.5. Software component specification document

11.5.1. *Objective*

Figure 11.3 shows an example of architecture: the software application has been broken down into three components (C1, C2, C3); there are interfaces between the environment (E1, E2, S1, S2) and the components and interfaces between components. For each component, the list of requirements to be taken into account is provided.

The purpose of the design phase is therefore to shift from this architecture to a decomposition describing all functions and algorithms as well as data.

---

1 The project glossary is to be updated throughout the whole of the software application implementation. New concepts could emerge at every level.

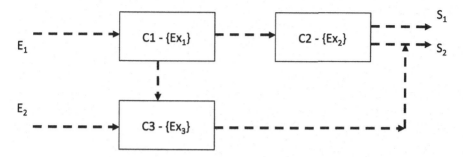

Figure 11.3. *Example of a software component architecture*

11.5.2. *Constraint on the methodology*

A so-called critical software application is associated with a safety level (SSIL[2]). This safety level requires that a number of constraints be taken into account.

One of these constraints is intended to avoid the introduction of defects; to this end, it is important to preserve the formalism introduced in the software application architecture (SwAD and SwCD) within the software application component design. This means that if the architecture of the software application (SwAD and SwCD) introduces states machines or an object-based approach, it would be preferable to use a similar formalism within the design. It should be noted that this constraint will also apply to the choice of language[3]. It is important to limit the number of defects introduced following changes in formalism.

A second constraint concerns error detection: it is important to detect errors as early as possible and as a result, it would be desirable that there is an approach that enables error detection at the earliest stages. The design is intended to describe the algorithms of each component function: a formal approach (see Chapter 6) based on the SCADE [DOR 08] or the B method

---

2 In order to characterize a safety level, we employ the notion of SIL (Safety Integrity Level) which ranges from 0 (no safety impact) to 4 (death of several people). With regard to software, we use the acronym SSIL for Software SIL.

3 As an example, suppose that the SwRS introduces state machines as a means of specification, that the SwAD and SwCD employ a service-oriented approach and that an object-oriented language is chosen for the implementation. This approach requires two changes in semantics that could lead to introducing defects in the software.

[ABR 96, BOU 13] would allow for verifications of the design. A graphical tool-based approach (for example VISIO or UML) does not allow for detecting errors.

This second constraint will also imply that we will have to justify that the language actually makes it possible to discover errors at the earliest stage. Every language is different: due to a flaw in C semantics, a C compiler is able to compile incorrect programs (bad use of the assignment in place and location of the comparison, for example). This topic will be addressed in Chapter 14.

In conclusion, it is very important to use a programming language with good properties:

1) well-defined syntax;

2) well-defined semantics;

3) with a return of experience.

In general, points 1 and 2 can be fulfilled if the language has an associate standard (ANSI C, ADA, etc.).

11.5.3. *Methodology characteristic*

According to the software safety integrity level, the chosen design method should provide characteristics that facilitate:

– abstraction;

– modularity and other characteristics for controlling complexity. Spaghetti code programming is to be avoided (the code appears as an inextricable confusion); to this end, factorization and a decomposition into subfunctionality must be implemented. Furthermore, it is important to avoid the use of global variables and to use clear object names specifying:

- the clear and accurate expression of the following elements:

1) the functionality;

2) the information flow between components;

3) sequencing and time information;

4) the parallelism (whether possible);

5) the data structure and properties. Some internal data can be managed in the component;

- human understanding: the automatic generation of documentation from code (with a tool such as DOXYGEN) does not guarantee human understanding. *A posteriori* generation of documentation is a path that will not make it possible to guarantee independence (the documentation is made based on the code that will enable the production of test cases; the results from the tests show the flaws in the software or that the latter works correctly);

- verification (static through new reading, or dynamic through component testing) and software maintenance.

11.6. Software component specification document

11.6.1. *Principles*

As shown in Figure 11.4, component design is carried out following the architecture phase. Consequently, a document describing the architecture (SwAD and SwCD) and a software integration testing specification (S/S and S/H ITS) must be available as inputs to the component design.

The purpose of design is to describe the behavior of each basic element (function or procedure). For each component (Cij), the SwCS contains a set of functions/services/methods denoted by {Fij} that must be implemented.

However, mastering a detailed design involves the management of design quality; this is why it will be necessary for there to be a guide presenting safety principles and a guide for the design describing naming conventions, decomposition rules, rules related to the description of algorithms, etc.

With regard to certifiable software applications, it is necessary to keep in mind that there are several objectives that must be achieved such as testability, maintainability and the ability to perform analyses to implement proofs of safety.

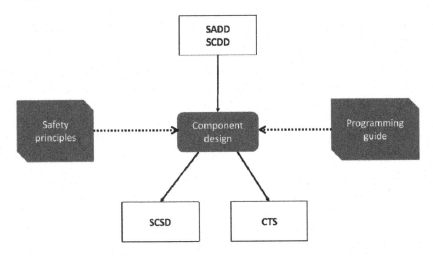

Figure 11.4. *Preliminary design phase*

Maintainability requires that modules be loosely coupled. The low coupling (see section 9.4.6.4) is related to the fact that a component should not make its implementation dependent on the implementation of another component.

Testability requires that behaviors be observable. The observation of a behavior is only possible if it is not hidden by another behavior. If the behaviors of functions F and G (see Figure 9.15) result in developing the variable X, then the execution of the statement "F; G" is not observable, because the effect of function F on variable X is not visible since the value of X is overwritten by the execution of G.

The capability to perform analyses on the design requires that this design be clear and accurate and that the documentation be sufficient. The notion of sufficient documentation refers to the fact that the role of documentation is to explain the choices as opposed to only serving as documentation. It is important to understand that the documentation is one of the major points. A sufficiently detailed documentation must be available to enable the maintenance of the software application or, in the worst-case scenario, for us to be able to rebuild the component.

The design is a stage of the implementation that makes it possible to finalize the decomposition of components into functions. In the end, every component (C_{ij}) is associated with a set of requirements denoted by $\{Ex_{ij}\}$ and a set of functions/services/methods denoted by $\{F_{ij}\}$.

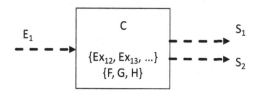

Figure 11.5. *Preliminary design phase*

For an interface *I*, we have to describe at least:

– the list of data exchanged and for each data element:

- the name;

- the family and/or the type;

- units (if necessary);

- the range of acceptable values;

- values identifying an error;

– real-time characteristics (time constraint, protocol, etc.);

– error handling:

- Is the interface capable of detecting errors during exchanges?

- If yes, what are the associated behaviors?

- Is there an exception handling mechanism?

– memory management:

- Is there memory allocation?

- Is there a buffer? If yes, what happens when it is full?

- If there is no memorization mechanism, what happens if several data elements are received at the same time?

11.6.2. *Functional decomposition*

The detailed design phase is intended to identify the algorithms and data structures for each service (Fi). The algorithms must be consistent with the needs identified by the associated requirements (Ex).

The construction of these algorithms can impose the implementation of additional services internal to this component.

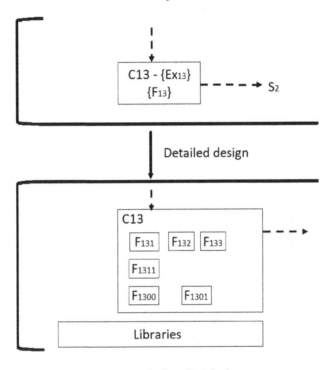

Figure 11.6. *Detailed design*

Figure 11.6 shows how function F13 of component C13 has been broken down into three functions F131, F132 and F133. The subfunction F131 relies on an internal service F1311 and the three functions F131, F132 and F133 rely on two internal functions F1300 and F1301. We have also introduced the fact that all of the services of component C13 may rely on one or more libraries.

Figure 11.7 represents the call graph of function F131.

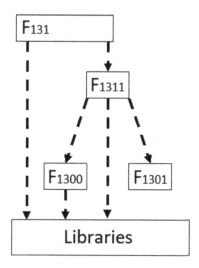

Figure 11.7. *Function F131 call graph*

11.6.3. *Modular or programming unit decomposition*

The software component is a group of programming units that allow its implementation. Programming units will depend on the design methodology being used.

They can either be modules (in the sense of independent files), packages (as understood in ADA; they are then composed of a specification part and a design part), classes (in the sense of object-oriented programming) and/or components (in the sense of the literature of components that describes the component as an autonomous independent entity).

11.6.4. *Data description*

As already stated, it is necessary to describe the data set used at the component level, namely:

– the list of the parameters used by the component functions. For every parameter, properly recall: the name, the type, units, functional values and error values;

– the list of local variables. For each local variable, properly recall: the name, the type, the restrictive value to apply to the initialization, units, functional values and error values;

– the list of global variables. For each global variable, properly recall: the name, the type, the restrictive value to apply to the initialization, units, functional values and error values.

Concerning global variables, it will be necessary to justify their usefulness and to propose a mechanism to protect the access (see sections 9.4.6.3.3 and 9.4.6.3.4).

For local variables of the component, a safety[4] mechanism will have to be provided for detecting corruptions (memory error, external disturbance, etc.) in addition to a mechanism for preventing the use of an obsolete value (if necessary).

11.6.5. *Description of the algorithms*

As already indicated, it is necessary to describe in the SwCS the algorithms associated with every function and procedure identified in the component. The description can be textual or graphic.

With regard to textual approaches for the description of algorithms, a pseudo-language is employed. Figure 11.8 shows an example of an algorithm in pseudo-language.

There are several pseudo-languages; here, we have decided to describe inputs, outputs, pre- and postconditions in addition to the algorithm.

The algorithm representation may be graphic. Grafcets can be used, or state machines, sequence diagrams, etc.

---

4 Redundancy information such as CRC-based may be used. The CRC (Cyclic Redundant Code), Hamming codes and/or checksums are mechanisms for protecting one or more data elements (for more information, see [BOU 09a, BOU 11c]).

Input   : A and B of natural integer type
Output   : Q and R of natural integer type
Precondition: A and B are positive

Algorithm:
Begin
        Q := 0
        R := A
        While (R>B) do
                Q :=- Q+1;
                R := R-B
        End While
End

Postcondition: Q and R are positive and A = B*Q+R

Figure 11.8. *Example of an algorithm*

11.6.6. *Requirement traceability*

Table 11.1 shows an example of traceability between the SwCD and SwCS. The purpose of this traceability is to demonstrate that all requirements of the upper level have been taken into account. In this example, there is a requirement that has not been included; it is required to add an explanation that justifies that the requirement SwCD_EX_2 is fully taken into account during the software application architecture phase.

SwCD	SwCS
SwCD_EX_1	SwCS_EX_11, SwCS_EX_12, SwCS_EX_13
SwCD_EX_2	
SwCD_EX_3	SwCS_EX_11

Table 11.1. *Example of SwCD/SwCS traceability*

As a general rule, a requirement associated with a component at the architecture level must be covered by requirements at the design level.

Table 11.2 shows an example of traceability between the SwCS and SwCD. The purpose of this traceability is to demonstrate that there is no untraceable design element with a need.

SwCS	SwCD
SwCS_EX_11	SwCD_EX_1, SwCD_EX_3
SwCS_EX_12	SwCD_EX_1
SwCS_EX_13	SwCD_EX_1
SwCS_EX_14	

Table 11.2. *Example of SwCS/SwCD traceability*

In the example, the requirement SwCS_EX_14 is not traceable with the architecture requirements of the software application. We must then identify the need associated with this requirement:

– this may be a requirement related to methodological processes (quality control, tool qualification, use of a language, etc.) and there should be a requirement at the architecture level that indicates the safety level (hence needs for quality control or language choice), the quality level (at least the application of the ISO 9001:2015 standard), standards to be satisfied and business processes;

– this may be a so-called "design" requirement; this would then be a design choice. A design choice (decomposition, redundancy, etc.) allows us to either address a safety goal, for example code segregation is a mechanism to avoid the propagation of defects, or a functional purpose, for instance reusing a component can be a means to address the functional need. In general, this type of requirement makes it possible to establish the connection between different design requirements to implement an architecture requirement as shown in Figure 11.9.

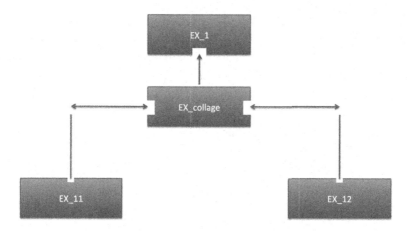

Figure 11.9. *Detailed design phase*

11.7. Design verification

The design (SwCS) should be verified. It is important to verify that the architecture is not too complex, that it is balanced, that it is testable and that it makes it possible to assume the requirements identified in the architecture.

For a balanced architecture, it is necessary to verify that the distribution of requirements onto the functions is homogeneous, and that there is no function accumulating all of the requirements. Conceivably, the number of requirements per function could be counted and it could be verified that there is no function with little or too many requirements. If such functions are identified, analysis and justification are necessary.

The complexity of the design is to be compared to the complexity of the functions. For every function, metrics can be measured and it should be verified whether some functions are more complex than others. Again, for each complex function, an analysis will have to be carried out. It is worth noting that complexity will affect testability (more tests) and also maintainability; the complexity of a complex function will increase progressively with the software development.

REMINDER.– Metrics are indicators: they can be seen as being able to identify what is complex, but they should not be turned into sanctions. It is important to analyze and justify but not absolutely necessary to transform the code (*a priori* functional decomposition to reduce the complexity).

The feasibility is based on the preparation of the component tests specification (SwCTS). In fact, if the tester is capable of preparing the SwCTS, it will then be possible to implement a software application that meets the software requirements.

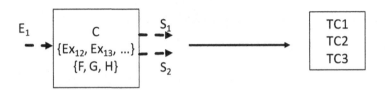

Figure 11.10. *Relationship between SwCS and SwCTS*

As shown in Figure 11.10, the preparation of the tests of software components based on the design (SwCS) allows us to identify observability and complexity problems as early as possible. The preparation of component tests (CT) is described in Volume 4 [BOU 19].

The verification of the design stage of a software specification will be presented in Chapter 12.

11.8. Consideration of COTS and reused components

11.8.1. *Introduction*

The preliminary and detailed design phases can rely on components that have already been used in other projects and/or with off-the-shelf components (COTS). As shown in Figure 11.7, a library has to be used.

If code or a library is reused to implement a function, it is necessary to demonstrate that the code or the library can actually be employed.

The code and/or reused libraries need to be identified (name, reference and version) and it has to be demonstrated that it is used in a similar context. Demonstration that the operating framework is similar must be based on the identification or not of the functions, on the constraints of use and on the impact of existing anomalies.

11.8.2. *Preexisting code*

Code and/or a preexisting library will at least have to provide the elements needed such as a set of interfaces, a set of functions and for each function a set of requirements characterizing their behaviors, but it must also be defined through a version and a set of assumptions for use.

Assumptions for use must allow for ensuring the proper operation of this component within the whole.

These assumptions should describe:

– hardware-related constraints (memory size, cache size, number representation, addressing, CPU load, etc.);

– real-time constraints;

– safety-related constraints (safety level, safety requirements, etc.).

As has been stated, it is required that the elements available are able to demonstrate that the code and/or the library assume the requirements associated thereto. Items of proof can be in the form of documentation but feedback could also be of interest. Feedback should then be formalized (project list, project type, safety level, operating environment, number of operating hours, distance traveled, etc.) and should demonstrate that the component has incurred no defect.

11.8.3. *COTS*

A COTS is a black box provided by a third party, which means that there is little documentation available and that there are concerns about the implementation and V&V processes.

For every COTS, a qualification document has to be available that indicates the functions that can be used, the safety levels that can be associated, constraints for use and existing anomalies. It is then required to show that the inclusion of COTS in the project satisfies the constraints of the qualification file.

In general, an encapsulation of the COTS is implemented (see Figure 11.11) which limits the functions that can be employed but which also limits the effects of the defects of this COTS. Figure 11.11 shows that the COTS has three functions AA, BB, CC that can be called by functions F1 and F2 of component C1.

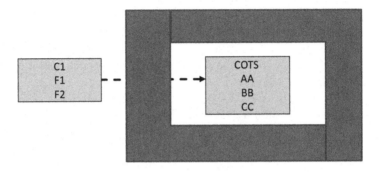

Figure 11.11. *COTS encapsulation*

11.9. Conclusion

The design of software components enables us to get close to the code; however, this is not yet code. This phase can be rather abstract (description of algorithms) or quite practical (process of modeling algorithms which will allow their simulation and/or proof activities).

12

Software Application Component Design Phase Verification

12.1. Introduction

The design phase of software components must enable the identification of the data set manipulated by the component and every function implemented by the component in order to meet the requirements. For each function of the component, it is necessary to define their behavior, which means that associated algorithms have to be described.

The verification of the software component design should verify that the component as it is described will actually assume the requirements associated with it. Part of this verification is based on the notion of component testing. For every function, one will have to produce test cases that will demonstrate that the component after implementation performs the requirements and the algorithms that have been defined.

12.2. Verification

12.2.1. *Reminder*

As presented in Chapter 11 of Volume 2 [BOU 17], verification can be done by means of static analysis and/or dynamic analysis.

Since the object here consists of verifying the component design of a software application, static methods prove more suitable.

12.2.2. *Software application component design phase verifications*

12.2.2.1. *Context*

The software component specification (SwCS) document describes the data, functions and algorithms implemented by the component. This document should at least provide a graphic vision of what is a structured model. The models at least contain boxes (functions) and links (interfaces).

It is however possible to improve the modeling a little further and, for each function, it is possible to achieve a more or less formal model of the algorithm. We can start from a representation in natural language and move toward a B-method [ABR 96, BOU 13] and/or Safety Critical Application Development Environment (SCADE)-based formalization [DOR 08].

12.2.2.2. *Methodology*

The SwCS verification may be achieved through several activities:

– the design review (new reading, using checklists, etc.) which can be more or less formal (see sections 12.2.2.3 and 12.2.2.4);

– the preparation of testing specifications (see section 12.2.2.5).

As indicated in Chapter 4 of Volume 2 [BOU 17], verification processes are carried out by a dedicated team. This team must be independent from the production team (see Figure 7.1). The verification team includes testers (TST), integrators (INT) and verifiers (VER).

However, the verification team is not the only one involved; as a matter of fact, it is necessary to verify that the SwCS meets the company's quality criteria. For this purpose, we will resort to the QUA (see Table 7.1).

Similarly, the architecture must be verified by the safety team (SAF). The safety team must verify that:

– the data being processed are of the right safety level;

– stored data are properly used and protected;

– safety requirements have been taken into account when defining the algorithms;

– safety principles are respected. Safety principles are issued from system documents, from the documents describing the physical architecture and safety principles.

12.2.2.3. *Design review*

The verification of a phase requires the verification of the implementation of quality requirements (procedures application, compliance of formats, etc.), the application of processes (compliance with plans, compliance with the organization, etc.), the correction of activities and that safety requirements are properly taken into account.

Concerning the design phase, methodological guides related to modeling, design conventions, architecture principles, etc., will be included in input documents, therefore there will be additional verifications.

The modeling rules include:

– naming conventions for all objects (constants, global variables, interfaces, local variables, software parameters, function parameters, functions, modules, etc.);

– documentation-related rules;

– design-related rules;

– decomposition rules.

12.2.2.3.1. Documentation review

The documentation review is then conducted through a quick reading (walkthrough) or a design review (formal design review). The documentation review was presented in detail in section 7.2.2.2.1.

This verification must have an objective. This objective may be formalized in the form of a checklist (control list).

12.2.2.3.2. Quality activity

This activity has been discussed in section 7.2.2.2.2.

12.2.2.3.3. Verifier

As already stated, the software component design verification (SwCS) must be made by a verifier (see Figure 7.1 for the organization). The verifier (see Table 7.3) shall verify the technical content of the document (see section 7.2.2.2.3 for more information).

12.2.2.3.4. Software component design verification

As it has been stated, the description of the design of a software component must define:

– external stored data (global variables);

– the parametrization data used by the component and these functions;

– stored data (local variables), their protections and access means.

For each function, we need to identify:

– the interfaces being used;

– the requirements to assume and their traceability with the requirements of the SwCD;

– the algorithms.

On this basis, it is possible to implement several verifications of the SwCS:

– verify that all the external interfaces are connected. There is at least one internal component that makes use of the information circulating through each external interface[1];

– verify that the use of global variables is justified;

– verify that the use of global variables is protected[2].

– verify that the use of local variables is justified;

– verify that local variables are protected[3].

And for each function of the component:

– verify that all input interfaces appear at least once in a function as input. If an input interface is not included, then it will not be used;

– verify that all output interfaces appear at least once inside a function as output. If an output interface is not included, then it will not be used;

---

1 At the component design level, all interfaces are seen as being external.

2 In order to protect the global variables, it is possible to implement a directory which will be responsible for verifying that only authorized components have access to global variables.

3 To protect local variables, it is possible to implement information redundancy in the form of information coding or in the form of a duplication of variables (for more information, see [BOU 09a, BOU 11c]).

– verify that all software parametrization data are at least included once in a component requirement. If a software parametrization data element were not included, it would then not be used;

– verify that all requirements are traceable with the SwCS;

– verify that all the functions utilize interfaces as inputs, otherwise the requirement is not observable;

– verify that all the functions utilize interfaces as outputs, otherwise the requirement is not observable;

– verify that all requirements identify the states in which they are applicable. Otherwise, there would be a possible ambiguity.

This is a first verification set that ought to be completed by your feedback. It is very important to put in place a Return of Experience (REX) approach, when some defects are not detected early; it is also very important to verify if it is not possible to improve the verification and the checklist used during verification.

12.2.2.3.5. Software component design complexity verification

At the architecture level, the complexity was linked to the distribution of requirements onto the components. At the software component design level, the complexity concerns several aspects:

– the number of requirements per function;

– the complexity of each function;

– the number of interfaces per function;

– the number of data handled by every function.

The design complexity of a software component can be analyzed through several topics:

– analysis of the distribution of requirements per function: Figure 12.1 presents an example that shows that functions F4 and F5 support more requirements than others. It is necessary to verify whether this is normal. It is preferable to have a balanced distribution of requirements within the architecture;

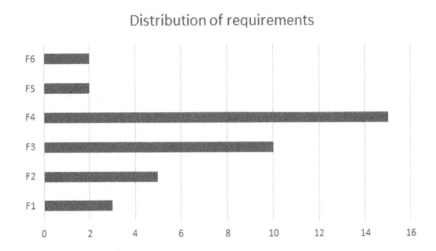

Figure 12.1. *Example of requirement distribution management per function*

– analysis of function complexity: the project must define metrics that must be measured from the component functions in order to be able to identify complex functions. Figure 12.2 shows an example where functions F3 and F5 exhibit significant complexity;

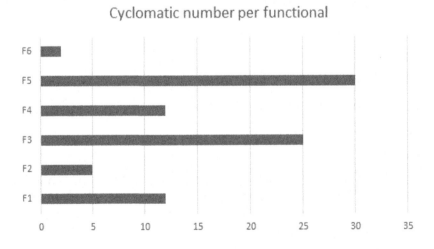

Figure 12.2. *Example of functional complexity control*

– analysis of interface distribution: as for the requirements, it is necessary to verify that the interfaces are evenly distributed onto all of the components;

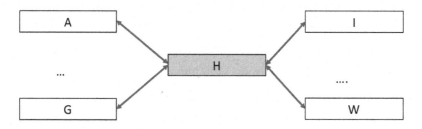

Figure 12.3. *Example of strong functional coupling*

– coupling analysis: it is necessary to verify that there is no coupling in the point architecture. Functional coupling is characterized by the number of functions in direct relationship (see Figure 12.3). We must therefore measure the coupling of each component and look for critical points. Strong coupling is similar to a spaghetti plate. It introduces a difficulty in performing integration tests and mainly in carrying out component maintenance. Each change of function H has a lot of impact;

– data coupling analysis: as shown in Figure 12.4, a stored data element can be used by several functions. An implicit link is seen to appear between functions, which is not good for maintainability.

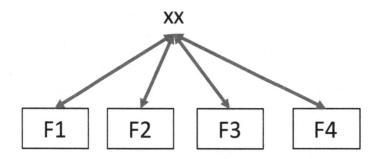

Figure 12.4. *Example of datum coupling*

12.2.2.3.6. Verification of requirement traceability

In order to cover the needs for requirement completeness and consistency, it will be necessary to put in place a requirement verification phase for each phase of the implementation process, such as defined in section 7.2.2.2.6.

12.2.2.3.7. Checklists for design verification

Requirement verification can be achieved using a checklist. This checklist (see, for example, Table 12.1) will have to define control points. These latter are related to the knowledge of the types of errors that can be introduced during the activity that has produced the documents to be verified.

Point	Rule	Status OK/KO	Comment
R_1	All the requirements of the SwCD must be laid out with the SwCS or a justification must be given		
R_1_1	If a requirement of the SwCS is not traced, a judgment on the justification will have to be provided		
R_2	All the requirements of the SwCS must be laid out with the SwCD or a justification must be given		
R_2_1	If a requirement of the SwCS is not traced, a judgment on the justification will have to be provided		
R_3	All interfaces introduced for this component in the SwCD are repeated in the SwCS		
R_3_1	If an external interface is not used (no connection), a justification and a control mechanism must be present		
R_4	All the parameters introduced in the SwCD are inserted again in the SwCS		
R_4_1	If a parameter is not used, there must be a justification as well as a control mechanism		
R_5	All local variables are defined, justified and initialized		

Table 12.1. *Example of checklists concerning a component*

In Table 12.2, we introduced some rules related to algorithm verification.

Point	Rule	Status OK/KO	Comment
R_60	All algorithms are clearly defined		
R_61	All data produced in algorithms are used		
R_62	All data consumed by algorithms are produced		
R_63	Complexity for algorithms respect the design standard		
R_64	Formalism used to define algorithms are completely defined		

Table 12.2. *Example of checklist concerning the component and algorithm*

12.2.2.4. *Model implementation*

The architecture of a software application is a model that is at least *structured* (see the notion of structured method, Chapters 5 and 6). As already mentioned in Chapters 9 and 11, it is necessary that modeling guidelines should be created that explain how a model can be implemented and how can it be read. In CENELEC 50128 [CEN 01, CEN 11], such guidelines are highly recommended.

At the component design level, it will be necessary to verify that the type of modeling implemented is consistent with the type of problem. As an example, a railway signaling system can be seen as a set of state machines, thereby a model in the form of an automaton would allow us to avoid the introduction of biases during the implementation, the bias being introduced during the change of formalism.

It will be important to put in place an activity for verifying that the model is consistent with this modeling guide.

12.2.2.5. *Component testing preparation*

12.2.2.5.1. Tester

The selection of test cases is carried out by a person who is not the one who wrote the SwCS. This person is called TESTER (TST) as for the software requirements test.

Table 7.7 describes the role of the TST by introducing the responsibilities and skills expected.

12.2.2.5.2. Principles

Initially, an architecture would be broken down into modules, accompanied by all the questions surrounding the definition of module (see Chapter 8). Therefore, there is the notion of module testing but also the concept of unit testing. Module testing is a functional entity based on the function, but very quickly the module becomes the compilation unit (file, package, class, etc.). In the end, it is difficult to comprehensively test a module (how can we test internal functions or specific code branches?); this is why the concept of a unit test has been introduced. The purpose of the unit test is to test a specific portion of code.

Unit tests and module tests are generally considered to be low-level tests. Actually, they allow for testing portions of code that do not always represent a function.

In the component-based approach, tests are functional tests. The objective is to verify the behavior of the component and that this behavior is in accordance with the requirements associated with it.

12.2.2.5.3. Reminder

As already explained, based on the definition of the algorithms of the functions of the SwCD, test cases are identified (TC_x); test cases describe a situation to be achieved, this situation being linked to an equivalence class. From the test cases, it is possible to prepare testing scenarios (TS_x), a test scenario describing a situation. A test case may therefore be included in several scenarios.

Since, at this level, the only input element is the SwCS, we are actually in the process of specifying black box testing (without knowledge of the implementation).

12.2.2.5.4. Verification example

The first verification consists of asserting that all interfaces are associated with at least one integration test, or more specifically, it is important to verify that the whole algorithm is associated with at least one test.

Similarly, as in section 7.2.2.5.2, we had verified that a requirement did not result in too many tests and that a test did not require too many requirements; it is necessary to verify that there is a balance at the function level.

The number of tests allocated to each interface should be similar. If an interface appears to be more complex than others (too many tests associated), one should verify whether this situation is acceptable (risk of non-maintainability).

Conversely, if a test requires a large number of interfaces, it is necessary to verify whether this is acceptable, because it seems that there is strong coupling between these interfaces and therefore a risk of non-maintainability.

12.2.3. *Synthesis*

The requirement specification phase of the software application requires the implementation of different skills:

– the DES is responsible for design management;

– the TST is responsible for component testing techniques management;

– the VER is responsible for verification management;

– the QUA and the VAL are responsible for standard and process control;

– safety management done by the SAF.

This is the reason why it will be necessary to ensure that the people involved clearly satisfy the skills requirements (see Chapter 4 of Volume 2 [BOU 17]).

When the verification process is finalized, it is necessary to produce a verification report called DES_VR (Design–Verification Report):

– which identifies the inputs and outputs of the stage;

– which identifies the means being used (people, tools, etc.);

– which describes the activities carried out, the results of these activities, the anomalies detected, the remaining open topics;

– which concludes with the possibility of moving on to the next phase.

This report is generally written by the VER and the QUA and verified by the VAL and under the approval of the project manager (PM).

12.3. Conclusion

Verification is a topic that is not always easy, and these chapters are intended to provide objectives for the verification of each phase of the software application implementation lifecycle.

In this chapter, we have thus provided the elements that make it possible to verify that an architecture is correct. As for the other chapters related to the verification, this chapter is an attempt to introduce elements based on feedback.

13

Software Application Coding

13.1. Introduction

There was a time when coding a software application was an activity restricted to a small elite. Moreover, a computer was needed for this purpose and then one had to have access to tools and information to develop a program. Since then, computer science has become widespread and it is now very easy or even trivial to develop a computer program (see, for example, the production of websites and/or how to program a small robot (Lego style)).

Languages allowing abstraction, encapsulation and supporting various types of programming (application, functional, object oriented, etc.) have emerged and allowed for a broad democratization of the development of a software application. Tools for generating executables (compiler, linker, etc.) have undergone improvements in terms of efficiency but one of the most significant advances was the development of integrated development environments (IDEs), which have made it possible to simplify programming (for example, by providing all the elements for building a graphical interface) or even to replace programming by an assembly process (website generators, for instance).

Another avenue for the evolution of the development of software applications concerns model-based automatic code generation. The automatic generation of code is seen as a means to dispense with the activity of programming, the fundamental activity being that which consists of creating a model.

The development of a software application is now accessible to everyday people, but we should not forget that ultimately it is code that will be compiled and executed on a target processor and that developers will have to be able to maintain this code for some time.

It is important to remember that all the tools used for the development of a software application (IDE, generating code, compiler, linker, testing tool, coverage measurement tools, etc.) are also the product of a development process and that in turn they can make use of other tools.

Therefore, it will have to be demonstrated that the tools used are "acceptable" for the development of our application. The acceptability of a tool will give rise to a qualification activity that is presented in Chapter 13 of Volume 1 [BOU 16].

Regardless of the means implemented to develop a software application, the code remains a product that will be manipulated; there are therefore a certain number of rules that it has to follow.

13.2. Coding phase objective

In the cycle of the development in V (see Figure 1.3), the coding stage is implemented once the (preliminary and detailed) design phase has been completed. The coding phase thus consists of translating the detailed design elements (functions, algorithms, data structures, etc.) into a software application.

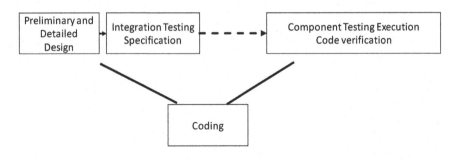

Figure 13.1. *Bottom of the V-cycle*

The coding activity involves transforming a component and algorithm view into source code under the constraint of following several methodological guides and a goal that is to only do what is asked. If there were difficulties during coding requiring the completion of design documents, the person in charge of developing the code should report it and any choice to be achieved must be formalized.

Figure 13.1 highlights that the code generated is verified in the context of the ascending stage of the implementation cycle of the software application. The verification will be made by way of two activities: code verification and executing component testing. Code verification concerns the good application of programming conventions and complexity control.

It should be noted that in this approach, developers do not have to prepare tests for the verification of their code but the tests prepared during the descending phase of the cycle will be executed.

For the component coding phase, the inputs are:

– the plans:

- Software Quality Assurance Plan (SQAP);

- Software Verification and Validation Plan (SVVP);

- Software Configuration Management Plan (SCMP);

– project documents:

- Software Component Design Document (SwCD);

- Glossary (GL);

– methodological guides:

- Coding guide[1].

The output of the software application architecture stage is:

– the code managed by configuration.

---

1 The coding guide will take into account the language that has been chosen by the project.

13.3. IMPlementer

As indicated in Chapter 4 of Volume 2 [BOU 17], the activities related to the implementation of software components are carried out by the developer (whom we refer to as the Implementer).

Role: Implementer: IMP

Responsibilities are as follows:
   – transform design solutions into data/source code/other design representations;
   – transform the source code into executable code/other design representation;
   – apply safety design principles;
   – apply the specified standards for preparation/data encoding;
   – develop and maintain the implementation documentation including the methods, data types and applied listings;
   – maintain traceability to and from the design;
   – maintain code/data generated or modified under changes and configuration management.

Main skills are as follows:
   – proficient in the appropriate application field engineering;
   – competent in the implementation of language and tools;
   – able to apply specified coding standards and programming styles;
   – understand all the constraints imposed by the hardware platform, the operating system and interfacing systems;
   – understand industry standard requirements applicable to the project and/or the company.

Table 13.1. *Implementer*[2]

13.4. Code production

13.4.1. *Manual coding or automatic generation*

The coding process may be manual or automatic (see Figure 13.2). In the context of a manual coding activity (Figure 13.2(a)), it is necessary to implement a certain number of rules to ensure that the requirements defined in the design are indeed taken into account (traceability) and that the code will be testable and maintainable (readability, clarity, etc.) (see Chapters 11 and 12).

---

2 This description of the role of the DES (DESigner) is taken from the CENELEC 50128:2011 standard [CEN 11].

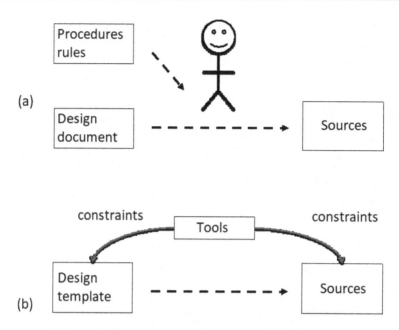

Figure 13.2. *Two examples of generation processes*

If a process of automatic code generation (see Figure 13.2(b)) is implemented, there will be a model on input (see Chapter 5) and it must be demonstrated that the tools used correspond to the safety level that must be attained (we talk about tool qualification in Chapter 13 of Volume 1 [BOU 16]).

Code generation can be comprehensive – see the example of code generation implemented in the SCADE environment[3][4] [DOR 08] – or partial – see, for example, code generation performed with UML tools [OMG 11, ROQ 07].

It should be noted that very often we find mixed processes or that manual code is interfaced with generated code; in this case, it will be required to fully master the interfacing devices.

---

3 SCADE has been presented in Chapter 6.
4 SCADE is distributed by the ANSYS (see: https://www.ansys.com).

If automatic code generation is used, it is requested to explain in the SQAP the impact in the software lifecycle. Figure 1.3 introduced the software V-cycle generally used for a safety-critical application; in the case where code generation replaces manual coding, we have different possibilities:

– code is completely generated and the tools are qualified and we can remove some activities done on the code (programming rules and metrics verification, etc.);

– code is completely generated and the tools are not qualified; we need to demonstrate that the code fulfills the SwCD. Traceability, programming rules and metrics verification plus component testing are needed;

– code is partially generated; we need to explain how IMP can update the code (whether it is allowed or not);

– code is manually produced and the complete V-cycle is applied.

13.4.2. *Executable generation sequence*

During the coding phase, the sequence generating the executable will have to be implemented. The executable generation sequence can be a more or less complex process.

Figure 13.3 illustrates two examples of the executable generation process. Version (a) is a linear sequence in which a single executable is produced from sources, unlike version (b), which presents the production of two executables.

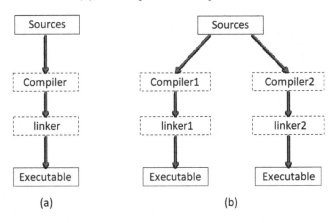

(a)   (b)

Figure 13.3. *Two examples of compilation processes*

The generation of an executable may be a more or less complicated process and may involve several tools.

The source code must satisfy certain criteria:

– it must be readable and understandable;

– it must be documented and comments should be useful (no description of the code itself, etc.);

– it must be managed by configuration;

– it must comply with methodological guides (naming conventions, coding conventions, constraints of the compilation process, etc.).

13.5. Principles to be implemented in the context of the coding phase

The implementation of a safety-related application must follow two principles:

– principle 1: the coding phase is intended to only implement what is established in the SwCD. Therefore, there must be no further addition or removal;

– principle 2: the coding phase relies on a set of programming rules that have to be respected. Any exception to the application of a rule must be justified and compensatory measures can be implemented.

13.5.1. Compliance with the SwCD

With respect to the SwCD (principle 1), it is necessary to implement a vertical traceability between the code and the SwCD that shows that all of the needs of the SwCD have been taken into account during the coding phase, and that each code element is justified by a need.

The vertical traceability between the SwCD and the code is a means to demonstrate that all services and all requirements have been implemented.

Vertical traceability between the code and the SwCD indicates that there is no code associated with unspecified services and that there is no code that cannot be executed. This process is a design activity that must be performed at the same time as the code.

13.5.2. *Programming rules*

13.5.2.1. *Identification of need*

As we have mentioned above, software source code must be legible, comprehensible and likely to be tested. For example, Table A.4 (Table 13.2) of the CENELEC 50128: 2011 standard [CEN 11] introduces several requirements:

– lines 1, 2 and 3 unveil the need that there is at least one structured model (SSIL2) or of modeling (SSIL3–SSIL4). It is worth noting that the need is more constrained than for the architecture (see Table 8.3). As this is visible in this section, an architecture actually requires a structured model (box, interface or connector), but it is possible to go further in the modeling because we dispose of data structures, information about the sequencing, etc.;

– lines 4, 5, 10, 12 and 13 are linked to the programming paradigm implemented. The CENELEC 50128:2011 [CEN 11] standard recommends to implement a component-based approach but it must be accompanied by a coding approach that is compliant with modularity, which is supported by a programming language and which may be procedural and/or object-oriented;

– lines 7 and 8 are a reminder that a design methodology has to be chosen enabling the detection of anomalies at the earliest (by means of typing) and analysis. It is possible to strengthen these properties through the definition of a subset (line 11) and/or through design and coding conventions.

Measure	SSIL0	SSIL1 SSIL2	SSIL3 SSIL4
1) Formal methods	R	R	HR
2) Modeling	R	HR	HR
3) Structured methodology	R	HR	HR
4) Modular approach	HR	M	M
5) Components	HR	HR	HR
6) Design and coding rules	HR	HR	M
7) Analyzable programs	HR	HR	HR

8) Strongly typed programming language	R	HR	HR
9) Structured programming	R	HR	HR
10) Programming language	R	HR	HR
11) Language subset	–	–	HR
12) Object-oriented programming	R	R	R
13) Procedural programming	R	HR	HR
14) Meta-programming	R	R	R

Table 13.2. *Table A.4 of the CENELEC 50128:2011 standard [CEN 11]*

Table A.12 of the CENELEC standard 50128:2011 (Table 13.3) identifies measures that the methodology must respect but also a set of programming rules to be implemented. The programming guide should identify the programming rules and rules should be justified. It is necessary to understand the purpose of each rule and the impact in the event of non-compliance.

Table A.12 (Table 13.3) of the CENELEC 50128:2011 standard [CEN 11] has been improved (compared to the 2001 version) concerning various points:

– line 8 reveals the need for code complexity control;

– line 9 refers to the fact that it is necessary to manage the exit points of a code unit; the C language allows executing the *return* statement almost anywhere, which introduces an exit point and which increases the cyclomatic complexity (Vg) by 1 for every *return*. The addition of exit points tends to introduce non-testable pathways;

– line 10 is redundant with line 3 of Table A.20 which is related to components;

– line 11 is important and its objective is to avoid developing spaghetti code (code that is not separable into parts). This rule has to be linked to the need for encapsulation, which was mentioned in Table A.20.

Measure	SSIL0[5]	SSIL1 SSIL2	SSIL3 SSIL4
1) Coding standard	HR	HR	M
2) Coding style guide	HR	HR	HR
3) No dynamic objects	–	R	HR
4) No dynamic variables	–	R	HR
5) Limited use of pointers	–	R	R
6) Limited use of recursion	–	R	HR
7) No unconditional branches	–	HR	HR
8) Limited functions, subroutines and methods size and complexity	HR	HR	HR
9) I/O points strategy for methods, subroutines and functions	R	HR	HR
10) Limited number of subprogram parameters	R	R	R
11) Limited use of global variables	HR	HR	M

Table 13.3. *Table A.12 of the CENELEC 50128:2011 standard [CEN 11]*

13.5.2.2. *Quality control*

The software design methodology must therefore be described (modeling guide, design guide and coding conventions) and it must be justified. The justification must be part of the SQAP or a specific document. That is why the coding phase must rely on programming conventions that have to be part of the company's quality standard.

The notion of a company quality standard is important because it is related to the training and management of skills. As a result, a coder is a person who has followed a training process and who knows the programming conventions of the company. This point is a sensitive one when it comes to using the provision of services in a project and/or when a policy is put in place for the relocation of coding activities.

Chapter 14 discusses the notion of programming rules.

---

5 The CENELEC 50128 railway standard [CEN 01, CEN 11] as well as the IEC 61508 standard [IEC 11] introduces the notion of SIL that can take four values from 1 to 4. To learn more about managing the SIL, we recommend reading Chapter 7 of Boulanger [BOU 11c]. The notion of SSIL (Software SIL) concerns the allocation of a safety level to software aspects. The SSIL level concerns systematic failures.

13.6. The choice of design language

13.6.1. *Introduction*

The typical development process of a software application is based on the use of a programming language such as Modula2, Ada, C and/or C++. Although these languages exhibit a certain level of abstraction compared to the code executed on the final computer, they require that lines of code be written. That is why the choice of the programming language must be mastered and justified. It is therefore important to choose a language that will allow one to detect abnormalities at the earliest.

13.6.2. *Essential properties*

13.6.2.1. *Strong typing*

Most standards do not recommend a language but the characteristics that the language must have. The characteristic that most often comes across in the first place is *strong typing*; in the second place, the need for disposing of a standard describing the language can be found.

	SSIL1	SSIL2	SSIL3	SSIL4
Appropriate programming language	HR	HR	HR	HR
Strongly typed programming language	HR	HR	HR	HR
Language subset	–	–	HR	HR

Table 13.4. *Table A.3 of the IEC 61508 standard, part 3 [IEC 11]*

Table 13.4 is taken from the IEC 61508 standard [IEC 11]. It highlights the need for choosing an appropriate language for the software application to be developed and the need for a strongly typed language (see Definition 13.1). The third point that concerns the definition of a subset of the language is present in different areas, because despite the fact that a language should be well-defined, there are still language elements that could have an impact on readability, maintainability, testability, etc.

DEFINITION 13.1 (Strong Typing).– *A language is said to be strongly typed if it is possible to define the type of each variable during compilation.*

Modula2, Pascal and Ada languages are included in the languages considered as being strongly typed; this is why they have been initially used in the implementation of critical software applications (SACEM uses Modula2, TVM 430 uses Ada, etc.)

```
type Age is range 0 .. 125;

procedure EX is
  my_age: Age
begin
    my_age := -1
end
```

Figure 13.4. *Example of strong typing*

Figure 13.4 illustrates an example that shows that a type (age) has been defined and that a data element of such type is not properly valued. The compiler will detect this error during compilation but it could also detect it during execution.

13.6.2.2. *Language standard*

Computer languages all have a more or less different background (created by industry, search engine, etc.) but for them to be fully recognized, it is necessary that formal elements are available to make it possible to describe them and their behavior. In order to obtain a consensus, a standardization phase is required whose objective will be to formally define the outline of the language.

The Ada language has always been accompanied by a standard characterizing it, whereas for the C language, it has been necessary to subsequently involve a standardization phase that has resulted in certifying only part of the language (the so-called ANSI[6] part).

The lack of a standard for a language gives rise to doubts about the capability to demonstrate that two implementations can result in the production of the same executable.

---

6 American National Standards Institute.

It should be recalled that standards allow the language to be defined but also exceptions such as runtime errors (division by 0, etc.).

13.6.3. *Analysis of languages*

13.6.3.1. *Introduction*

It is not possible to analyze all existing programming languages and for every area, therefore in the remainder of this section, we will analyze developments that may have taken place in the railway sector.

The conventional development process of a software application is based on the use of a programming language such as the Ada, C and/or C++ languages. Although these languages are of a certain level of abstraction compared to the code executed on the final computer, they require that lines of code be written and contribute to introducing defects in the code.

Table A.15 of the CENELEC 50128:2001 standard [CEN 01] had taken into account feedback from the beginning of the 2000s; this is why C and C++ were unacceptable without restriction.

	SSIL0	SSIL1 SSIL2	SSIL3 SSIL3
ADA	R	HR	R
MODULA-2	R	HR	R
PASCAL	R	HR	R
C or C++ unrestricted	R	–	NR
C or C++ subset	R	R	R

Table 13.5. *Table A.15 of the CENELEC 50128:2001 standard [CEN 01]*

13.6.3.2. *The ADA language*

13.6.3.2.1. Presentation

The first railway applications in France were programmed the mid-1980s with the language Modula 2. However, since then the Ada 83 language [ANS 83] has become the language of reference for the development of critical applications [RIC 94]. As shown in Table 13.5, in applications involving a high level of criticality (SSIL3/SSIL4), the Ada language itself is just R (Recommended), a subset of the language has to be implemented so that the utilization of the Ada language be HR.

The Ada language was designed at the initiative of the D.O.D. (USA Department of Defense) to unify more than 400 languages or dialects used by this body in the 1970s.

```
with Ada.Text_IO;
procedure Hello is
begin Ada.Text_IO.Put_Line("Hello, world!");
end Hello;
```

Figure 13.5. *Ada code example*

The Ada language is widely used in embedded software applications in avionics (Airbus), aerospace (the Ariane rocket) and the railway sector. The main characteristic of these systems is that they require a correction of the execution.

The Ada 83 language has evolved into a second major standard, the Ada 95 [ISO 95], then into Ada 2012 [ISO 12], which was the first standardized object-based language. It provides the ability to build object-oriented models. The latest up-to-date version is called Ada 2005.

DEFINITION 13.2 (Certification).– *The certification consists of achieving a certificate that is a commitment that the product satisfies a normative standard. The certification is based on the results of an evaluation and on the production of a certificate.*

Regarding the certification of Ada compilers, the existence of a standard and a fairly fine semantic of the Ada language has helped define a process of certification of a compiler.

This process has been implemented on different compilers. It is based on a testing suite named ACATS (Ada Conformity Assessment Test Suite) (see the standard [ISO 99a]). To learn more, readers can refer to Ada Resource Association [ADA 01].

For now, these new versions of the Ada language have not been adopted in the field of embedded systems because of the object-oriented aspect. However, in view of their efficiencies, the Ada 95 compilers are used for compiling knowing that we are merely addressing a subset of the language, which does not make use of "object-oriented" features.

In the article ADACORE, John Barnes made a presentation of the strengths of the Ada 2005 language (syntax and semantics, strong typing, pointer safety and memory management, etc.) and the impact of its implementation on the demonstration that the software is safe.

13.6.3.2.2. Language restriction

The "object-oriented" aspect is not taken into account by the CENELEC EN 50128 [CEN 01, CEN 11], DO 178 [ARI 92, DO 12], CEI/IEC 61508 [IEC 11] and ISO 26262 [ISO 11] standards applicable to critical applications.

In order to avoid this pitfall, the ISO 15942 standard [ISO 00] defines a restriction on the constructs of the Ada 95 language and defines the rules for use (programming style) that allow a so-called certifiable application to be achieved.

DEFINITION 13.3 (Certifiable Application).– *A certifiable software application is a software application that has been developed such as to be certified.*

13.6.3.2.3. SPARK Ada

The SPARK Ada [BAR 03] language is a programming language that is a subset of Ada. All complex structures of ADA that are considered to be risky or do not allow for an easy demonstration of safety are not encountered in SPARK Ada. A mechanism enabling the addition of annotations in the code has been implemented.

The SPARK Ada tools contain a compiler but also an annotation verifier. It should be noted that there is a free version of SPARK Ada tools[7]. Chapter 7 of [BOU 11a] is dedicated to the presentation of the SPARK Ada toolkit as well as to industrial implementation examples.

---

7 To learn more about AdaCore and free versions of tools such as GNAT and SPARK Ada, visit: www.libre.adacore.com.

In the 2014 version of SPARK Ada, a realignment with the 2012 version of the Ada language has been achieved. The 2012 version allows us to describe "pre" and "post" conditions characterizing a service just as the behavior can be described through invariants.

That is the reason why SPARK Ada 2014 introduces the ability to verify these elements by way of a prover.

13.6.3.3. *The C language*

13.6.3.3.1. Presentation

The C[8] language [KER 88] is one of the first languages that has been made available to developers to build complex applications. The main difficulty of the C language lies in the partial definition of the language, which makes that different compilers generate an executable with different behaviors. The C language has since been submitted to a process of normalization by the ANSI [ISO 99].

13.6.3.3.2. Language restriction

Regarding the use of the C language [ISO 99], depending on the desired safety level, the CENELEC EN 50128 standard [CEN 01] recommends the definition of a subset of the language (see Table 13.2) whose execution would be manageable.

	SSIL0	SSIL1	SSIL2	SSIL3	SSIL4
ADA	R	HR	HR	HR	HR
MODULA-2	R	HR	HR	HR	HR
PASCAL	R	HR	HR	HR	HR
C or C++	R	R	R	R	R
C#	R	R	R	R	R
JAVA	R	R	R	R	R

Table 13.6. *Table A.15 (partial) of the CENELEC 50128: 2011 standard [CEN 11]*

---

8 Although Kerdigan and Ritchie [KER 88] do not describe the ANSI C language, their book remains one of the most interesting on the subject.

Table 13.6 (excerpt from the new version of the CENELEC EN 50128 standard [CEN 11]) shows that it has been considered that there was enough feedback for the Ada, C and C++ languages, which made it possible to no longer explicitly mention the notion of a language subset because it is taken for granted.

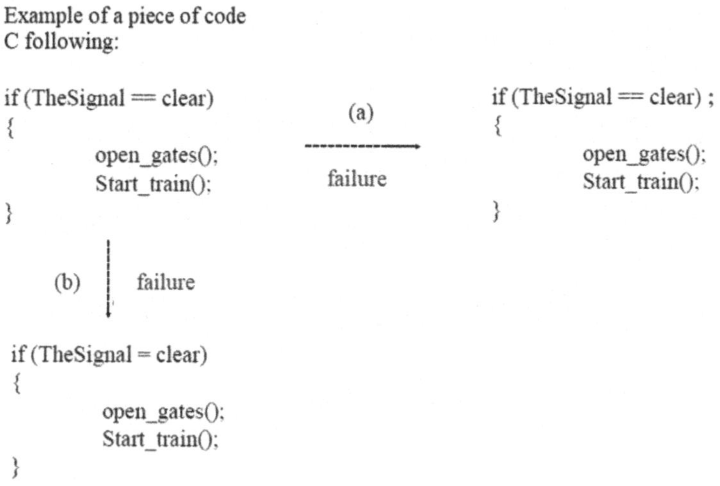

Example of a piece of code
C following:

```
if (TheSignal == clear)                              if (TheSignal == clear) ;
{                           (a)                      {
        open_gates();       -------------->                  open_gates();
        Start_train();      failure                          Start_train();
}                                                    }


    (b)  |   failure

if (TheSignal = clear)
{
        open_gates();
        Start_train();
}
```

Figure 13.6. *Example of failure in C*

Figure 13.6 shows a piece of C code that can result in two different codes depending on the anomaly (a) or (b), which is being implemented. This example highlights the weaknesses of the C language; small programming errors are not detected in the compilation. It should be noted that this type of error is detected if the programming language used is Ada.

Some of the weaknesses of the C language can be circumvented by putting in place programming rules; for example, to avoid an anomaly of the type if (a = cond) instead of if (a == cond), it would be possible to implement a rule of the form "when performing a comparison with a variable, the latter must be in the left-hand side of the expression".

As early as 1994, based on the feedback concerning the implementation of the C language (see, for example, Hatton and Safer [HAT 94]), it has been showed that it was possible to define a subset of C that can be used to develop software applications that have to provide a high level of safety (SSIL3–SSIL4).

13.6.3.3.3. MISRA-C

In fact, for the C language, the MISRA-C standard [MIS 04] has become a *de facto* standard that was developed by the Motor Industry Software Reliability Association (MISRA[9]).

MISRA-C [MIS 04] specifies programming rules (see examples in Table 13.7) as mechanisms to avoid runtime errors caused by ill-defined constructions, unexpected behaviors (a number of structures of the C language are not completely defined) and misunderstandings between the people responsible for the implementation (readable code, code which is implicit, etc.). Several tools enable the automatic verification of the MISRA-C rules.

Id	Statuses[10]	Description
Rule 1.1	Required	All code must comply with the ISO 9899:1990 standard "Programming languages – C", amended and corrected by ISO/IEC9899/COR1:1995, ISO/IEC/9899/AMD1:1995 and ISO/IEC9899/COR2:1996.
Rule 5.4	Required	Each tag is a unique identifier.
Rule 14.1	Required	There should be no dead code.
Rule 14.4	Required	No goto in programs.
Rule 14.7	Required	A function must have a single exit point at the end of the function.
Rule 17.1	Required	Pointer arithmetic can only be used for pointers, which address a table or an array element.
Rule 17.5	To be dealt with	An object declaration should not contain more than two levels of pointer indirection.

Table 13.7. *A few MISRA-C:2004 rules[11] [MIS 04]*

---

9 To learn more, visit: www.misra.org.uk/.
10 A MISRA rule may be "required" or "to be dealt with" (advisory). A "required" rule must compulsorily be implemented by the developer and a rule "to be dealt with" cannot be ignored even if it is not mandatory to implement it.
11 MISRA [MIS 04] introduces 122 "required" rules and 20 "to be dealt with" rules.

The MISRA-C standard [MIS 04] includes rules (see rules 14.4 and 14.7, for example) that are explicit in several standards:

– Rule 14.4 in the EN 50128 standard – Table A.12 or the IEC 61508 standard – Table B.1;

– Rule 14.7 in the EN 50128 standard – Table A.20 or the IEC 61508 standard – Table B.9.

MISRA-C [MIS 98] was created in 1998, updated in 2004 [MIS 04] then in 2012 [MIS 12], which shows that the feedback provided is certain.

The main difficulty of the C language remains the choice of a compiler having sufficient feedback for the chosen target and the safety level to be achieved. In the absence of an accurate and comprehensive standard, there is no certification process for C compilers, even if there are initiatives such as those shown in Leroy [LER 09][12].

13.6.3.3.4. Example of rule

Rule_x: All blocks must be indicated with a beginning and an end

The structure

```
for ( i=1; i<= length; i++ )
   x = i + 3;
```

is to be replaced by

```
for ( i=1; i<= length; i++ )
{
   x = i +3;
}
```

---

12 It is worth noting that Leroy [LER 09] presents a verification work for a small C compiler, but when the term certification is introduced, it is not a certification provided by an external body. The certification does not only concern the demonstration that the compiler is correct but should also apply to the process being implemented, to the elements produced (documents, sources, etc.) and to the tools employed (Ocaml, Coq and other free tools must be demonstrated as being safe).

13.6.3.4. *Object-oriented languages and the C++ language in particular*

13.6.3.4.1. Presentation

As mentioned earlier, the "object-oriented" aspect is not taken into account by the CENELEC EN 50128 [CEN 01, 11], DO 178 [ARI 92, DO 12], CEI/IEC 61508 [IEC 11] and ISO 26262 [ISO 11] standards applicable to applications.

The object-oriented aspect is mentioned in the CENELEC EN 50128 standard [CEN 01, CEN 11], but the constraints that apply to the languages do not allow the development of critical applications (SSIL3 and SSIL4) with this type of language (see Table 13.8).

	SSIL0	SSIL1 SSIL2	SSIL3 SSIL4
No dynamic objects	–	R	HR
No dynamic variables	–	R	HR
Limited use of pointers	–	R	R

Table 13.8. *Table A.12 – CENELEC 50128:2001 [CEN 01]*

As shown in Tables 13.5 and 13.6, the C++ language [ISO 03, ISO 06] is cited as being applicable but there are some recommendations that are not compatible with the use of an object-oriented language, as shown in Table 1.4.

The C++ language has been developed during the 1980s; it is an improvement on the C language. C++ introduces the notions of class, inheritance, virtual functions and overloading. It has been standardized by the ISO in 1998 and 2003 [ISO 03].

13.6.3.4.2. Return of experience

C++ was used for SSIL1–SSIL2 for railways (and in a similar way in aeronautics) and from different projects, some points emerge:

– due to the use of interface classes and inheritance, the size of the C++ code grows and in general the size is between 1.5 to twice the size if we used a non-OO language;

– due to the use of inheritance and the OO-based approach, method complexity is very small (in general we extend/specialize the mother method with some simple statement) but coupling between classes increases. The cyclomatic number is not a good metric for OO applications;

– due to inheritance and the OO-based approach, we have no view of the complete method; it is difficult to carry out a code review or a safety analysis;

– due to polymorphism, during the code review it is difficult to analyze one method behavior if some methods are polymorphic; we need to study all possible behaviors.

13.6.3.4.3. Programming rules

Since the beginning of the 2000s, several works have been undertaken in order to define a framework for using the C++ language [ISO 03, ISO 06] in the context of the development of high-safety level applications (SSIL3–SSIL4).

We should mention the works of:

– the OOTiA[13] (Object-Oriented Technology in Aviation) which has published several guides [FED 04a, FED 04b, FED 04c, FED 04d];

– the JSF++ (Join Strike Fighter C++) which has published a guide [LM 05] focusing on development with C++. This guide revisits existing works and in particular the MISRA-C standard [MIS 98];

– the MISRA which has developed the MISRA-C++:2008 standard [MIS 08]; Table 13.9 presents examples of MISRA-C++:2008 rules.

Id	Statuses[14]	Description
Rule 0-1-1	Required	Software programs must not contain unreachable code.
Rule 0-1-2	Required	Software programs must not contain non-executable code.
Rule 1-0-1	Required	All code must comply with the ISO/IEC 14882:2003, "the C++ standard incorporating Technical Corrigedum1".

13 To learn more, visit: http://www.faa.gov/aircraft/air_cert/design_approvals/air_software/oot/.
14 A MISRA-C++ rule may be "required" or "be dealt with" (advisory) or a "document". A "required" rule must be compulsorily implemented by the developer, a rule "to be dealt with" cannot be ignored even if it is not mandatory to implement it and a "document" rule is compulsory.

Rule 2-10-4	Required	Names for "class", "union" or "enum" must be a unique identifier.
Rule 5-2-3	To be dealt with	The "cast" operation from a base class to a derived class must not be performed with polymorphic types.
Rule 15-5-1	Required	A class destructor should not return with an exception.
Rule 17-0-4	Document	All libraries must comply with MISRA-C++.
Rule 18-0-1	Required	The C library should not be used.

Table 13.9. *A few MISRA-C++:2008 rules[15] [MIS 08]*

The C++ language [ISO 03, ISO 06] is thus a fairly old language. Approaches identifying the weak points of C++ and proposing rules have appeared at early stages [SCO 98, SUT 05], but the definition of a framework for using C++ for high safety level applications is quite recent [FED 04a, FED 04b, FED 04c, FED 04d, LM 05, MIS 08], which explains that applications in C++ are found up to the safety level SSIL2.

As shown in Table 13.9, the MISRA-C++:2008 standard [MIS 08] introduces a certain number of rules based on those existing for the C language, but they do not allow all the difficulties of the C++ language to be taken into account.

Due to pressures of different kinds (decrease in the number of Ada and C programmers, for example) the updating of standards such as the CENELEC EN 50128 or the DO 178 standards has given rise to initiatives aiming to introduce object-oriented languages.

	SSIL0	SSIL1	SSIL2	SSIL3	SSIL4
Classes should only have one objective.	R	R	R	HR	HR
Inheritance is only used if the derived class is a refinement of its base class.	R	HR	HR	HR	HR
Depth of inheritance limited by coding standards.	R	R	R	HR	HR
Neutralization of operations (methods) under strict control.	R	R	R	HR	HR
Multiple inheritance is only used for interface classes.	R	HR	HR	HR	HR
Inheritance from unknown classes.	–	–	–	NR	NR

Table 13.10. *Table A.23 – CENELEC 50128:2011 [CEN 11]*

---

15 MISRA [MIS 08] introduces 198 rules.

Therefore, the new version of the CENELEC EN 50128 standard [CEN 11] has extended the list of object-oriented languages that can be used with JAVA and C# as shown in Table 13.6. However, this new version of the standard introduces some restrictions (limitations on inheritance), as shown in Table 13.10.

The C version of the DO 178 standard [DO 12] includes a specific appendix for the purpose of defining the implementation constraints of an object-oriented language for the development of a critical application; this appendix is extremely restrictive and even inapplicable.

As for C, the difficult point with C++ remains the demonstration that the compiler for the chosen target and associated libraries meet the safety objectives, which have been defined by the safety studies. Given that there is no existing certification for C++ compilers, it will be required that a justification based on feedback and/or qualification should be implemented.

13.6.3.5. *Programmable logic controller development*

The execution means can be commercial platforms and/or specific platforms. In [BOU 09a] and [BOU 11c], we have introduced different execution platforms.

There is a type of platform that is used in several areas known as programmable logic controllers (PLCs). The interest of these platforms lies in the fact that there is a compliance certificate (see Definition 13.2) of these platforms to the 61508 standard [IEC 11].

The use of a certified platform makes it possible to focus on the production of the software application. For this type of application, a 61131-3 standard [IEC 13] has been defined. This standard defines 7 languages (IL[16], ST, FBD, LD, grafcet, etc.) for the development of an application for a PLC.

It should be noted that the CONTROLBUILD tool provided by the Dassault System is capable of building a model in 1131 and generating C code. The code generator is certified for a SSIL2 level.

13.6.3.6. *Programming rules*

The topic of programming rules is covered in more detail in Chapter 14.

---

16 IS for Instruction List, FBD for Functional Block Diagram, LD for Ladder Diagram.

13.7. Consideration of COTS and reused components

During the coding process of an algorithm, it is possible to use COTS or preexisting code. As for the other phases of the software application implementation cycle (especially for the design, see section 11.8), it is important:

– to properly include all the elements in the configuration;

– to dispose of a set of elements that can demonstrate that the element can be used in this application, these elements concerning: the specification of reused elements, the identification of component interfaces, the identification of assumptions for use.

The assumptions for use must allow for ensuring the proper operation of this component within the whole. These assumptions should describe:

– hardware-related constraints (memory size, cache size, number representation, addressing, CPU load, etc.);

– real-time constraints;

– safety-related constraints (safety level, safety requirements, etc.).

The code and/or reused libraries need to be identified (name, reference and version) and it has to be demonstrated that it is used in a similar context. The demonstration that the operating environment is similar must be based on the identification of the functions that are or are not employed, on the constraints of use and on the impact of existing anomalies.

13.8. Coding phase verification

The verification of the coding stage of a software specification will be presented in Chapter 16 of this volume.

13.9. Conclusion

This chapter has enabled a recall of the constraints linked to the production process of the code. We are reminded that it is possible to choose any language provided that answers can be given to the following questions:

– Is there a standard for the chosen language?

– Is the chosen language a programming language?

– Do you have a set of recognized programming rules?

– Do you have a set of metrics for the detection of complex elements for your language?

– Is the language used easily testable?

– Is the language used easily analyzable?

– Does the language being used include recognized and qualifiable tools?

14

Programming Rules

14.1. Introduction

As we have mentioned previously, software source code must be readable, comprehensible and testable. The first challenge is thus to choose a programming language (see Chapter 13) and the second challenge consists of defining a methodology for limiting the risks of introducing defects in the code. That is why the coding phase must rely on programming rules that must be integrated in the company's quality standard. In the end, the choice of programming language should be justified in the Software Quality Assurance Plan (SQAP); it must be associated with the implementation of a guide to coding and a set of programming rules.

The notion of company quality standard is important because it is linked to the notion of training and skills management. Moreover, an IMP (short for implementer) is a person who has followed a training process and who knows the programming rules of the company. This becomes a sensitive issue when outsourcing processes (to someone outside of the company) in a project and/or when a policy for relocating coding activities is put in place (organization external to the company).

14.2. Characteristics of programming rules

14.2.1. *Introduction*

The different standards recommend formalizing programming and coding rules in the form of a guide. Coding rules must be developed and specified by:

– good programming practices. We want to develop a code that is maintainable, verifiable and testable;

– measures to avoid or detect errors that may be committed in the application of the language and which are not detectable during the verification (variable aliasing, bad memory management, etc.). Such failures can be identified through risk analysis on the set of characteristics of the language;

– the description of procedures for the documentation of the source code: the source code is a deliverable that must have its own documentation.

The choice of coding rules must be justified within the limits required by the software safety integrity level. It is thus possible to define a guide that covers different safety levels. Coding rules should be used for the development of all software programs (regardless of the safety level) and require that they be referenced in the SQAP of the project.

These encoding rules should cover different points:

– formatting rules (tabulation, structure of header files, etc.);

– documentation rules (comments format, comments objectives, SwCD/Code traceability links, etc.);

– software engineering conventions: all objects must be names, typed and initialized; every constant, quantity and/or specific value of the system must have a unique identifier, etc.;

– conventions related to safety principles: defensive programming, assertion-based programming, safety variables protection, etc.;

– definition rules for the subset of the language being used;

– language-specific rules and/or rules specific to the compiler used.

Rules are generally formalized by way of a programming guide. This programming guide must be defined for every programming language that can be used for the development of safety-related software applications.

The programming rules will be presented in the following way:

RULE_<Number> : <Title> (<Type>)
<Text>

where:

- Number: a unique number;

- Title: a summary of the rule;

- Type: the type of the rule, I for Imperative and R for Recommended;

- Text: the description of the rule, eventually with an example.

This first formalism for programming rules may be completed in order to take into account different points of view. Table 14.1 introduces an example of a table for the description of programming and coding rules.

Rule name	A unique identifier for each rule
Safety level	Each rule can be associated with one or more safety levels: SSIL0/SSIL2/SSIL4[1].
Description	The description of the rule can be the text used in the standard.
Explanation	The description can be very brief and an explanation can help with understanding.
Examples	For each rule, it is necessary to introduce at least an example of correct use and a counterexample.
Type	The function of this attribute is to indicate whether the rule is mandatory (*Required*) or recommended (*Advisory*). It is possible to define additional values in order to identify rules that have an impact on the form or on other aspects.
Verification	Type of the verification to be implemented: new reading, manual verification, automatic verification, etc.
Traceability	We outline here using the various standards: – MISRA-C, – MISRA-C++, – CENELEC 50128, – JSF++.
Impact	Here, we will indicate the impact that non-compliance with the rule can have: impact on safety, impact on testability, impact on verification, impact on maintainability, etc.

Table 14.1. *Example of the description of rules*

1 As an example of safety level, here we have chosen the SSIL used in the rail industry but we could take the DAL x (aeronautics sector) or the ASIL x (automotive sector).

As introduced several different times in this chapter, programming and coding rules must cover different areas:

– formatting rules;

– good practice definition rules;

– language subset definition rules.

14.2.2. *General rules*

Code production needs to verify a certain number of detailed rules but it is also possible to introduce a few general rules such as:

RULE_01: Language convention (I)
English will be used for naming objects (functions, services, procedures, packages, files, variables, etc.) and for every comment.

RULE_02: Language convention (I)
The code must meet the standard of the chosen language[2].

Since programming conventions are mandatory, it is necessary to have access to a formal procedure allowing us not to follow them.

RULE_03: Rule method 1:
Whenever a rule is not followed, this must be clearly justified.

This is part of a set of examples to be completed depending on our needs and feedback.

14.2.3. *Compilation rules*

Compilers are tools that still have a strong impact on the executable. Compilation options are mechanisms to influence the structure of the executable. This is why it is necessary to identify all options in the manual

---

2 For the C language, the ISO C standard [ISO 99b] standard will be the reference. For the ADA language, the ISO/IEC 8652:1995 [ISO 95] and ISO/IEC 8652:2012(E) [ISO 12] standards will be the reference. For programming programmable logic controllers, the IEC 61131-3 standard [IEC 13] is to be followed.

describing the generation of the executable and to apply a number of rules, such as:

RULE_04: Warnings management:
Always compile with the highest possible alert level in order to eliminate as many warnings as possible.

RULE_05: Options management:
The implementation of compilation options must be formalized in the executable generation manual.

RULE_06: Optimization management:
Optimization options should be used only as needed. When using them, it is the optimized executable that will have to undergo so-called validation tests.

This is part of a set of examples to be completed depending on our needs and feedback.

14.2.4. *Formatting rules*

Formatting rules must enable that a controlled and known structure be given to source files; for this purpose, we will define tabulation rules, the structure of header files, the decomposition into files, etc.

The comment contains:

– the copyright;

– the name of the project;

– the name of the set module or module which is the name of the file;

– a description of the content;

– the name of the project;

– the configuration management history;

– the definition of whether this is a theme or a function;

– added information related to changes taken into account.

14.2.5. *Documentation conventions*

It is necessary to document the source code in order to allow any developer to easily access the code. Comments must be compact, clear and easy to identify.

Documentation conventions must describe the format of the comments, the objectives of the different types of comments, the definition of SwCD/Code traceability links, etc.

Regarding the comments, a rating for comments can be introduced in order to provide a metric for verification. This rating can be defined in the form of a percentage of line of comment / number of lines in the code. It is however important to correctly define what is accounted for in the number of lines of code.

```
/* the file is named toto.c */.

/* the next function is named auntie * /.
/* it has a parameter: aa */
/* parameter aa is of type int */.
void auntie (int aa)
{
/* i is printed out for i varying from i to 0 to 9 */.
for (int i++, i=0, i<10)
  printf (i)
}
```

Figure 14.1. *Example of commented code*

The implementation of rating for comments sometimes results in the creation of comments that are useless, or even inadequate as shown in Figure 14.1. In a very large number of programs (even in safety-critical software), comments are futile and have no purpose.

14.2.6. *Software engineering conventions*

It should be reminded that the rules related to the state of the art of software engineering must be part of the programming rules. In the following, we are going to present a set of rules which is not meant to be exhaustive, but which allows the identification of the type of rule that is expected for this part.

Code maintainability will take precedence over its optimization. This rule can be circumvented if and only if there is a performance problem. Rules can be separated into two sets: the rules indicating what has to be done and the rules indicating what should not be done.

As part of the development of a software application, *we should*:

– give a name to all elements (constant, variable, function, procedure, program, class, instance, etc.) that are manipulated in a software application. In addition, the name has to have a meaning (see section 13.2.6);

– so-called "magical" numbers must be avoided in the code. These are fixed numbers that are used anywhere in the code;

– define a type for each element manipulated by the software application;

– define an initialization for each element manipulated by the software application;

– avoid the use of global variables. Global variables should not be used to implement temporary local processes or for performing exchanges of information between services;

– implement data encapsulation. The purpose of encapsulation is to implement access mechanisms to non-volatile variables. These accesses can be achieved by local or external services;

– control code complexity:

    - a component (function, procedure, service, module, etc.) must have a maximum number of lines. The size in number of lines of a component is a factor which influences and maintains readability;

    - a component must have a maximum number of input and output parameters. The number of input and output parameters of a component is linked to the complexity of use of this component;

    - a component must utilize a maximum number of local variables;

    - the cyclomatic complexity of a component must be limited (between 10 and 15).

As part of the development process of a software application, *we should not*:

– duplicate code. Copies of code fragments will be avoided;

– have (too) strong coupling between elements (procedures, functions, classes, programs, etc.) of a software application (the class managing error message is used by all other classes, and any change leads to the recompilation of the whole);

– have (too) low cohesion. Low cohesion means that local variables and/or methods within the same module are not sufficiently linked;

– introduce unnecessary parameters.

14.2.7. Object names

14.2.7.1. Naming

According to the first rule that we had set out, a name has to be given to the various objects manipulated by the application software. In this explanation, the notion of object covers variables, constants, functions, procedures, programs, classes, methods and data as well as all of the elements manipulated by the software application.

RULE_11: Every object must be declared before being used.

RULE_12: Every object must be defined only once.
Example:

```
int i;
int i;
```

These are a number of examples to be completed depending on our needs and feedback.

14.2.7.2. Naming management

Naming objects is an important activity that can incur consequences on maintenance. Simple naming rules make it possible to characterize the objects being manipulated. For example, constants and variables have a name of the form C_xxx and V_xxx, respectively. With respect to variables, naming can be used to identify the context of use, V_xxx_g for a global variable and V_xxx_l for a local variable.

```
MACHINE
      BOOKING
CONSTANT
Max
PROPERTIES
Max ∈ NAT ∧ Max > 10
VARIABLES
places
INVARIANT
places ∈ 0 .. Max
INITIALIZATION

places:= ??
OPERATIONS
reservation =
???
cancel =
???
END
```

Figure 14.2. *Naming example. For a color version of this figure,*
see www.iste.co.uk/boulanger/applications3.zip

However, as shown in Figure 14.2 (inspired by [IDA 06] – Example 1.1), naming objects may raise issues. Furthermore, the machine BOOKING manipulates the variable *places*; when there is no information available (and after tests on six generations of students during my lectures on the B-method[3] at the UTC[4]), it emerges that one half of people think that the variable *places* represents free places and that the other half thinks that the variable *places* represents occupied places.

This type of ambiguity will allow defects to be introduced during development or maintenance. This is the reason why it is important that the name of the variables is chosen according to their uses. Figure 14.3 illustrates an attempt at modeling free places. We have introduced constants to manage high and low limits.

---

3 The B-method was presented in Chapter 6 of this volume; for more information see [BOU 14].
4 University of Technology of Compiègne: https://www.utc.fr.

```
MACHINE
     BOOKING
CONSTANTS
     C_max,
     C_lower_limit = 0,
     C_upper_limit = 10,
PROPERTIES
C_max ∈ NAT ∧ C_max > C__upper_limit
VARIABLES
V_free_seats
INVARIANT
V_free_seats ∈ C_lower_limit . . C_max
INITIALIZATION
V_free_seats := C_max
OPERATIONS
reservation =
PRE V_free_seats > C_lower_limit THEN
V_free_seats := V_free_ seats - 1
END
cancel =
PRE V_free_seats < C_max THEN
V_free_seats := V_free_seats + 1
END
END
```

Figure 14.3. *Example of explicit naming*

14.2.7.3. *Name size*

RULE_22: Name size
The name of the objects (internal or external to the application) is limited to 31 characters.

These are some of a number of examples to be completed depending on our needs and feedback.

14.2.8. *Variables management*

14.2.8.1. *Introduction*

Data management can be achieved through the use of variables that can be local or global. The use of variables is a common practice except for languages known as functional (LISP, OCAML, etc.); however, it can introduce problems with testability (no observability following the overwriting of a variable), maintenance (no access to stored data) or even safety (poor management of accesses to the variables). Therefore, it is required that management rules be put in place for the variables whether they are local or global.

14.2.8.2. Global variables management

Initially in embedded software applications, the recovery of the internal state of a software application by a maintenance tool was achieved by recovering memory blocks. Under these conditions, the use of global variables was recommended in order to have the maximum amount of data in the same block of data.

In general, the use of global variables introduces a bias in the design because it is then very easy to define a set of so-called "catch-all" variables that can be used to store different types of information that have no consistency between them. This will result in maintenance and testability issues for the software application. The use of global variables creates non-reentrant functions (values would be updated by another function).

RULE_33: Global variables
The use of global variables must be justified and ought to be subject to a specific control.

In the CENELEC 50128:2011 standard [CEN 11], it is highly recommended that the usage of global variables be limited (which means that all utilizations of global variables should be justified).

Reading and writing rights management is another issue related to the use of global variables. The management of access rights to global variables can be carried out through the implementation of a specific library responsible for managing directories.

14.2.8.3. Local variables management

14.2.8.3.1. Introduction

The notion of local variable is necessary for the implementation of algorithms, but some programming languages have rules more or less constrained concerning accesses to local data from one code unit to another (components, modules and functions). That is the reason why software engineering conventions introduce the concepts of encapsulation and information hiding.

14.2.8.3.2. Protected data

Information hiding is a principle that advocates that local data have to be made inaccessible. The C language introduces the notion of protected variables. A protected variable is inaccessible outside of the code unit. This practice is good from the application safety perspective but not so good from the testability and/or defect analysis perspective.

Data protection (*hiding variables*) is a technique supported by programming languages through the use of *private* and/or *protected* instructions. Although useful, this approach has a direct impact on observability. The datum no longer being observable, there will be problems during testing and especially during defect analysis phases that could emerge during operation.

It should be noted that in the railway sector, the CENELEC EN 50128 standard in its 2011 version [CEN 11] requires developers to not use data hiding.

Data protection should not be used in the context of so-called critical software applications: it must be replaced by *data encapsulation*.

14.2.8.3.3. Data encapsulation

Encapsulation is a principle that indicates that data cannot be directly accessed but we must employ specific services such as *set* (to change values) or *get* (to retrieve values).

Thereby, the CENELEC 50128:2011 standard [CEN 11] identifies information hiding as a technique with almost no interest, whereas encapsulation is seen as highly recommended.

Data encapsulation requires at least the reading function (get) which could be used by the maintenance tool to enable access to internal data in the event of operating issues.

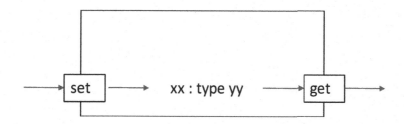

Figure 14.4. *Encapsulation*

14.2.9. *Rules related to safety principles*

14.2.9.1. *Managing the range constraining a type*

With respect to the ranges constraining a type (table, etc.), there is a lower bound and an upper bound. There are several policies that exist; bounds can be included or excluded from the range.

The recommended strategy consists of having an inclusive lower bound and an exclusive upper bound. For example, for the range *0..size* defining the indices of a table, the bound 0 is included and the size bound is excluded, which is consistent with the definition of the table.

It is important that such recommendations be defined, applied and verified.

14.2.9.2. *Language-specific rules*

In Chapter 13, we presented coding standards dedicated to languages such as MISRA-C, MISRA-C++ and JSF++.

For ADA [ISO 12], we have a specific subset of the language, known as the Ravenscar profile (see [ISO 00]). This language subset can be extended with some additional rules such as:

RULE_40: "When others" is not allowed
The "when others" clause in case statements is not allowed. It is necessary to explicitly cite all alternatives in case.

14.2.9.3. *Floating-point management*

Within the context of applications that are known as safety critical, whenever possible integers are used (large integers make it possible to avoid floating-point numbers), but it is now increasingly common to develop software applications that manipulate floating-point numbers.

It will be necessary to put in place specific rules that aim to control miscalculations with floating points, such as:

RULE_41: Precision
It is required that computation errors do not affect the result in the context of floating-point computations.

RULE_42: Comparison operators
The use of comparison operators between floating-points must be limited.

These are some of a number of examples to be completed depending on our needs and feedback.

14.3. Programming rules verification

As was presented as part of Chapter 11 of Volume 2 [BOU 17], the verification can be done through static analysis and/or dynamic analysis. For programming rules, it is a static analysis. Programming rules can be verified manually or automatically.

More and more, we prefer to use a tool to do automatic verification. In fact, some rules (see in MISRA-C) can be very difficult to verify. Programming rules are formally verified by the VER (short for verifier; see Table 7.3).

But from the point of view of process, it is very important that the IMP have access to the tool that verified the programming rules and IMP will check that the code is correct. It is possible that some programming rules are not fulfilled and in this case IMP can add some justification (by using comments) to explain why the programming rules are not fulfilled and VER will check if the comments are acceptable.

Checking programming rules is a verification process and it will be discussed in Volume 4 [BOU 19], which is related to verification and validation.

14.4. Conclusion

Choosing a language is not an easy task; as we have already mentioned, a standard, strong typing and a collection of recognized programming rules must be available.

Strong typing is not achievable in every language, and that is the underlying reason why it is possible to add programming rules and to define a subset of the language to enable the reduction of the scope of the language and thus to render it acceptable for the implementation of a safety application.

15

Coding Verification

15.1. Introduction

The activity of coding the software application must include a verification stage. The verification must be able to show that the code is in compliance with the Software Component Design (SwCD), that coding rules have been satisfied and that quality processes have been followed.

Code verification is done by a verifier (VER) that is independent from the software implementer (IMP).

This verification is part of the demonstration that the software is maintainable. Indeed, during this verification, we verify the programming rules and the complexity. Complexity management and programming rules help us to be sure that a new team can update the code.

15.2. Verification

15.2.1. *Reminder*

As presented in Chapter 11 of Volume 2 [BOU 17], verification can be carried out by means of static analysis and/or dynamic analysis.

Since the objective here consists of verifying the quality of the code of a software application, static methods are more suitable.

15.2.2. *Methodology*

15.2.2.1. *Method*

Code verification may be achieved through several activities:

– the design review (new reading, using checklists, etc.) which can be more or less formal;

– the verification of programming rules;

– the verification of complexity.

As indicated in Chapter 4 of Volume 2 [BOU 17], verification processes are performed by a dedicated team. This team must be independent from the development team (see Figure 7.1). The verification team includes testers (TST), integrators (INT) and verifiers (VER).

Nevertheless, the verification team is not the only one involved; as a matter of fact, it is necessary to verify that the code meets the company's quality criteria. For this purpose, we will resort to the QUA (see Table 7.1).

Similarly, the design must be verified by the safety team (SAF). The safety team must verify that;

– the manipulated data are of the right safety level;

– stored data are properly used and protected;

– safety requirements have been taken into account during the definition of the algorithms;

– safety principles are followed (safety principles are issued from system documents, from the documents describing the physical architecture and safety principles).

15.2.2.2. *Verifier*

As already stated, the verification of the software code must be made by a verifier (see Figure 7.1 for the organization). The verifier (see Table 7.3) is responsible for verifying the technical content of the document (at this level in the source file) (see section 7.2.2.2.3 for more information).

15.2.2.3. *Objective of the design review*

The verification of a phase requires the verification of the implementation of quality requirements (application of procedures, compliance with formats, etc.), the application of processes (compliance with plans, compliance with the organization, etc.), the correction of activities and that safety requirements are properly taken into account.

Concerning the design phase, methodological guides related to modeling, design rules, principles of architecture etc., might be included as input documents; as a result, there will be additional verifications.

In general, rules include:

– naming conventions for all objects (constants, global variables, interfaces, local variables, software parameters, function parameters, functions, modules, etc.);

– documentation-related rules;

– design-related rules;

– decomposition rules.

The design review can have different objectives:

– to demonstrate that some rules are assumed by the code;

– to demonstrate that the code implements all functions defined in SwCD;

– to demonstrate that all safety requirements are implemented;

– to demonstrate that the safety principles[1] are implemented (in the case of a safety-critical system, a safety concept can be introduced and some safety-principle will need to be fulfill, for example some data must be protected, a watchdog will need to be refreshed, etc.).

15.2.2.4. *Critical Code Review*

A new reading of the code must be put in place in order to show that the functions implemented during the coding phase correspond to needs identified in the SwCD. We call this review a Critical Code Review (CCR).

---

1 During the design of safety-critical systems, it is necessary to design a safety platform and safe software. Different mechanism can be used such as redundancy and diversity. For more information on safety platform, see [BOU 09a, BOU 11c].

The review is then conducted by way of a quick reading (walkthrough) or through a design review (formal design review). A documentation review has been presented in detail in section 7.2.2.2.1, but in the case of a code, we need to introduce an adapted process.

This verification must have an objective. This objective may be formalized in the form of a checklist (control list).

During a CCR, we can check:

– that all source files fulfill the style rules (naming, structure, comments, etc.);

– that in all source files, comments are useful (sometimes, the implementer adds a comment just to fulfill the rule that requests x% of comments in source code);

– that all source files fulfill the coding rules or if a coding rule is not respected a comment exists to explain why;

– that in all source files, defensive programming is used and commented. It is necessary that the implementer commented the defensive programming part;

– that all parameters defined during software design are implemented and used;

– that all functions, operations and/or services identified in the SwCD are implemented and fulfill the SwCD (signature, algorithm, etc.);

– that all safety requirements are correctly implemented;

– that all design choices are explained in source files.

This is a first verification set that ought to be completed by the feedback. It is very important to put in place a Return of Experience (REX) approach, when some defects are not detected early, it is very important to verify if it is not possible to improve the verification and the checklist used during verification.

15.2.3. *Compliance with coding rules*

The topic covering coding rules has been mentioned in Chapter 14 of this volume. The definition of a subset of the programming language and the definition of a set of coding rules are a first step that must be accompanied by the verification of the effective compliance by the code with aforementioned rules.

The implementation of the verification that the code follows the rules that have been defined may be performed manually if the number of rules is limited and/or the size of the code is not too large. One should bear in mind that this verification step must be auditable, meaning there should be a formal record of the verification. In order to ensure the maintenance of the software application, this review must be reproducible.

This is the reason why it is preferable that this type of verification be assisted by tools. The tool must be able to analyze the code for the language under consideration and it must be possible to define the rules to be verified.

As we saw in previous sections, there are sets of recognized rules such as:

– for ADA, you can use [BAR 03, ISO 00];

– for C, you can use MISRAC [MIS 98, MIS 04, MIS 12];

– for C, you can also use [HAT 94] or [PLU 89];

– for C++, you can use MISRA-C++ [MIS 08] or JSF++ [LM 05][2];

– for C++, you can also use [SCO 98] and [SUT 04];

and one must also be able to define one's own rules.

As an example, Figure 15.1 is a screenshot of the execution of the application QAC on a P program written in C.

15.3. Dead code and unreachable code

15.3.1. *Introduction*

The coding phase should be a phase that is implemented quite easily. As a matter of fact, algorithms and data of the design stage simply have

---

2 For C++, JSF++ is more relevant than MISRA-C++ and now JSF++ is used in many domains and is well implemented in tools.

to be transformed into sections of code. This work could be performed by the designer or a person responsible for coding.

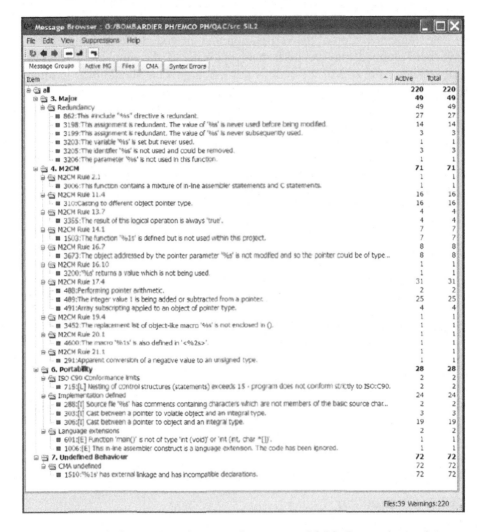

Figure 15.1. *Screenshot of the overview screen of QAC. For a color version of this figure, see www.iste.co.uk/boulanger/applications3.zip*

In fact, this is not that simple because while the coding phase might allow us to write code, it is also possible to use sections of code commercially available (COTS) or to reuse preexisting software programs.

15.3.2. *Unreachable code*

It is possible to produce code that contains unreachable parts (see Figure 15.2).

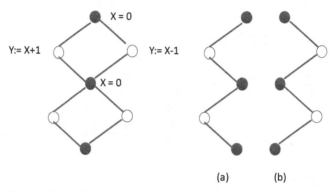

Figure 15.2. *Example of a code including unreachable portions*

The code in Figure 15.2 can give rise to executions (a) and (b) but since variable *x* does not change its value inside the first IF, it is not possible to execute two paths following through the diagonals.

15.3.3. *Dead code*

It is possible that some portions of code are not executable because they are never called at any instant in the software application. This is referred to as dead code. However, there are other cases where dead code is executed but whose results are not employed.

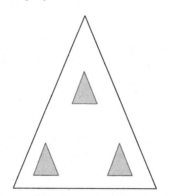

Figure 15.3. *Example of dead code*

In Figure 15.3, the gray areas define code that is not called from within the application.

Dead code is a threat to the software application; as a matter of fact, the code has never been tested and may thus contain flaws.

15.3.4. *Inhibited code*

It is possible to define a generic software application having optional functionality. Therefore, during the implementation of the specific application, we will use a parametrization that can inhibit certain services as shown in Figure 15.4. The inhibited code has been fully tested during the development of the generic application.

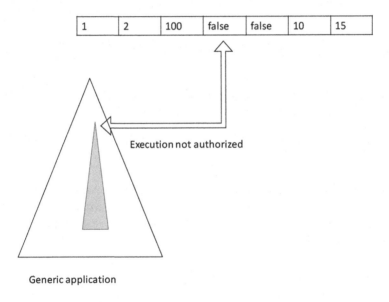

Figure 15.4. *Example of inhibited code*

15.4. Conclusion

In this chapter, we have presented verification activities to be implemented at the code level. The main verifications concern the programming rules, code complexity and traceability with the SwCD.

Version Sheet of the Software Application

16.1. Introduction

Once the development of the software application is completed, it is necessary to guarantee that the latter can be identified and it must be possible to identify whether the correct version is exchanged and/or installed. The software application design process contains many documents and many tools; it is very important to be sure that the software executable we deliver can be reproduced. On the other hand, we need to manage the software (exchanged by USB key, exchanged by email, installed with tools, installed by copy, etc.) and we need to verify that the software effectively installed in the final system is the correct version. To this end, a software version sheet (SwVS) has to be implemented.

At the center of the different quality standards (ISO 9001 [ISO 15], CMMI, Spice, etc.), we find once again the need to manage the configuration of a software application and to practically identify the version.

However, it is important to remember that it is essential to be able to reproduce the same executable; therefore, the capability of regenerating the same executable must be attached to the identification process.

16.2. Generating the executable

16.2.1. *Principles*

Within the context of Chapters 11 and 12 of Volume 1 [BOU 16], we mentioned tool and qualification management. Nonetheless, part of these tools, those related to generation and compilation, requires specific management. This is referred to as the executable generation process.

During the coding phase, the sequence generating the executable will have to be implemented. The executable generation process can be a more or less complex process. Figure 16.1 illustrates two examples of the executable generation process. Version (a) is a linear sequence in which a single executable is produced from the sources, unlike version (b) which presents the production of two executables.

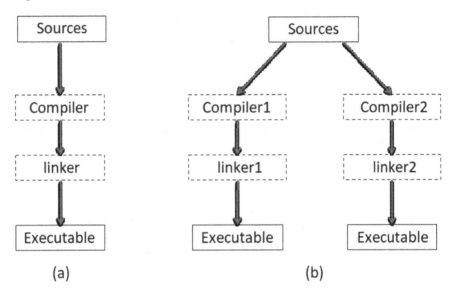

Figure 16.1. *Two examples of compilation processes*

It is necessary to formalize this process and to properly make sure that all tools are identified, no step should be forgotten. The formalization of the executable generation process can be done in a specific document or in SwVS. Figure 16.2 is an example of the executable generation process.

The executable generation process must be analyzed in order to verify whether it makes it possible to build a single executable. The use of tools that introduce dates in source files, in intermediate files or in binary should be avoided. As an example, some compilers such as Visual-C add the compilation dates to the executable.

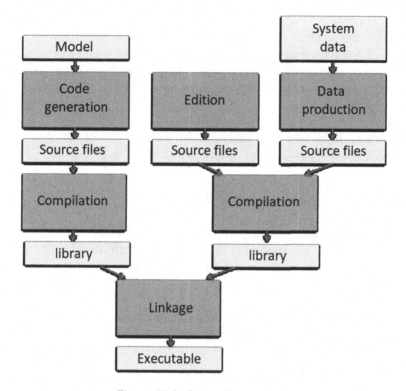

Figure 16.2. *Generation process*

This process of generating the executable should be subject to a safety study designed to identify mitigations to be put in place to manage the potential risks induced by tools. This safety study is part of the tools qualification process (see Chapter 13 of Volume 1 [BOU 16]).

In a number of areas, such as railways, the client may ask to install the design environment on a new computer (generally empty), as well as the executable generation process, in order to verify that it generates the same executable that was delivered. For example, it is difficult to identify the Windows version used on the design computer; we know that we installed Windows 7 but we apply numerous patches (or they are automatically applied), and during the installation of tools an old library can sometimes be installed. Another example is Cygwin.

16.3. Identification of the executable

16.3.1. *Introduction*

Within the context of critical applications, the identification of the version of a software application is essential because it helps determine the constraints of associated use. In general, every piece of software has known bugs and for safety-critical software known bugs are linked to constraints of use.

However, it is also necessary to be able to detect changes in the executable (memory issues, transmission problems, etc.).

16.3.2. *Identification of the executable*

Once the installation of the software application is achieved on a specific hardware platform, it is important to be able to identify the installed version; for this purpose, the application software must be capable of providing an identifier.

This identifier could be displayed on screen or on any another display (for example through the front LEDs of the equipment) and/or sent on the output linked to maintenance.

16.3.3. *Executable protection*

The executable of a software application must be protected so that we can verify that during transport and various downloads, the version has not been altered. We are in the domain of safety-critical systems and are interested in detecting unintentional corruption.

The protection for the executable is a specific code[1] such as a checksum, Message Digest 5 (MD5)[2], etc.

---

1 Redundancy information may be used based on the checksum. The CRC (Cyclic Redundant Code), Hamming codes and/or checksums are means for protecting one or more data elements (for more information, see [BOU 09a, BOU 11c]).
2 The MD5 algorithm is a hash function. In a safety-critical system, it is used as a checksum to verify data integrity.

16.4. Version datasheet of the application software

16.4.1. *Presentation of the need*

After reaching the final steps of the implementation of the software application, it is necessary to make a reference version of the software application available. This version should be identified and formalized through a SwVS. This activity is carried out using the process known as *delivery* (see Figure 16.3).

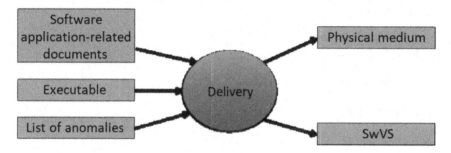

Figure 16.3. *Creation of the SwVS*

This SwVS must make it possible to identify the software application in a unique way. Therefore, the reference of the application software and its version are not sufficient: a mechanism has to be provided (for example a checksum verification) that makes it possible to verify the integrity of the software application.

This verification is necessary because this software application will be delivered by means of a physical medium (USB key, CD, DVD, etc.) and will be transferred onto the final system via a download tool.

16.4.2. *Implementation*

The creation of the SwVS includes the analysis of:

– the scope of the version;

– the configuration (software, documents, tools, etc.);

– residual defects;

– derogations related to the non-application or partial application of the design process.

The SwVS will have to identify:

– the compatibility between the software and hardware;

– the compatibility between the software generated and other software (for example OS version, version of the maintenance tool, etc.);

– the version of the executable, the version of the sources and the version of the applicable documents;

– the identification of the software, and elements allowing us to verify that the software is the one that should be installed;

– limits and restrictions of use;

– constraint of uses.

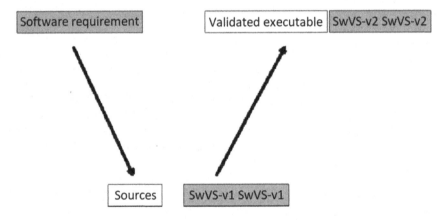

Figure 16.4. *V-model and two versions of the SwVS*

With regard to the V-model conventionally used (see Figure 16.4), it is necessary to produce at least two versions of the SwVS. A first version of the SwVS has to be published at the end of the descending phase in order to provide a version of the software application for the purpose of performing the V&V activities. The first version will make it possible to define the version of the sources in the configuration and V&V activities will be able to clearly identify the elements being analyzed. The second version will be produced at the end of the ascending phase.

16.4.3. *Compatibility*

It should be noted that the CENELEC EN 50128: 2011 standard [CEN 11] identifies specific needs that the SwVS must take into account in order to be able to proceed to the deployment of the new version. The needs include the need to identify the compatibility between the software application and other software and with different hardware platforms.

16.4.4. *Summary*

The SwVS is an essential document for the management of the software application and its control. The SwVS is a document that must identify:

– the input version of the maintenance process;

– the list of changes taken into account (corrected anomalies and/or change requests taken into account);

– the characterization of the version:

- list of project documents (complete list or list of modified documents),

- list of sources files and versioning,

- identification of the version x.y.z. (see configuration management),

- protection of the executable;

– the list of known anomalies;

– the list of restrictions of use (function not implemented, limit, etc.).

16.5. Conclusion

The SwVS is essential for managing the software application (knowledge of the scope, identification of limits, etc.) and predominantly for the deployment of a new version.

Version management relies on the notion of configuration management, which is addressed in Chapter 7 of Volume 1 [BOU 16].

16.6. Appendix: SwVS

An SwVS comprises the following:

– identification of the software application: name, reference and version;

– identification of the configuration associated with this version: a configuration can be based on several tools located at different places; a configuration may be characterized by a specific tag, etc.;

– identification of the version's content:

- list of documents and associated versions,

- list of sources files and associated versions,

- list of result files and associated versions,

- list of tools with their reference and their associated version;

– identification of limits and restrictions of use;

– identification of constraints of use;

– identification of known defects;

– identification of the executable generation process;

– identification of interfacing software applications (other software, maintenance software, etc.) and compatible versions;

– identification of supporting compatible hardware platforms;

– identification of interfacing hardware elements (measuring tools, maintenance pc, etc.) and compatible versions.

Conclusion

Conclusion and Perspectives

The first volume of this series [BOU 16] has enabled us to present the link that must be implemented between the system and software applications through the architecture stages. Furthermore, it is necessary to ensure that the software application is operating correctly within an environment that is generally quite complex. In the context of complex systems such as those in transport, energy and production, the safety, availability, reliability and maintainability of the system directly depend on the software application. We have presented the implementation process of a software application taking into account the set of constraints linked to safe and certifiable complex systems.

The second volume [BOU 17] allowed us to identify and describe supporting processes that have to be to put in place to build a certifiable application. These include quality assurance, configuration management, change management, the definition of versioning, archiving, V&V and data preparation, as well as the management and qualification of tools and audits. These processes are essential but, in general, are rarely or poorly applied. It is therefore necessary to build a system for quality management that covers all of the support processes by defining procedures, templates, generic plans, a quality assurance manual, guides and all the elements for facilitating the implementation of a new project.

The third volume (the present book) is dedicated to presenting the activities to be established during the descending phase of the V-model of the implementation of the software application. We have retained the V-model as the central axis, but we have shown that there are in fact several V-models based on the architecture phase. The central element of our presentation is the notion of component. The software component has good property that will make it possible to implement a high rate of reutilization but that will also enable us to manage obsolescence. The notion of component makes it possible to limit the impact of changes and thus avoids the problem of spaghetti code (when altering a single line of code affects the whole software).

We have introduced verifications within the implementation cycle of the software application which can detect anomalies at the earliest moment. It is very important to have a useful process that help us to detect anomalies but not at the end of the process. We just recall that a big part of software costs are related to the correction of bugs. Each new version has a cost and a cost that clients do not want to manage.

Volume 4 [BOU 19] will be dedicated to V&V; we will introduce and explain verification techniques such as review, testing and proof, and study their application to safety-critical software.

Glossary

2oo2: Architecture 2 out of 2

2oo3: Architecture 2 out of 3

ACATS: Ada Conformity Assessment Test Suite

AM: Abstract Model

AMN: Abstract Machine Notation

ANSI: American National Standards Institute

AON: All or Nothing

API: Application Programming Interface

APTE: Application to Entreprise Techniques (*Application aux Techniques d'Entreprise*)

ASA: Automata and Structured Analysis

AUTOSAR: AUTomotive Open System ARchitecture

BDD: Binary Decision Diagram

BoP: Burden of Proof

CAS: Computer-Aided Specification

CCR: Critical Code Review

CENELEC[1]: European Committee for Electro-technical Standardization

CF: Constraint Function

CM: Concrete Model

CMMi[2]: Capability Maturity Model for integration

COTS: Commercial Off The Shelf software

CRC: Cyclic Redundant Code

CT: Component Testing

D: Dependability

DAL: Design Assurance Level

DD: Data Dictionary

DES: DESigner

DEV: DEVeloper

DFD: Data Flow Diagram

FMEA: Failure Modes and Effects Analysis

FTA: Fault Tree Analysis

GL: Project Glossary

GUI: Graphical Unit Interface

HMI: Human/Machine Interface

---

1 See: http://www.cenelec.eu.
2 For more information, see the *Software Engineering Institute* website at: www.sei.cmu. edu/cmmi/.

HR : Highly Recommended

IDE: Integrated Development Environment

IdM: Model Engineering (Ingénierie des Modèles)

IEC[3]: International Electrotechnical Commission

IMA: Integrated Modular Avionics

IMAG: Institute of Applied Mathematics of Grenoble

IMP: IMPlementer

INT: INTegrator

IRIS[4]: International Railway Industry Standard

IS: Interpretation Semantic

ISO[5]: International Organization for Standardization

IT: Integration Testing

ITS: Integration Test Specification

ITSD: Integration Testing Specification Document

LAV: Light Automatic Vehicle

MBD: Model-Based Development

ME: Model Engineering

MEMVATEX: Modeling Method for Requirement Validation Traceability

METEOR: East-West Fast METro (*METro Est Ouest Rapide*)

---

3 See: http://www.iec.ch/.
4 See: http://www.iris-rail.org/.
5 See: http://www.iso.org/iso/home.htm.

MF: Main Function

MISRA[6]: Motor Industry Software Reliability Association

MT: Modular Testing

MVC: Model-View-Controller

NooM: N out of M

OMG[7]: Object Management Group

OS: Operating System

PDL: Project Documentation List

PM: Project Manager

QAM: Quality Assurance Manual

QMS: Quality Management System

QUA: QUAlity manager (project quality manager)

RAM: Reliability, Availability and Maintainability

RAMS: Reliability, Availability, Maintainability and Safety

REQ: REQuirement

REX: Return of EXperience

RQM: ReQuirement Manager

SEEA: Software Error Effect Analysis

S/H: Software/Hardware

S/H ITS: Software/Hardware Integration Testing Specification

---

6 See: www.misra.org.uk/.
7 See: http://www.omg.org/.

S/S: Software/Software

S/S ITS: Software/Software Integration Testing Specification

SA: Structured Analysis

SACEM: Driver Assistance, Operation, and Maintenance System

SAD: Software Architecture Document

SADD: System Architecture Description Document

SADT: Structured Analysis and Design Technique

SAET: Train Operation Automation System

SAF: SAFety

SART: Structured Analysis for Real-Time systems

SCADE: Safety Critical Application Development Environment

SCDD: Software Component Design Document

SCMP: Software Configuration Management Plan

SCT: Software Component Testing

SCTS: Software Component Testing Specification

SDD: Software Design Document

SDP: Software Development Plan

SIL: Safety Integrity Level

SM: Source Model

SQAP: Software Quality Assurance Plan

SS_VR: Software Specification Verification Report

SSIL: Software SIL

SVaP: Software Validation Plan

SVeP: Software Verification Plan

SVVP: Software Verification and Validation Plan

SwAD: System Architecture Description

SwCD: Software Component Design

SwCS: Software Component Specification

SwCTS: Software Component Testing Specification

SwOTS: Software Overall Testing Specification

SwRS: Software Requirement Specification

SwRTS: Software Requirements Testing Specification

SwVS: Software Version Sheet

SyAD: System Architecture Description

SyRS: System Requirement Specification

SysML: System Modeling Language

TC: Test Case

TM: Target Model

TS: Test Scenarios

TST: TeSTer

UML: Unified Modeling Language

UT: Unit Testing .

V&V: Verification and Validation

VAL: VALidator

Val P: Validation Plan

VDM: Vienna Development Method

VER: VERifier

Ver P: Verification Plan

VR: Verification Report

VT: Validation Test

VVP: Verification and Validation Plan

WP: Weakest Precondition

xx_VR xx: Verification Report

Bibliography

[ABR 91] ABRIAL J.R., LEE M.K.O., NEILSON D.S. *et al.*, "The B-method", *VDM'91*, pp 398–405, 1991.

[ABR 92] ABRIAL J.R., "On constructing large software systems", *IFIP 12th World Computer Congress*, vol. A-12, pp. 103–112, 1992.

[ABR 96] ABRIAL J.R., *The B-Book*, Cambridge University Press, 1996.

[ADA 01] ADA RESOURCE ASSOCIATION, Operating procedures for Ada conformity assessments, Version 3.0, available at: www.ada-auth.org/procs/3.0/ ACAP30.pdf, 2001.

[AFN 90] AFNOR, NF X 50-150, Analyse fonctionnelle du besoin – Guide pour l'élaboration d'un Cahier des Charges Fonctionnel, European standard, 1990.

[AFN 91] AFNOR, NF X 50-151, Analyse de la Valeur, Analyse Fonctionnelle – Expression Fonctionnelle du besoin et Cahier des Charges Fonctionnel (CdCF), European standard, 1991.

[AFN 96] AFNOR, NF EN 1325-1, Vocabulaire du management de la valeur, de l'analyse de la valeur et de l'analyse fonctionnelle - Partie 1: analyse de la valeur et analyse fonctionnelle, European standard, 1996.

[AFN 01] AFNOR, NF EN 13306, Terminologie de la maintenance, European standard, 2001.

[AFN 05] AFNOR, NF EN 1325-2, Vocabulaire du management de la valeur, de l'analyse et de la valeur et de l'analyse fonctionnelle – Partie 2: management par la valeur, European standard, 2005.

[AFN 07] AFNOR, NF X 50-152, Management par la valeur – Caractéristiques fondamentales de l'analyse de la valeur, European standard, 2007.

[AFN 09] AFNOR, NF X 50-153, Analyse de la valeur – Recommandations pour sa mise en œuvre, European standard, 2009.

[AFN 11] AFNOR, NF X 50-100, Management par la valeur – Analyse fonctionnelle, caractéristiques fondamentales – Analyse fonctionnelle : analyse fonctionnelle du besoin (ou externe) et analyse fonctionnelle technique/produit (ou interne) – Exigences sur les livrables et démarches de mise en œuvre, European standard, 2011.

[AFN 13] AFNOR, NF EN 16271, Management par la valeur – Expression fonctionnelle du besoin et cahier des charges fonctionnel – Exigences pour l'expression et la validation du besoin à satisfaire dans le processus d'acquisition ou d'obtention d'un produit, European standard, 2013.

[ANS 83] ANSI, Ada programming language, Military standard MIL-STD-1815A-1983, 1983.

[ARI 92] ARINC, *Software Considerations in Airborne Systems and Equipment Certification*, Guideline, no. DO 178B, EUROCAE, no. ED-12B, 1992.

[ARI 11] ARINC, *Software Considerations in Airborne Systems and Equipment Certification*, Guideline, no. DO 178C, EUROCAE, no. ED-12C, 2011.

[AUT 17] AUTOMOTIVE SPICE, Quality management in the automotive industry, Automotive SPICE®, Process assessment model, Version 3.1, 2017.

[BAI 08] BAIER C., KATOEN J.P., *Principles of Model Checking*, The MIT Press, Cambridge, 2008.

[BAR 03] BARNES J., *High Integrity Software: The SPARK Approach to Safety and Security*, Addison-Wesley, Reading, 2003.

[BAU 10] BAUFRETON P., BLANQUART J.P., BOULANGER J.-L. *et al.*, "Multi-Domain Comparison of Safety Standards", *ERTS2*, Toulouse, France, 2010.

[BEH 93] BEHM P., "Application d'une méthode formelle aux logiciels sécuritaires ferroviaires", *Atelier Logiciel Temps Réel, 6es Journées Internationales du Génie Logiciel*, Nantes, France, 1993.

[BEH 96] BEHM P., "Formal development of safety critical software of METEOR", *First B Conference*, Nantes, November, 1996.

[BEH 97] BEHM P., DESFORGES P., MEIJA F., "Application de la méthode B dans l'industrie ferroviaire", *ARAGO 20*, pp. 59–88, 1997.

[BEN 03] BENVENISTE A., CASPI P., EDWARDS S.A. *et al.*, "The synchronous languages 12 years later", *Proceedings of the IEEE*, vol. 91, no. 1, pp. 64–83, 2003.

[BLA 18] BLANQUART J.P., LEDINOT E., GASSINO J. *et al.*, "Software Safety – A Journey Across Domains and Safety Standards", *ERTSS*, Toulouse, 31 Jan-2Feb, 2018.

[BON 03] BON P., BOULANGER J.-L., MARIANO G., "Semi formal modelling and formal specification: UML & B in simple railway application", *CNAM-Paris, ICSSEA*, Paris, 4-6 Nov, 2003.

[BOU 99] BOULANGER J.-L, DELEBARRE V., NATKIN S., "METEOR: Validation de Spécification par modèle formel", *Revue RTS*, vol. 63, pp. 47–62, 1999.

[BOU 00] BOULANGER J.-L., GALLARDO M., "Processus de validation basée sur la notion de propriété", *Lambda Mu 12*, March, 2000.

[BOU 04] BOULANGER J.-L., BON P., "B-Rail: requirement analysis", *FORMS'04*, 2004.

[BOU 05] BOULANGER J.-L., BERKANI K., "UML et la certification d'application", *ICSSEA*, CNAM, Paris, 2005.

[BOU 06a] BOULANGER J.-L., Expression et validation des propriétés de sécurité logique et physique pour les systèmes informatiques critiques, PhD thesis, Université de Technologie de Compiègne, May 2006.

[BOU 06b] BOULANGER J.-L., BON P., "B-Rail: Analyse et modélisation des exigences", *Revue génie logiciel*, vol. 79, pp. 18–24, 2006.

[BOU 07a] BOULANGER J.-L., BON P., "BRAIL : d'UML à la méthode B pour modéliser un passage à niveau", *Revue RTS*, vol. 95, pp. 147–172, 2007.

[BOU 07b] BOULANGER J.-L., "UML et les applications critiques", *Proceedings of Qualita' 07*, pp. 739–745, Tangier, 2007.

[BOU 07c] BOULANGER J.-L., PHILIPPE L., "A generic process and its tool support towards combining UML and B for safety critical systems", *CAINE*, San Francisco, 2007.

[BOU 08] BOULANGER J.-L., "RT3-TUCS: how to build a certifiable and safety critical railway application", *17th International Conference on Software Engineering and Data Engineering*, pp. 182–187, Los Angeles, 2008.

[BOU 09a] BOULANGER J.-L. (ed.), *Sécurisation des architectures informatiques – exemples concret*, Hermes-Lavoisier, 2009.

[BOU 09b] BOULANGER J.-L., "Le domaine ferroviaire, les produits et la certification", *Journée "ligne produit"*, 2009.

[BOU 11a] BOULANGER J.-L. (ed.), *Utilisations industrielles des techniques formelles – interprétation abstraite*, Hermès-Lavoisier, Paris, 2011.

[BOU 11b] BOULANGER J.-L. (ed.), *Techniques industrielles de modélisation formelle pour le transport*, Hermès-Lavoisier, Paris, 2011.

[BOU 11c] BOULANGER J.-L. (ed.), *Sécurisation des architectures informatiques industrielles*, Hermés-Lavoisier, Paris, 2011.

[BOU 12] BOULANGER J.-L. (ed.), *Outils de mise en œuvre industrielle des techniques formelles*, Hermès-Lavoisier, Paris, 2012.

[BOU 13] BOULANGER J.-L. (ed.), *Mise en œuvre de la méthode B*, Hermès-Lavoisier, Paris, 2013.

[BOU 14] BOULANGER J.-L., BADREAU S., *Ingénierie des exigences – méthodes et bonnes pratiques pour construire et maintenir un référentiel*, Dunod, Paris, 2014.

[BOU 16] BOULANGER J.-L., *Certifiable Software Applications 1 : Main Processes*, ISTE Press, London, and Elsevier, Oxford, 2016.

[BOU 17] BOULANGER J.-L., *Certifiable Software Applications 2 : Support Processes*, ISTE Press, London, and Elsevier, Oxford, 2017.

[BOU 19] BOULANGER J.-L., *Certifiable Software Applications 4*, ISTE Press, London and Elsevier, Oxford, forthcoming, 2019.

[BOW 95] BOWEN J.P., HINCHEY M.G., *Applications of Formal Methods*, Prentice Hall, New York, 1995.

[CEN 00] CENELEC, Applications Ferroviaires. Spécification et démonstration de la fiabilité, de la disponibilité, de la maintenabilité et de la sécurité (FMDS), EN 50126, 2000.

[CEN 01] CENELEC, Railway Applications – Communications, Signalling and Processing Systems – Software for Railway Control and Protection Systems, EN 50128, 2001.

[CEN 03] CENELEC, Applications ferroviaires: systèmes de signalisation, de télécommunications et de traitement systèmes électroniques de sécurité pour la signalisation, NF EN 50129, European standard, 2003.

[CEN 11] CENELEC, Railway Applications – Communications, Signalling and Processing Systems – Software for Railway Control and Protection Systems, EN 50128, 2011.

[CHO 01] CHOVEAU E., DE CHAZELLES P., "Application de l'ingénierie système à la définition d'une démarche d'ingénierie des exigences pour l'airbus A380", *Génie logiciel*, vol. 59, pp. 13–18, 2001.

[COP 95] COPLIEN J.O., SCHMIDT D.C., *Pattern Languages of Program Design*, Addison-Wesley, 1995.

[COU 77] COUSOT P., COUSOT R., "Abstract interpretation: a unified lattice model for static analysis of programs by construction or approximation of fix points", *Conference Record of the 4th Annual ACM SIGPLAN-SIGACT Symposium on Principles of Programming Languages (POPL'77)*, ACM Press, pp. 238–252, 1977.

[COU 00] Cousot P., "Interprétation abstraite", *TSI*, vol. 19, available at : www.di. ens.fr/~cousot/COUSOTpapers/TSI00.shtml, 2000.

[DE 00] DE LA BRETESCHE B., *La méthode APTE: Analyse de la valeur, analyse fonctionnelle*", Pétrelle, 2000.

[DIJ 76] DIJKSTRA E.W., *A Discipline of Programming*, Prentice Hall, New York, 1976.

[DIL 95] DILLER A., *Z,: An Introduction to Formal Methods*, John Wiley & Sons, 1995.

[DOR 08] DORMOY F.X., "Scade 6: a model based solution for safety critical software development", *Embedded Real-Time Systems Conference*, Toulouse, 2008.

[EIA 98] EIA, Processes for engineering a system, Technical report, EIA-632, 1998.

[FAV 06] FAVRE J.-M., ESTUBLIER J., BLAY-FORNARINO M., *Ingénierie dirigée par les modèles : au-delà du MDA*, Hermes-Lavoisier, Paris, 2006.

[FED 04a] FEDERAL AVIATION ADMINISTRATION (FAA), Handbook for Object-Oriented Technology in Aviation (OOTiA), Volume 1: Handbook Overview, Revision 0, 2004.

[FED 04b] FEDERAL AVIATION ADMINISTRATION (FAA), Handbook for Object-Oriented Technology in Aviation (OOTiA), Volume 2: Considerations and Issues, Revision 0, 2004.

[FED 04c] FEDERAL AVIATION ADMINISTRATION (FAA), Handbook for Object-Oriented Technology in Aviation (OOTiA), Volume 3: Best Pratices, Revision 0, 2004.

[FED 04d] FEDERAL AVIATION ADMINISTRATION (FAA), Handbook for Object-Oriented Technology in Aviation (OOTiA), Volume 4: Certification Practices, Revision 0, 2004.

[GAM 95] GAMMA E., HELM R., JOHNSON R. *et al.*, *Design Patterns – Elements of Reusable Object-Oriented Software*, Addison-Wesley, 1995.

[GUI 90] GUIHOT G., HENNEBERT C., "SACEM software validation", *Proceedings of the 12th IEEE-ACM International Conference on Software Engineering*, Nice, 1990.

[HAD 06] HADDAD S., KORDON F., PETRUCCI L., *Méthodes formelles pour les systèmes répartis et coopératifs*, Hermès-Lavoisier, Paris, 2006.

[HAL 91] HALBWACHS N., CASPI P., RAYMOND P. *et al.*, "The synchronous dataflow programming language Lustre", *Proceedings of the IEEE*, vol. 79, no. 9, pp. 1305–1320, 1991.

[HAL 05] HALBWACHS N., "A synchronous language at work: the story of Lustre", *MEMOCODE '05 Proceedings of the 2nd ACM/IEEE International Conference on Formal Methods and Models for Co-Design*, Verona, 2005.

[HAT 94] HATTON L., SAFER C., *Developing Software for High-integrity and Safety-critical Systems*, McGraw-Hill, New York, 1994.

[HIN 95] HINCHEY M.G., BOWEN J.P. (eds), *Applications of Formal Methods*, Prentice Hall, 1995.

[HOA 69] HOARE C.A.R., "An axiomatic basis for computer programming", *Communications of the ACM*, vol. 12, no. 10, pp. 576–580, 1969.

[HUL 05] HULL E., JACKSON K., DICK J., *Requirements Engineering*, Springer, Berlin, 2005.

[IDA 06] IDANI A., B/UML: Mise en relation de spécifications B et de descriptions UML pour l'aide à la validation externe de développements formels en B, PhD thesis, Joseph Fourier University, 2006.

[IDA 07a] IDANI A., BOULANGER J.-L., PHILIPPE L., "A generic process and its tool support towards combining UML and B for safety critical systems", *CAINE*, San Francisco, 2007.

[IDA 07b] IDANI A., OKASA OSSAMI D.D., BOULANGER J.-L., "Commandments of UML for safety", *2nd International Conference on Software Engineering Advances*, IEEE Computer Society, Cap Esterel, 2007.

[IDA 09] IDANI A., BOULANGER J.-L., PHILIPPE L., "Linking paradigms in safety critical systems", *Revue ICSA*, vol. 16, no. 2, pp. 111–120, 2009.

[IEC 06] IEC, "IEC 60880: Centrales nucléaires de puissance – instrumentation et contrôles-commande importants pour la sécurité. Aspects logiciels des systèmes programmés réalisant des fonctions de catégories A", International standard, 2006.

[IEC 08] IEC, "IEC 61508:2008: Sécurité fonctionnelle des systèmes électriques électroniques programmables relatifs à la sécurité", International standard, 2008.

[IEC 10] IEC, "IEC 61508: Sécurité fonctionnelle des systèmes électriques électroniques programmables relatifs à la sécurité", International standard, 2010.

[IEC 11] IEC, "IEC 61508: Sécurité fonctionnelle des systèmes électriques électroniques programmables relatifs à la sécurité", International standard, 2011.

[IEC 13] IEC "IEC 61131-3, Automates programmables – Partie 3: Langages de programmation", International standard, 2013.

[IEC 15] IEC, "IEC 61508: Sécurité fonctionnelle des systèmes électriques électroniques programmables relatifs à la sécurité", International standard, 2015.

[IEE 04] IEEE, 1474.1, IEEE Standard for Communications-Based Train Control (CBTC) Performance and Functional Requirements, IEEE, 2004.

[ISO 95] ISO, ISO/IEC 8652:1995, Information Technology – Programming Languages – Ada, 1995.

[ISO 99a] ISO, ISO C Standard 1999, Technical report, available at http://www.open-std.org/jtc1/sc22/wg14/www/docs/n1124.pdf, 1999.

[ISO 99b] ISO, ISO/IEC 18009:1999, Information Technology – Programming Languages – Ada: Conformity Assessment of a Language Processor, 1999.

[ISO 99c] ISO, ISO/IEC 9899:1999, Programming languages – C, 1999.

[ISO 00] ISO, ISO/IEC TR 15942:2000(E) Information Technology – Programming Languages – Guide for the Use of the Ada Programming Language in High Integrity Systems, 2000.

[ISO 03] ISO, ISO/IEC 14882:2003(E), Programming Languages – C++, American National Standards Institute, New York, 2003.

[ISO 04a] ISO, ISO 9126:2004, Information Technology – Software Product Evaluation – Quality Characteristics and Guidelines for Their Use, 2004.

[ISO 04b] ISO, ISO/IEC 15504-x Information Technology — Process Assessment, 2004.

[ISO 04c] ISO, ISO/IEC 90003:2004, Software Engineering : Guideline for the Application of ISO 9001:2001 to Computer Software, 2004.

[ISO 06] ISO, ISO/IEC 14882:2003(E), Programming Languages – C++, American National Standards Institute, New York, 2006.

[ISO 08] ISO, ISO 9001:2008, Systèmes de management de la qualité – Exigences, 2008.

[ISO 11] ISO, ISO 26262, Road Vehicles – Functional Safety, 2011.

[ISO 12] ISO, ISO/IEC 8652:2012(E), Ada 2012 Language Reference Manual, 2012.

[ISO 14] ISO, ISO/IEC 90003:2014, Software Engineering – Guideline for the Application of ISO 9001:2001 to Computer Software, 2014.

[ISO 15] ISO, ISO 9001:2015, Systèmes de management de la qualité – Exigence, 2015.

[JON 90] JONES C.B., Systematic Software Development Using VDM, 2nd ed., Prentice Hall, 1990.

[KER 88] KERNIGHAN B.W., RITCHIE D.M., The C Programming Language, 2nd ed., Prentice Hall, New York, 1988.

[LAN 96] LANO K., *The B Language and Method: A Guide to Practical Formal Development*, Springer Verlag, London, 1996.

[LEC 96] LECOMPTE P., BEAURENT P.-J., "Le système d'automatisation de l'exploitation des trains (SAET) de METEOR", *Revue générale des chemins de fer*, no. 6, pp. 31–34, 1996.

[LER 09] LEROY X., "Formal verification of a Realistic Compiler", *Communications of the ACM*, vol. 52, no. 7, pp. 107–115, 2009.

[LIS 90] LISSANDRE M., *Maîtriser SADT*, Armand Colin, Paris, 1990.

[LOC 05] LOCKHEED MARTIN CORP., Joint strike fighter air vehicle C++ coding standards for the system development and demonstration program, Document no. 2RDU00001, Revision C, December 2005.

[MAT 98] MATRA, RATP, "Naissance d'un Métro. Sur la nouvelle ligne 14, les rames METEOR entrent en scène. PARIS découvre son premier métro automatique", *La vie du Rail & des transports*, special edition, no. 1076, 1998.

[MEI 02] MEINADIER J.P., *Le métier d'intégration de systèmes*, Hermes-Lavoisier, Paris, 2002.

[MEM 05] MeMVaTEx, Glossary, version 0.88, 2005.

[MEY 98] MEYERS S., *Effective C++: 50 Specific Ways to Improve Your Programs and Design*, 2nd ed., Addison-Wesley, Reading, 1998.

[MIS 98] MISRA, *MISRA-C:1998: Guidelines for the Use of the C Language in Vehicle Based Software*, 1998.

[MIS 04] MISRA, *MISRA-C:2004: Guidelines for the Use of the C Language in Critical Systems*, 2004.

[MIS 08] MISRA, *MISRA-C++:2008: Guidelines for the Use of the C++ Language in Critical Systems*, 2008.

[MIS 12] MISRA, *MISRA-C:2012: Guidelines for the Use of the C Language in Critical Systems*, 2012.

[MON 00] MONIN J.-F., *Introduction aux méthodes formelles*, Hermes Sciences, Paris, 2000.

[MOR 90a] MORGAN C., *Programming from Specifications*, Prentice Hall, Hemel Hempstead, 1990.

[MOR 90b] MORGAN C., *Deriving Programs from Specifications*, Prentice Hall, London, 1990.

[MOT 05] MOTET G., "Vérification de cohérence des modèles uml 2.0", *1ère journée thématique Modélisation de Systèmes avec uml, SysML et B-Système*, Association française d'ingénierie système, Toulouse, France, June 2005.

[NIE 93] NIELSEN J., *Usability Engineering*, Morgan Kaufman, 1993.

[OBS 97] OBSERVATOIRE FRANÇAIS DES TECHNIQUES AVANCÉES (OFTA), *Applications des Méthodes Formelles au Logiciel*, ARAGO, vol. 20, Masson, Paris, 1997.

[OKA 07] OKALAS OSSAMI D.D., MOTA J.M. *et al.*, "A method to model guidelines for developing railway safety-critical systems with UML", *ICSOFT'07 – International Conference on Software and Data Technologies*, Barcelona, 2007.

[OMG 07] OMG, Unified Modeling Language (UML), Version 2.1.1, February 2007.

[OMG 11] OMG, Unified Modeling Language (OMG UML), Infrastructure, Version 2.4.1, August, 2011.

[OSS 07] OSSAMI D.O., MOTA J.M., BOULANGER J.-L., "A model process towards modeling guidelines to build certifiable UML models in the railway sector", *7th International SPICE Conference (Software Process Improvement and Capability Determination)*, Seoul, 2007.

[PLU 89] PLUM T., *C Programming Guidelines*, 2nd ed., Plum Hall Inc., 1989.

[POH 10] POHL K., *Requirements Engineering: Fundamentals, Principles, and Techniques*, Springer, Berlin, 2010.

[RAH 08] RAHUL G., Avionics Industry Moving Towards Open Systems Integrated Modular Avionics (IMA), White paper, HCL Technologies, 2008.

[RAM 09] RAMACHANDRAN M., ATEM DE CARVALHO R., *Handbook of Research on Software Engineering and Productivity Technologies: Implications of Globalization*, IGI Global, 2009.

[RAM 11] RAMACHANDRAN M., *Knowledge Engineering for Software Development Life Cycles: Support Technologies and Applications*, IGI Global, 2011.

[RAS 08] RASSE A., BOULANGER J.-L., MARIANO G. *et al.*, "Approche orientée modèles pour une conception UML certifiée des systèmes logiciels critiques", *Conférence Internationale Francophone d'Automatique (CIFA)*, Bucharest, 2008.

[RIC 94] RICHARD-FOY M., LEGOFF G., "On-board with safety critical software: implementing safety critical software for high-speed railway transportation", *Alsys World Dialogue*, vol. 8, no. 2, 1994.

[ROQ 07] ROQUES P., *UML 2 – Modéliser une application Web*, Eyrolles, Paris, 2007.

[RTC 11] RTCA, DO 178: C, Software Consideration in Airbone Systems and Equipment Certification, Version C, 2011.

[SCH 01] SCHNEIDER S., *The B-Method: an Introduction*, Palgrave, 2001.

[SPI 89] SPIVEY J.M., *The Z Notation – a Reference Manual*, Prentice Hall, London, 1989.

[SUT 04] SUTTER H., ALEXANDRESCU A., *C++ Coding Standards, 101 Rules, Guidelines and Best Practices*, Addison-Wesley, Reading, 2004.

[THE 94] THE STANDISH GROUP, The chaos report, Technical report, 1994.

[THE 01] THE STANDISH GROUP, Extreme chaos, Technical report, 2001.

[WAE 95] WAESELYNCK H., BOULANGER J.-L., "The role of testing in the B formal development process", *ISSRE'95*, Toulouse, October 1995.

[WOR 96] WORDSWORTH J., *Software Engineering with B*, Addison-Wesley, 1996.

Index

A, B

abstraction, 11, 49, 54, 76, 77, 80–85, 90, 131–133, 194, 214, 236, 261, 271, 273
assessment, 55, 274
availability, 14, 55, 56, 62, 156
B-method, 24, 68, 87, 92, 95, 97, 121–126, 130, 131, 148, 149, 152, 250, 295

C, D

CBTC, 148, 149
CENELEC, 5–7, 32, 45–48, 70, 80, 93, 94, 141, 149–153, 161, 176–181, 187, 194, 196, 199, 257, 264, 268–270, 273, 275–277, 280–283, 289, 297, 298, 317
certification, 29, 141, 142, 274, 275, 279, 283
compilation, 63, 64, 130, 174, 228, 258, 267, 271, 272, 277, 290, 291
compiler, 142, 152, 177, 211, 236, 261, 262, 272–279, 283, 288, 290
compliance, 5, 95, 131, 133, 138, 140, 150, 157, 217, 251, 267, 269, 283, 289, 303–307
COTS, 70, 209, 210, 246, 247, 284
dependability, 37, 45, 56

development cycle, 29, 123, 125, 126, 131, 140, 155, 215

E, F, G

evaluation, 29, 161, 168, 226, 274
event, 12, 17, 23, 34, 49, 50, 54, 105, 120, 141, 150, 177, 197, 205, 269, 298
exploration, 105
FAA, 281
failures, 12, 37, 48, 61, 62, 65, 70, 71, 95, 102, 113, 134, 141, 193, 194, 202, 211, 270, 277, 288
fault, 37, 69, 187, 195
formal method, 70, 95, 121, 144–148
graph, 61, 120, 136, 240, 241

H, I

HMI, 166
IEC, 5, 7, 46, 48, 93, 95, 96, 136, 150, 152, 161, 176, 270, 271, 275, 278–281, 283, 290
implementation, 2, 24, 35, 85, 144–146, 264, 267, 315
independent, 1, 33, 49, 54, 96, 128, 137, 156, 176, 216, 241, 250, 303, 304
INT, 145, 156, 157, 216, 226, 228, 230, 250, 292, 294, 304

interpretation, 11, 78, 81, 89
  abstract, 97, 121, 144, 151, 152,
    153,
ISO, 4, 5, 7, 9, 31, 32, 46, 48, 142,
  149–152, 159, 199, 207, 244, 274–
  276, 278, 280–282, 290, 299, 307,
  311
IT, 2, 14, 36, 142, 146, 155, 184–186,
  208, 209, 215, 222, 226–229, 232,
  237, 255, 258, 262

M

machine, 68, 80, 95, 119–121, 125–
  128, 131, 133, 142, 151, 166, 188,
  224, 228, 235, 242, 257, 295, 296
maintainability, 4, 14, 48, 49, 55, 57,
  156, 157, 174, 175, 182–184, 190,
  193, 203, 205, 206, 214, 229, 237,
  238, 245, 255, 259, 271, 289, 293
methodology, 187, 235, 236, 304
model,
    -checking, 121, 130, 147, 148,
      152, 153
    transformation, 78, 82–84, 90, 96
modular, 54, 141, 176–179, 191, 241,
  268
    architecture, 176

P

petri net, 80, 93–95, 121
PM, 157, 171, 230, 260
program, 10, 12, 78, 123, 126, 130,
  152, 176, 261, 293, 307
proof, 81, 97, 121–125, 131–134,
  140–143, 150, 161, 210, 247, 248
    burden of, 132, 134
protection, 55, 181, 194, 195, 196,
  200, 211, 252, 288, 298, 314, 317
prover, 134, 152, 153, 276

R

railway, 32, 48, 57, 65–67, 70, 81,
  84, 97, 100, 105, 107, 124, 136,

  148, 151, 174, 189, 196, 199, 224,
  257, 270, 273, 274, 280, 289, 298,
  313
RAMS, 55, 56, 150, 156, 157
RATP, 24, 104, 123, 136, 144
refinement, 15, 91
reliability, 14, 38, 45, 48, 49, 55–57,
  124, 140, 156, 278
risk, 48, 55, 109, 127, 140, 161, 200,
  228, 229, 259, 275, 287, 288, 313

S

S/H ITS, 36, 215, 237
S/S ITS, 36, 215
SACEM, 70, 105, 123, 124, 151, 272
SAET-METEOR, 24, 105, 124, 125,
  144, 148, 152
safety requirement, 45, 48, 51, 53,
  56, 64, 140, 141, 210, 217, 247, 250,
  251, 284, 304–306
SAGA, 134
SCADE, 97, 121, 123, 134–142, 149,
  151, 152, 188, 235, 250, 265
SIL, 55, 161, 189, 224, 235, 270
SSIL, 81, 161, 189, 224, 235, 270,
  289
static analysis, 156, 171, 216, 249,
  300, 303
structured method, 94, 102

T, U

TC, 40, 75, 87, 109, 110, 113,
  168–171, 205, 226, 229, 237, 249,
  257, 258
THALES, 136
traceability, 18, 243
train, 64, 65, 68, 69, 84, 107, 114,
  116, 123, 125, 127, 144, 148, 149,
  224, 225, 277
UT, 14, 87, 122, 146, 179, 233, 258

V

V&V, 33, 35, 37, 39, 48, 51, 56, 87,
    88, 90, 91, 125, 150, 185, 210, 212,
    233, 247, 263, 300, 316
VER, 77, 140, 156, 157, 160–162,
    167, 170, 171, 216, 217, 230, 250,
    251, 259, 260, 275, 300, 303, 304
V-model, 2, 3, 5, 35, 36, 39, 136,
146, 149, 155, 184, 215, 316